TIMPSON'S
TIMEPATHS

TIMPSON'S TIMEPATHS

Eight journeys through history, from stone age to steam

JOHN TIMPSON

With photographs by Peter Anderson

BBC Books

PAGE 1 *Bridge at Blaenycwm on the
old Aberystwyth mailcoach run.*

Published by BBC Books,
a division of BBC Enterprises Limited,
Woodlands, 80 Wood Lane
London W12 0TT

First Published 1994

© John Timpson 1994
The moral right of the author has been asserted.

ISBN 0 563 36791 1

Additional research by Mark Kershaw
Maps by John Woodcock
Designed by Grahame Dudley Associates

Set in Aldus by Goodfellow & Egan Ltd, Cambridge
Printed in Great Britain by Cambus Litho Ltd, Glasgow
Bound by Hunter & Foulis Ltd, Edinburgh

CONTENTS

INTRODUCTION

The name is invented, but the 'Timepaths' are genuine, the routes which our forebears used at different eras in our history. They varied over the centuries according to the type of transport that was available – from Shank's pony to the four-legged ones, sailing ships to stage-coaches, canal boats to steam locomotives. *Timepaths* rolls back the layers of later years to trace these original routes, to follow them where it is still possible, and – this is the fun bit! – to see what has happened to them today, through the eyes of those earlier travellers, from Stan the Stone Age Man to Sandy the Steam.

Take the Icknield Way, for example, the earliest Timepath of them all; it was first used in the Neolithic Age, 5000 years ago, and much of it is still used today. Some sections remain as just bridle paths or green lanes, but elsewhere the Romans straightened it out and modern road-builders added dual carriageways, while settlements became villages and villages became towns. Stan, our travelling salesman from the Stone Age, would find himself dragging his sledge of fur samples through the middle of Luton…

The Fosse Way still cuts diagonally across Britain from the Devon coast to Lincoln, never varying more than six miles either way, but Len the Roman Legionary would be a little confused – as indeed I was – by the six-lane round-abouts of Leicester's 'Fosse Way Industrial Estate'. Vic the Viking would be impressed, I hope, by the Humber Bridge as he sails up the Ouse to York, but Paul the Bearer might be a little irritated by all the happy hikers on the Corpse Trail in Swaledale. Dai the Welsh Drover would be even more put out to discover that Halfpenny Green, where he paid a halfpenny a head to graze his cattle overnight, is now a busy airport on the outskirts of the Birmingham conurbation, while Bill the Blunderbuss, riding shotgun on the Aberystwyth mailcoach, would pass a much larger airport as he heads out of London, with the M4 beside him and the M25 ahead. But at least they do not block his way; Ben the Bargee would have to thread his barge through a 3-foot culvert every time a hump-backed road bridge has been levelled across the old Wey & Arun Canal.

Only Sandy the Steam would find his track unchanged on the West Highland Line to Mallaig; it still survives after so many others succumbed in the sixties to the Beeching Axe. But its freight traffic has gone, most of its stations are unstaffed, only the tourists keep it in business – and the new road being built beside it may succeed where Beeching failed.

I have no claim to being an historian, and this is not a history book, though it is based on historical events. Nor is it primarily a travel book, though it provides the information to follow these routes if you wish. But I like to discover the more unusual features of the British countryside and delve into the curious tales behind them, and this has given me another opportunity to do so.

The stories of how our ancestors created these routes, and what they were used for, are fascinating in themselves. But to follow in their footsteps after all these centuries, to spot the sometimes bizarre reminders that are left behind – an 1820s canal bridge marooned, canal-less, in the middle of a modern housing estate, a 10-foot signpost which is far too high for a motorist but just right for the driver of a stage-coach, a farm deep in the Welsh mountains on the drovers' road to Smithfield which is still called Little London – and then to turn the next corner and be plunged back into the twentieth century... Well, that's really what *Timpson's Timepaths* is all about.

THE ICKNIELD WAY

*England's Oldest Road
with Stan the Stone Age Man*

PREVIOUS PAGES *Cymbeline's Castle, ancient earthwork on the route of the much older Icknield Way.*

THE GREEKS, OF COURSE, had a word for the Icknield Way era, and so we have been stuck with it too; they called it the Neolithic Age. It came after the Mesolithic and the Paleolithic, real mouthfuls which could put most people off early history for good, but they just mean New, Middle and Old, and they all refer to what we usually think of, rather more simply, as the Stone Age.

During the Old Stone Age our forebears got the hang of using stone tools and weapons to go hunting and fishing, and started thinking about moving out of their caves and building their own homes. It took them half a million years or so, but in the Middle Stone Age they finally got around to it, and during the New Stone Age, about four thousand years ago, the more enterprising of the fishermen and hunters went in for farming and mining too. They began to live in communities, and some early entrepreneur got the idea of swopping flint axes for sheepskins, and leather thongs for bags of corn. England's first travelling salesmen

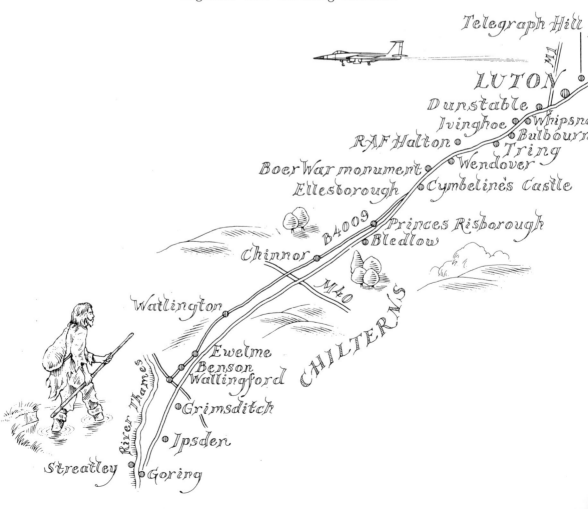

Telegraph Hill

M1

LUTON

Dunstable

Ivinghoe   Whipsna

RAF Halton   Bulbourne

Tring

Boer War monument   Wendover

Ellesborough   Cymbeline's Castle

B4009   Princes Risborough

Bledlow

Chinnor

M40

CHILTERNS

Watlington

Ewelme
Benson
Wallingford

Grimsditch

River Thames

Ipsden

Streatley   Goring

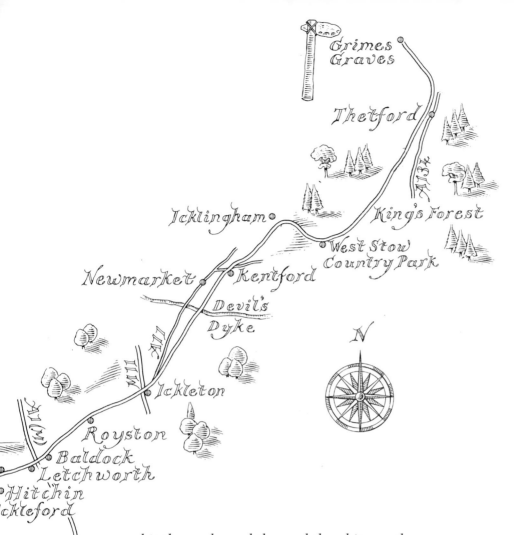

       hit the road – and the road they hit was the Icknield Way.

Actually 'road' is putting it a bit high. The Icknield Way was a skein of parallel tracks along a natural belt of open country, a chalk ridge which divided the dense forests on the higher ground from the marshes below. It provided a convenient grazing area for the settlements that grew up along it, and a natural route for Stone Age commercial travellers. In later eras it was used by drovers taking their cattle from one community to the next.

There are those who argue that the Icknield Way runs from Wiltshire to the Norfolk coast, but the western section, from Salisbury Plain to the Thames, is more generally known as the Ridgeway, and the Norfolk section is so closely associated with the much later and straighter Peddars Way that it is more Roman than prehistoric. For me it is the 140-odd miles from Goring, on the border of what used to be Mercia and Wessex, to the Norfolk-Suffolk border at Thetford, which qualifies as the Icknield Way, referred to in the reference books as England's oldest road.

I have to acknowledge, though, that the Ridgeway did provide the principal western destination for those who used the Icknield. Local traffic may have stopped at the Thames, but the dedicated long-distance Stone Age traveller kept going, because at the far end of the Ridgeway was a major community, which built up regular trading links with the substantial settlement at the Norfolk end of the Way.

They had developed simultaneously, but for different reasons. Salisbury Plain was great for farming, Norfolk was great for flints. Both the farmers and the miners used the same implement, a primitive pickaxe made from a deer-antler. In fact, antler picks were in such universal use during the New Stone Age that it's a pity nobody chipped off that period from the rest of the Stone Age and called it the Antler Age instead.

Up in Norfolk they used their picks in the flint mines, in the area now known as Grimes Graves, and you can still go down one of the mines and see the doodles they drew in the chalk during the tea-breaks. If you had been there three or four thousand years ago, you could have caught them knapping.

Grimes Graves looks like a series of bomb craters now, because in the Bronze Age which followed – and what a relief the Greeks never saddled us with a fancy word for Bronze – the mines were left derelict and farmers made use of the site for their livestock. It was Norfolk's earliest experience of land reclamation. In its time, though, this was the main centre in the whole of England for the manufacture of knives and axes and blades of all kinds; it was the Sheffield of the Stone Age.

Meanwhile, at the other end of the Ridgeway, they were using the picks on Salisbury Plain to dig furrows for their corn and clear ditches for drainage and defence. There was one particular ditch we know a great deal about today; it was circular, about 325 feet across, 20 feet wide and 6$\frac{1}{2}$ feet deep, the first stage of what we now call Stonehenge. The stones themselves were erected much later, great bluestone pillars which were hauled there, not along the Icknield Way, but from the other direction, the Welsh mountains.

People still argue about why they bothered. Whole books have been devoted to explaining what Stonehenge is all about. My favourite is called, unequivocally, *The Stonehenge Solution*, which argues that the stone circle represents the Earth Goddess, and the solitary upright stone between the Goddess and the rising sun is purely phallic; watch the way its shadow moves as the sun rises… On the other hand, a noted archaeologist has been quoted as saying: 'Most of what has been written about Stonehenge is nonsense or speculation.' I leave them to fight it out.

There is no dispute, however, about how the stones got there. Nobody had yet invented the wheel – not in backward Britain anyway – so the stones were levered on to wooden sledges, then hauled along on rollers made from treetrunks. That sounds quite straightforward, but each stone weighed up to 4 tons and needed 100 men to haul it.

This sort of transport, on a much smaller scale, was used on the Icknield Way. The original travelling salesmen probably hauled their samples on a one-man sledge. Subsequent bulk deliveries must have needed bigger sledges and more men, until 1000 years later their descendants caught up with the rest of the world and fitted their sledges with wheels. That was in the Bronze Age, but it wasn't until the Iron Age that someone had another bright idea, and attached his cart to a horse.

The actual dates are rather vague, of course, and this is the fascination of the Icknield Way. It is so extremely old that nobody can be quite certain about its precise route, or who used it, or even how it got its name. It sounds as if it is linked with the Iceni, the Norfolk tribe which produced the redoubtable Queen Boadicea, and indeed it is likely she followed the Way south against the Romans, earning her reputation as England's earliest and most dangerous lady driver. But that was many centuries after the Stone Age, and those earlier travellers would not have recognized the name. They may have called it the Flint Route, just as China, much later, had its Silk Route, but more likely, since there were no other routes to confuse it with, they just called it The Way.

It is no longer as simple as that. Apart from the fact that it consisted of several alternative tracks, strung out across the width of the chalk ridge, the Romans complicated the situation with their passion for straight lines. The Icknield Way was far too meandering for their liking, and along those sections which might prove useful to them they

'Romanized' it, either by smoothing out the bends or building a new road alongside.

When it reaches the Chilterns, for instance, the original Icknield Way potters gently up and down the hillside, which the Romans must have found irritating, because they built a new straight road on the flat plain below. In the Stone Age the plain was boggy and wellnigh impassable, but in due course it dried out and must have been very inviting to a Roman road engineer. Hence between Watlington and Ivinghoe Beacon we have been left with two Icknield Ways, the Upper and the Lower. Both are shown on maps in Gothic lettering, indicating an ancient route; it doesn't indicate that one of them is 2000 years more ancient than the other...

In more recent times, great chunks of the Icknield Way have been blotted out completely; it is somewhere underneath Luton and Dunstable and Letchworth Garden City. Other sections, originally straightened by the Romans, have been made even straighter and faster, like the A505 dual carriageway between Baldock and Royston. And finally there is the Icknield Way Long-distance Path, which begins, rather confusingly, part of the way along the original route, at Ivinghoe Beacon. There is another modern Path between Ivinghoe and the Thames, but to confuse you still further, this is called the Ridgeway National Trail, and it continues across the Thames on to the original Ridgeway.

The Icknield Way Path takes in the most scenic sections of the original route. That's the good news. The bad news, for anyone wanting to follow the Stone Age Way, is that the Path avoids all roads and built-up areas. For instance, it invents an entirely new route around Luton and Dunstable, which is all very well for the happy hiker, but not very helpful for the seeker after historical truth – and other titbits.

To be fair, the literature about the Path provided by the admirable Icknield Way Association does make it clear that it only 'shadows' the original Way. Be wary, therefore, of the 'Icknield Way' shown on maps in modern type. This is the gentrified version, adapted for ramblers who like quiet footpaths and nice views, just as the Romans adapted it for soldiers who could only march in straight lines.

I wanted to discover what had happened to the real Icknield. So yes – I did it my Way...

THE FIRST PROBLEM FOR Stone Age travellers joining the Icknield Way from the Ridgeway was to get across the Thames. In those days there would be nothing much along the Way except forest on one side, bog on the other, and some unpleasantly belligerent animals in between, but there was also the occasional settlement, and there were quite substantial ones where Streatley and Goring now face each other across the river. Three natural routes met at this point: the Ridgeway ended on the Berkshire side at Streatley, the Icknield Way began on the Oxfordshire side at Goring, and the Thames itself, with its water traffic, was the third. There have been Stone Age and Bronze Age artefacts discovered on both sides of the crossing, and a Bronze Age urn from Streatley, which always seems to be regarded as the more upmarket of the two, was rated good enough to be put in the Ashmolean Museum.

Soaring over Goring: a gilded fish now flies above the Icknield Way.

I have never understood why Streatley has always had a better press than Goring. One reputable guide states firmly: 'Streatley is the prettier of the two, with its delightful Georgian houses and cottages, and its old nineteenth-century gabled malthouse.' But Goring has its Georgian houses and cottages too, and as for the 'old nineteenth-century malthouse' (is nineteenth-century really 'old'?), Goring has a seventeenth-century mill on the site of one mentioned in the Domesday Book. Maybe the writer was influenced by the excellent fare at Streatley's expensive riverside restaurant – or maybe it is all too tempting to rhyme Goring, even subconsciously, with boring.

It is not surprising that a healthy rivalry existed until very recent times, and in the days when the river was the boundary between Wessex and Mercia, it was more like downright hostility. But Wessex and Mercia had not been invented in the Stone Age, and Goring only got its Anglo-Saxon name when a chief called Gara arrived, probably via the Icknield Way. Streatley, with the Latin 'strata' in its name, was probably colonized by the road-loving Romans. So when the first Stone Age wanderer turned up along the Ridgeway and told the locals he wanted to cross the river, I hope the two settlements were still on good terms. In later centuries they would probably have shoved him in.

Instead they should have directed our traveller – for simplicity let's call him Stan the Stone Age Man – to the ford which existed a little way downstream from the present bridge. Stan would have to go through a private back garden on the Streatley side to reach it today, but the Goring river-bank is still a public path – another bonus point for Goring.

There is no notice on the bank saying 'Stone Age Ford', but the Romans built a causeway at that point, and they no doubt had the sense to site it where the water was shallowest. Certainly until the last century it was shallow enough for the stones to be visible at low water.

The ford, and later the causeway, were the only link between the two settlements for 3000 years, maybe because they disliked each other so much that nobody wanted to cross the river anyway. Then in Norman times they finally got around to running a ferry. It was operated by the nuns of Goring Priory, who shrewdly acquired the exclusive rights and held on to them until Henry VIII dissolved the priory and in effect nationalized the ferry.

In spite of this link-up the two villages continued to be rivals – the word, after all, does come from 'rivalis', meaning 'dweller on a riverbank', so this sort of thing no doubt went on all along the Thames. In 1674, however, an effort was made to get together. A party of sixty men, women and children from Streatley – plus, unaccountably, a horse – crossed the river to join in the annual Goring Feast. The idea was to drown their differences, but perhaps the boatmen drowned theirs too thoroughly, because on the return journey the boat passed too close to the weir and overturned; all but fifteen of the party perished – including the horse. Alas, the reaction in Streatley, I am told, was that it served them right for going to Goring in the first place.

Crossing the river these days is less hazardous; there has been a bridge since 1837. Relations have greatly improved too, perhaps helped by the fact that Streatley folk have to pass through Goring to reach the railway. The GWR tactfully named the station Goring-and-Streatley, which may sound like a firm of shady solicitors, but it was music to the ears of a *Punch* contributor in 1904. His paeon of praise began:

> The Great Western Railway runs down to the West,
> Conveyance, like young Lochinvar's, of the best;
> And into the sunset it carries me fleetly,

Stone Age travellers forded the Thames here, between Streatley and Goring.

First a ford, then a ferry, now a bridge to link the Ridgeway with the Icknield Way.

But I never go further than Goring-and-Streatley.

Streatley, it seems, has much better rhymes than Goring; maybe that's its secret. 'The dusk falls discreetly', 'the sun shining featly', 'Even strawberries-and-cream do not sound half so sweetly'. And today, I can add, they're united – completely?

Stan the Stone Age Man knew nothing of all this, of course, as he splashed through the river, hauling his sledgeful of samples, and started off along the Icknield Way.

One can only guess at the path he took through the settlement, but he must have landed on the open area by the river which was used for archery practice in the Middle Ages, and he probably continued up the track which became Ferry Lane, where the ferryman's cottage has since been expanded unrecognizably into the sprawling Ferry House. This was where Oscar Wilde was living when he invented characters like Lord Goring and 'The Ideal Husband'; an imaginative fellow, but I wonder if he ever pictured Stan the Stone Age Man tramping past his door.

Air Chief Marshal 'Bomber' Harris lived here too in more recent years. If he ever had such a vision, he would doubtless have told Stan to get a crease in his sheepskins and smarten up the load on his sledge…

As an alternative to Ferry Lane, Stan may have stayed by the river and walked upstream for a while, in which case he would have been spotted, in later years, from Ye Miller of Mansfield. Ye twelfth-century miller, like Stone Age Stan, was a long way from home, and an inscription in the bar explains why. One night at his mill near Sherwood Forest he entertained a huntsman who had lost his way, feeding him venison pasty for dinner. The bad news was that the huntsman was Henry II, and in those days killing the King's deer was a hanging offence. The good news was that the King enjoyed his meal so much that he pardoned the miller and told him to open a hostelry at Goring, where he could drop in for a pasty more conveniently. There has been a Miller of Mansfield at Goring ever since.

I hope Stan managed to get the prehistoric equivalent of a venison pasty before he left the settlement and set off into the unknown along the Icknield Way. These days he might be tempted to continue upriver along a path which is

A comparatively late arrival on the Icknield Way – Goring's Ye Miller of Mansfield.

invitingly labelled 'The Ridgeway', but if he went up the main street, crossed the railway and turned along the B4009 he would find, among the jumble of roads on his right, the name that he was looking for. An inconspicuous lane that runs out of a modern estate and up into the hills above Goring is named Icknield Way.

It would have been a stiff climb for Stan with his sledge back in the Stone Age, and a lot less inviting than it is today, with its vista of well-manicured fields, neat hedges, and scattered farmhouses. One of these is right by the lane; it is called, encouragingly, Icknield Farm. Then the lane veers off to the right towards Ipsden, while Stan would have kept straight on across the fields, towards a dip which is known as Drunken Bottom – though I doubt that Stan can be blamed for that.

I imagine that Ipsden could originally have been Icksden. A number of villages along the route have an Ick in them (though Ickenham itself, on London's Bakerloo line, is nowhere near it). The various tracks that made up the Icknield Way covered such a broad swathe of country that one of them might well have passed through the village. If Stan had chosen that track today he would have come across a building which he might mistake for an entire settlement. Ipsden Farm has the biggest eighteenth-century barn in England, 365 feet long and incorporating so many timbers in its roof it must have been a major factor in reducing Oxfordshire from forests to fields.

Opposite, in pleasing contrast, is a neat little wooden granary on straddlestones, those stone mushrooms which keep out the rats and mice. And up the road is Ipsden House, where Charles Read wrote *The Cloister and the Hearth*, which is still well read, and *Hard Back*, which isn't – perhaps because it never went into paperback...

Back on his own track, Stan would have passed Drunken Bottom and crossed the present bridleway which is part of Grimsditch, the first of the many dykes that the Way traverses before it reaches Norfolk. Not that Stan would know about any of them, because they were dug long after he and his contemporaries were using the Way. Sections of Grimsditch also survive around Northchurch and Wendover, thirty-odd miles away, and the experts say it was probably dug as a major line of defence, about AD 800. That was a period when King Offa was in the ditch business in a big

Ipsden's timber and brick granary, set on straddlestones to foil the rats.

way, and Grimsditch is very similar to Offa's Dyke, on the Welsh border. He was active around the Chilterns so he probably dug this one as well. I would say it's the best bet, on Offa.

From Grimsditch Stan would have headed across open country today until he encountered a much more formidable obstacle than anything Offa could offer, the A423 trunk road from Oxford to Henley and ultimately the M4 motorway. Across it lies another modern development in transport which would baffle Stan even more, Benson RAF Station, home of some very noisy aircraft indeed.

Benson always struck me as an unlikely name for a village. I went to school with a boy called Benson, and I always associated the name with Biggs and Jenkins and Andrews-Jones, none of whom sounds like a village. However, Benson village dates back far beyond my schooldays. According to the Anglo-Saxon Chronicles the ditch-digging King Offa knew it well. 'In this year [AD 779] Cynewulf and Offa contended around Benson, and Offa took the village.'

I'm not sure he'd still want it if he could see how it has been transformed in recent years, but next along the Icknield Way is Ewelme, much more picturesque with its ancient church school and almshouses, still functioning in their original fifteenth-century buildings. They were founded by Lady Alice de la Pole, grand-daughter of Geoffrey Chaucer, and her tomb has pride of place in the adjoining church – which she rebuilt at the same time.

The church guidebook gives a useful tip on how to view the frescoes on the base of the tomb, which stands on little arcaded legs about a foot high. 'On a sunny day,' it says, 'the frescoes can be clearly seen by anyone who lies prone on the sanctuary floor and looks up at them through the arcades.' Each time I visit the church I hope to find a row of legs sticking out from under the tomb, but I suspect most people cheat and just look at the copy of the frescoes on the wall.

Stan would have bypassed Benson and Ewelme and taken the track along the edge of the hills, now confusingly called the Ridgeway Path. It is reassuring to find, where the track crosses the road from Watlington to Nettlebed, the more accurately named Icknield House, but there is more confusion to come. This is where the Icknield Way continues over the Chilterns, and the Romans built their own version down below.

One of the heavily decorated de la Pole tombs at Ewelme.

The so-called Lower Icknield Way may be straighter and faster but it is also a lot duller. It does boast the Icknield Nurseries near Kingston Blount, to console the historically minded, but its main feature after that is the cement works at Chinnor. Then you find yourself in the very modern environs of Weston Turville and Aston Clinton, where little of historical note survives.

Stan was happily unaware of the Romans' alternative route, and followed the original Way on to the hillside above Watlington. Today he would find himself on Christmas Common, a name he was 2000 years too early to understand, but he would be intrigued by a curious carving on the hillside called the White Mark. It may seem familiar, because it was once thought to date back to his own era, just as other hill figures have been attributed to prehistoric times. I would have liked to think it was the only surviving signpost on the Icknield Way, but alas, the White Mark turns out to be a much more recent creation, though it has a delightful story attached to it. According to local folklore, it is a detachable church spire.

There is, of course, the stuffy official version. The Victoria County History of Oxfordshire dismisses it as 'an eighteenth-century folly, originally intended to be an obelisk.' I much prefer the local story that a Mr Edward Horn decided Watlington Church would look better with a spire, so he had the White Mark cut in the hillside beyond the church, a tall triangle 36 feet wide at the base and 270 feet high. There is no denying that, from a certain position on the road out of Watlington, it looks exactly like a spire perched on top of the tower. If you prefer the tower without it, you just continue along the road until the White Mark is only a white mark again.

The Icknield Way ambles along the hillside through pleasant woods and past a nature reserve, and there is a convenient lane running parallel with it which crosses the M40 motorway. From the bridge you can look down on that astonishing ravine which did not exist in Stan's day, nor indeed in mine until a few years ago. This is the cutting for the M40 through the chalk cliff, which was so skilfully designed that it is hardly visible from the plain below. Stan would be quite impressed with that, but more so, perhaps, by the telecommunications tower just above him at Stokenchurch, which dominates that part of the Chilterns and

ABOVE *As the Icknield Way climbs into the Chilterns, a chance to send a postcard home.*

OPPOSITE *The Watlington White Mark, pointing (unintentionally) to the Icknield Way.*

makes a nonsense of the M40's efforts to be unobtrusive.

The original Icknield Way then converges with a line of communication that was created in the nineteenth century and abandoned in the twentieth. A railway used to run along the hillside between Watlington and Princes Risborough; it was taken over by the GWR in 1884 and abandoned by it in 1957.

The Ridgeway Path, as it is still called – the Icknield Way Association doesn't take over for a few miles yet – follows the line for a while, and passes uncomfortably close to Chinnor cement works and its quarries before it disappears into Bledlow Great Wood. The best-known feature of Bledlow is the Bledlow Ridge, and one might expect a ridgeway to go along the top of it, but actually the Ridge is at right-angles to the Way, and anyway it is not nearly as interesting as Bledlow itself. In spite of the gruesome origin of its name (it is said the Danes and Saxons fought here and called it Bloody Hill) the village could hardly be more peaceful. There is a cluster of Tudor cottages around an eighteenth-century Manor House and a Norman church, set on a little-used lane which loops above the main road. It is a different world from Chinnor and its cement works, only a mile or so away.

Stan was too early to see Bledlow, though the Great Wood and the Ridge existed even in his time. He wouldn't have seen the Bledlow Cross either, but then he'd have a job to see it today, it is so overgrown with beech scrub and juniper. Its twin further along the hillside, known as the Whiteleaf Cross, is in rather better shape, an impressive landmark 50 feet wide and 90 feet long. Some archaeologists say it goes back to Anglo-Saxon times, which would still be too late for Stan, but a favourite theory is that it was carved by local Royalists to celebrate a victory in the Civil War.

Certainly it existed before the reign of George IV, because at that time it was ordered to be preserved under a special Act, and the person ordered to preserve it was the Lord of the Hampden Estates. John Hampden was the local MP whose refusal to pay his taxes to Charles I helped to start the Civil War; if indeed the Cross is a Royalist relic, it was a nice irony that his successors had to look after it.

There is another theory, incidentally, that the Whiteleaf and Bledlow Crosses marked each side of a break in the hills called the Risborough Gap, but this would seem a little

The Whiteleaf Cross, another latter-day landmark on the Icknield Way.

unnecessary, since the gap is just as visible as the crosses. But then, people have carved out patterns on chalky hillsides for far less reason than that…

The Way crosses the Risborough Gap near Saunderton, now virtually a suburb of Princes Risborough, but once the centre for the oldest sheep, cheese and hop fair in the South of England. Stan, I think, would rather have enjoyed that – he might have traded a few of his hides to discover the pleasurable uses of hops. As it was, he continued along the hillside to the Whiteleaf Cross, where the little community of Whiteleaf is strung out along a lane high above the main road. Happily the lane has not been saddled with the inaccurate name of The Ridgeway; the Council has very correctly named it Icknield Way.

From Whiteleaf the Way dips down to join the Old Road at Ellesborough. It is a very old road indeed, the original Icknield Way, but there is little left as a reminder of its antiquity except for a remarkable grass mound that looms beside it, known as Cymbeline's Castle. Cymbeline, according to Shakespeare, was a British king in the first century who was a great chum of the Romans: 'Publish we this peace to all our subjects. Set we forward: let a Roman and a British ensign wave friendly together…' However, local legend has it that Cymbeline (or Cunobelinus, as he appears in the history books) actually fought the Romans here, and lost.

Archaeologists, on the other hand, say the mound is an Iron Age fort, and leave it at that. Personally I like to think it goes back even further, and marked a staging post where Stan got his breath back before pressing on to Wendover and the distant delights of Luton…

On the skyline is a much loftier landmark, the Boer War Monument on the summit of Coombe Hill, the highest point in the Chilterns. Rather less prominent, in fact tucked away out of sight in the beechwoods below, is Chequers Court, presented to the nation by Lord Lee in 1922 so that successive Prime Ministers could escape from the public eye and put their feet up. They usually go to church in Ellesborough when they are in residence, and their route takes them in Stan's footsteps along the Icknield Way.

Beyond Coombe Hill the Way goes straight through the centre of Wendover. It coincides at this stage with the modern version, which makes Wendover one of the few towns in

The Boer War Monument on Coombe Hill, hundreds of feet above the Way.

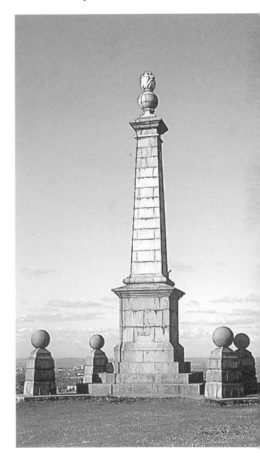

the country with an official Long Distance Footpath going down its main street. It still has a rural flavour, with a scattering of timbered cottages, one or two nice old pubs, and an ivy-covered lock-up, but it is on a busy main road which gets even busier as the Way continues past Halton RAF Station and joins the Roman Akeman Street, now the A41 trunk road from Aylesbury to London.

Happily it doesn't stay on it very far, just far enough to pass Icknield House (or so it says on the map – the house itself, very sensibly, conceals itself completely from the road). Then the way turns off through the industrial outskirts of Tring, a town which is much more historic than it looks. This was in fact where William the Conqueror finally conquered; the Battle of Hastings was only the beginning.

London was still held by the English, and they actually managed to repulse his first attack. So he tried a war of nerves instead; he went off on a tour of southern England, thumping every local he met and generally terrifying the populace. He crossed the Thames at Wallingford and joined the Icknield Way, following Stan's route along the Chilterns and still thumping as he went. He made sure that word of all this reached London, and it had the desired effect. By the time he reached Tring the chiefs of staff in London decided that enough was enough. They sent emissaries to meet him waving white flags, and William was the Conqueror at last. Tradition has it that the handover ceremony took place at nearby Berkhamsted, but if William was still on the Icknield Way when the first meeting took place, and the emissaries came from London along Akeman Street, then Tring can take some of the credit too.

Beyond Tring the Way is back in open country again. At Bulbourne it has its only encounter with a canal as it crosses the Grand Union, and not far ahead is Ivinghoe Beacon, where the so-called Ridgeway Path ends at last and the more accurately-named Icknield Way Path begins.

Everyone climbs to the top of the Beacon these days to admire the view, but I doubt that Stan the Stone Age Man was quite so enthusiastic. The view, after all, would have been obscured by forest, and the features that catch the eye today didn't exist. The windmill at Pitstone, for instance, reputed to be the oldest surviving postmill in England, only goes back some 370 years, which is a very small slice of

OPPOSITE *Wendover, on the original Way, has the official footpath down its main street.*

BELOW *The bridge at Bulborne where the Way crosses a later timepath, the Grand Union Canal.*

Pitstone postmill, reputedly the oldest in Britain – but way after the Way.

4000. And while an innocent visitor might fleetingly assume that the great chalk lion on the opposite hillside was a throwback to Stan's day, when wild animals roamed the area, he would soon realize that it is basically an advertisement for Whipsnade Zoo.

There is evidence of a Bronze Age fort on Ivinghoe Beacon, so somebody must have climbed it within a thousand years or so of Stan's arrival, but I suspect that Stan himself circled the Beacon and passed through what is now Ivinghoe village. Today he would find a vicious-looking object hanging on the churchyard wall which he might have wielded to some effect if the locals had turned nasty. It is a thatch-hook, used for pulling off the thatch if a cottage catches fire. On second thoughts, Stan would have had quite a job to brandish it single-handed; the handle is 18 feet long.

The Icknield Way – the genuine one – is now marked on the maps as the road leading straight to Dunstable, passing the Five Knolls burial ground where some of Stan's contemporaries were buried. However, the modern Path makes a diversion to take in the Tree Cathedral at Whipsnade, and I think Stan would have appreciated it too, even though he knew nothing of cathedrals. It was planted in the 1930s by Edmund Kell Blyth in memory of the friends he lost in the Great War, and it has been a place of peace and serenity ever since. Oaks form an archway at the entrance, the aisle is lined with limes, and the side chapels have cedar, rowan, elm and spruce. It is now owned by the National Trust, and although the Tree Cathedral has never been consecrated, occasional services are held there. It remains, one might say, a safe arbour.

Meanwhile the Way heads straight into Dunstable and Luton, neither of which one associates immediately with peace and serenity. The two neighbours have no history of animosity on the lines of Goring and Streatley, but somehow the names do not inspire the sort of eulogy that the *Punch* poet indulged in. He might try:

> *In all my travels I've been nowhere as wonderful*
> *As the charmingly picturesque Luton and*
> *Dunstable...*

Or perhaps:

> *Not even the genius of an Isaac Newton*
> *Could sum up the beauty of Dunstable and*
> *Luton...*

No, perhaps not.

The hikers on the Icknield Way Path have taken the easy way out and made a long detour through Wingfield and Toddington, an altogether more euphonious combination. Devoted followers of Stan the Stone Age Man must just keep on through both the towns – dual carriageway, M1 motorway junction and all. It was not ever thus, of course. Dunstable was once a Roman town on the junction of the Icknield Way and Watling Street, and later a stopping-place for Eleanor of Castile's funeral cortege, where her husband Edward I erected one of the famous Eleanor Crosses – later destroyed in the Civil War. Luton had its quieter moments too, when it was just the centre of the straw hat trade. But both are now dominated by cars, the people who make them and the people who drive them, and Stan is well out of it.

There are one or two reminders of his presence. Luton still has a road called Icknield Way, and I caught a glimpse of the Icknield Industrial Estate. He would also find signposts pointing to Streatley, which might confuse him, since that was where the Icknield Way began. This is a different Streatley, of course, just off the trunk road from Luton to Bedford, and the Way actually avoids it and cuts across country, via a convenient golf course, to become a green lane at last at Galley Hill.

Stan would notice something familiar about this hill, though the name only goes back to the fifteenth century, when a gibbet used to stand there. On the summit are two barrows, and one of them has been dated about 4000 BC, so it would certainly have been there when Stan tramped by. Inside it were found the chopped-up remains of two young men, which suggests that the locals had some rather unpleasant habits. I trust they didn't spot Stan.

From Galley Hill the Way leads to another hill with a modern-sounding name. Telegraph Hill was part of an Admiralty communication system between Great Yarmouth and London in the early nineteenth century. The telegraph followed the Icknield Way for part of its route, rather like

An unnerving sight for Stone Age travellers – the Icknield Way meets the M1.

telegraph poles alongside a road, except that the 'poles' were telegraph stations about ten miles apart, linked by manual signals instead of wires.

The station on Telegraph Hill looked rather like a king-size cricket scoreboard. It was a wooden hut with a huge frame on the roof, 20 feet high, containing six slatted shutters. The slats were opened and closed by the men inside the hut, and different combinations of shutters were used to send signals to the next station. There a man observed them through a telescope, and shuttered the message on. Each combination of shutters represented a different letter, but to speed things up there were some which conveyed complete phrases, like 'Steer to North' and, more ominously, 'Court Martial to Sit'. I hope they also had one which said 'England expects…'

This chain of rather primitive signal stations operated from 1796 to 1814, by which time the chaps must have been quite exhausted, hauling away on their shutters; shuttered, in fact. Happily a simpler system was then introduced, sending semaphore messages by moving two arms on a mast. In 1847 the new electric telegraph made all these stations redundant, and Telegraph Hill reverted to being just another landmark on the Icknield Way.

Between these two hills the Way crosses a lane which has a convenient car park for anyone following the route the easy way, by road. The modern Path has now rejoined it, and there is a useful noticeboard which explains, for instance, that Treasure's Grove, on the way to Telegraph Hill, is not the site of buried treasure but a memorial to a former deputy county planning officer, one George Treasure.

The board also records that the deep gullies on top of Telegraph Hill are caused 'by the passage of countless feet', and I assumed that Stan's feet were amongst them. The Icknield Way Association, however, offers a quite different explanation.

'The deep ruts that climb the ridge here,' says its handbook, 'are not prehistoric but were largely made by the carriages of the gentry attending the racecourse that once stood on the adjoining plateau.'

Does the notice mean, then, that the 'countless feet' are those of the hikers who now use the Icknield Way, plus any of the gentry who lost their shirts at the races and had to

The Icknield Way heads for Telegraph Hill…

… where Stone Age sledges may have made the original grooves.

walk home? Or is this another case of experts disagreeing, as they have done so often about the Icknield Way? Personally I think the gullies are due to Stan's sledge.

The racecourse referred to was on Lilley Hoo, and for a couple of hundred years it was virtually the Newmarket of Hertfordshire, until the races were moved to Brocket Hall. During its heyday there was a pub called the Running Horse where runners had to be entered, and it would be nice to think that this was the original name of the Lilley Arms, which in its time has also been the Sowerby Arms and the Sugar Loaf. The Arms, however, is down in Lilley village, a fair distance from the Hoo, so there may have been another by the course which has since disappeared. Hoo can say?

On the other side of Telegraph Hill the Way continues past Pirton, and yet another mound with a distinctive name, Toot Hill. I thought the Admiralty might have been here too, trying to communicate by sound instead of signal, but 'toot' just meant lookout, and the mound was actually used by the Normans as a stronghold.

Parallel with the Way at this point is another ancient route, the Hambridge Way. With great respect to Hambridge, it seems very likely that this was just one of the skein of tracks which made up the Icknield Way. It appears in any event that Icknield was the senior partner; the next village along the route is not Hambridge but Ickleford.

Apart from being on the Icknield Way, Ickleford has two other claims to fame. Its churchyard is the last resting-place of Henry Boswell, known as the Gypsy King. He lived to be ninety, through three reigns, and in that period he is said to have travelled every road in England. Stan would have found him a kindred spirit.

The village also stands on the River Hiz (I searched in vain for a River Herz) and this flows past Gerry's Hole. Gerry was one of the navvies who built the nearby railway, and the Hole is the pond which he drowned in after a heavy night with the boys. 'Today,' says the Icknield Way hand-book, 'the pond is an attractive spot with considerable wildlife interest.' Small consolation, I fear, for Gerry.

Until this century the Icknield Way would have contin-ued across open country, but then along came Ebenezer Howard and created Letchworth Garden City. Today the Way is one of its boulevards, which still retains its name but little else. From Letchworth onwards it is houses all the way

Gerry's Hole at Ickleford, where a hapless navvy drowned along the Way.

Straightened by the Romans, dualled by the Department of Transport: the Way near Royston.

to the A1(M) motorway and Baldock, which not even the modern Icknield Way Path can avoid.

Baldock could be a most attractive town, with its broad High Street made to measure for medieval markets, but even though it is no longer on the Great North Road it is still on a Fairly Great East Road, the original Icknield Way, and plenty of traffic pours off the motorway to head for Royston and points east – as in his own era, did Stan.

Today he would find a fast dual carriageway, thanks to Roman engineers and then more recent ones, who had plenty of land to play with alongside the original road – a throwback perhaps to Stan's day, when the Icknield Way was many tracks creating a broad swathe across the countryside. This road provides fast travel but a boring journey, and I have some sympathy with the Icknield Way Path, which takes a parallel route through a string of little villages which seem a hundred miles from the nearest dual carriageway – Wallington, Sandon, Kelshall and Therfield.

Wallington is the most attractive, with more than the usual share of thatched cottages for this part of Hertfordshire, and on a quiet day more ducks than people. One of the cottages was the home for a while of Eric Blair who, as George Orwell, wrote *The Road to Wigan Pier* there. He was married in the village church, and the enterprising parochial church council has put his marriage certificate on show, with replicas available for a modest fee. The Orwells ran a small village store from their cottage; I hope they exercised the same commercial acumen.

The Path rejoins the Way by descending Therfield Heath, described officially as 'a remarkable surviving piece of prehistoric landscape', though Stan might be bewildered by the bunkers, however royal and ancient golf may be. It remains notwithstanding the most extensive barrow cemetery in this part of England, and looming over the golfers are the most obvious of them, the Five Hills. They are easily visible against the skyline from the Icknield Way down below, and Stan, I am sure, would recognize them straight away.

Royston, like Dunstable, lies on a crossroads of the Icknield Way and a major Roman road, in this case Ermine Street, but the Romans don't seem to have been too excited about that, and nothing much happened until a Norman lady called Roisia erected a cross at the junction. The hamlet that grew up around it became known as Roisia's Town, and the contracted version of the name lives on. So too does the Cross, or at least the base of it, which still stands near the crossroads and features on the town crest. Also near the junction, and also attributed by some to Lady Roisia, is the Royston Cavern.

There have been so many theories about the Cavern since it was accidentally discovered in 1742, by workmen digging a hole for a post, that if I claimed Stan sheltered in it and drew some of the pictures on the walls, it might be difficult to prove me wrong. At various times it has been identified as a hermit's cell, as a secret headquarters of the Knights Templar, as Lady Roisia's secret retiring room, and as an ancient rubbish pit. The pit theory was put forward by a highly reputable scientist in 1852; he dug out a depression in the floor which was thought to be the grave of the cavern's occupant, and discovered fragments of iron, leather, bone and oak. To me that could have been the remains of a coffin and its contents, but to him it was an indication that the Cavern had been hollowed out from an ancient dump.

George Orwell's cottage, where he wrote The Road to Wigan Pier, *just off the Icknield Way.*

He was no more specific than 'possibly pre-Roman', which covers almost any era from the Iron Age backwards, so who knows if the ancient dump was there when Stan passed this way, and whether it provided him with a convenient night's shelter?

The Cavern is always described as bell-shaped, and so it is, but it is also the shape of an enormous septic tank, a device still indispensable in rural East Anglia, and since it is situated right in the middle of town it might also have been the central feature of an advanced sewage system. Certainly the chalk walls are absorbent, so the Cavern drains naturally; but there, I fear, credibility ends. Personally I go for the hermit theory. I only wish his wall drawings had included the odd mammoth, just to give a boost to my Stone Age story. But whatever its origin, it is a very odd thing to find underneath the Icknield Way.

Royston's other historic relic is better documented. James I had a palace-cum-hunting-lodge here, the main building of which can easily be spotted next to the fish-and-chip shop. Another part of the palace became a restaurant, boarded up when I last saw it, but still bearing a sign saying 'King James's House'. James enjoyed himself so much at Royston that he refused to return to London for important affairs of state. It was at Royston, for example, that Sir Walter

James I was a later traveller on the Way; he built a hunting lodge at Royston.

Strethall church, where the squire exhibited the body of a burglar at threepence a look.

Raleigh's death warrant was signed. But it all ended in tears for the Stuarts; James's son Charles I was eventually confined there as a prisoner, and didn't enjoy himself at all.

The Icknield Way Path follows Stan's route through the middle of Royston – another rare case of a Long Distance Footpath in a town's main street. It then crosses the Greenwich Meridian, though I doubt Stan realized he was walking from one half of the world into the other, and present-day ramblers only know by the notice on the pavement. They continue across country, bypassing Barley with its smart wooden lock-up on the village green, and head for the Heydon Ditch, one of the many dykes between here and Norfolk which straddle the Icknield Way. The Path turns to follow the Ditch to Heydon, but Stan would have kept on towards Ickleton – where else?

The Romans did a lot of roadbuilding in this area, and one road passed through the tiny village of Strethall, not far from the Way. Strethall is unusual for having no war memorial; it was one of only thirty-odd villages in the whole country which suffered no casualties in the two World Wars. It is also notable for the story of Nehemiah Perry of Strethall Manor, who shot and killed a gypsy attempting to burgle his house, and put the body on show in the church belfry, charging visitors threepence a look. Afterwards he sent it to Cambridge for dissection – in a game basket. I doubt Nehemiah would get away with that sort of thing today, but in 1849 nobody argued with the squire.

Strethall is still surrounded by open country, but Ickleton is surrounded by traffic, and these days Stan would have great difficulty in reaching it. It lies inside a square of roads and railways, with the main railway line to London on one side, the busy road from Cambridge to Chesterton on another, and the M11 motorway with its spur to the A11 forming the other two. Yet somehow it has managed to preserve the peaceful atmosphere of a traditional English village inside this stockade of fast-moving traffic; only the continuous hum from the motorway is a reminder of the hectic world outside.

In Stan's time the Icknield Way – the motorway of the Stone Age – went through the middle of the village, crossing the River Cam where a footbridge and ford still exist today. The traffic increased considerably when the Romans arrived and built a vast military station just across the river at Great Chesterford, with its accompanying road to London. There was local traffic too between the camp and a large villa on the edge of Ickleton itself, which may have been the headquarters of the station commander; it had a basilica, a sort of office block, where his staff could have worked. Ickleton, in fact, was very busy indeed, and apart from that distant hum it probably has less traffic now than at any time since Stan arrived on the Icknield Way.

The Way joins the Roman road, later the A11, at Stump Cross, which is still a busy roundabout today. Stan could have followed the A11 all the way to Newmarket, but I have driven that road so many times, and it is so excessively boring, that I prefer to think he took a parallel track through Linton, which is on the site of an Iron Age settlement and could easily have existed in Stan's day too. It also has a zoo, which might make him feel at home. What might comfort him still further is the milestone in Balsham, the next village along this route, which says 'Ridgeway 63' in one direction and 'Peddars Way 43' in the other. This is, of course, a very modern milestone (1992, in fact) but he would be relieved to know that he was on the right track — or at any rate one of the right tracks, the one selected by the Icknield Way Association.

Even so, he was wise not to be in Balsham in the wrong era, say about AD 1010, when the entire population was massacred by the Danes. The village sign depicts one of the locals defending himself in the doorway of the church. The actual church doorway bears the inscription: 'Ye shall keep My Sabbath and reverence My sanctuary', but I assume His sanctuary has not been reverenced enough, because, unfortunately for the Saxon defender and for present-day visitors, the door is kept locked.

Whichever route Stan took towards the Suffolk border, the A11 or Linton and Balsham, he could not have avoided, in later times, the Devil's Dyke. It extends from what used to be fenland at Reach to what used to be forest at Woodditton, completely spanning the belt of open chalkland which was the only access to East Anglia. It is now a Long Distance Footpath in its own right, and where it has been breached by the six-lane Newmarket bypass, walkers can cross in safety on a new concrete footbridge. They will then find themselves alongside Newmarket racecourse, where the

The Danes massacred everyone in Balsham, down to the last villager.

Devil's Dyke once blocked the Icknield Way; now it is a public footpath.

The packhorse bridge at Moulton, a later timepath which has also had its day.

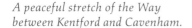

A peaceful stretch of the Way between Kentford and Cavenham.

Dyke provides a natural grandstand overlooking the track.

If Stan were following the scenic route on the Icknield Way he would have mounted a rise near Stetchworth and then descended to Cheveley. The Devil's Dyke runs along that rise, and on each side of the track Stan would have taken is this raised, wooded path, with a deep ditch on the southern side.

This was probably the main line of defence for the Iceni after Boadicea's onslaught on the Romans had finally been repulsed and they were driven back into Norfolk. Many Iceni coins and artefacts have been found on their own side of the Dyke, and very few on the southern side, but I am not sure if that was good news or bad news. Does it mean that none of the Iceni was caught on the wrong side of the Dyke, or did the Romans breach it, catch them all before they could retreat, and tell them to empty their pockets?

Either way it would not have bothered Stan, for whom the Dyke did not exist. He may have followed one of the tracks into Newmarket, but the town is still very congested in spite of the bypass and I prefer to think he kept to the pleasant paths and lanes which now lead to Moulton. Its picturesque packhorse bridge would be another mystery for Stan, who had not yet seen a packhorse, let alone a packhorse bridge, but today it is just history, another timepath which is almost as difficult to trace.

The Icknield Way Path diverts through Dalham, which has lots more bridges – little footbridges linking the main street with the adjoining cottages. Both routes, the old and the new, converge on Kentford, where the Ordnance Survey recognizes once again, after a long gap, the existence of the Way. Its name is on an innocuous-looking lane running from Kentford to Cavenham, and beyond it is the familiar-sounding village of Icklingham.

I can hardly leave Kentford without mentioning the gypsy boy's grave, a strange survival of a more heartless era, though Stan might consider it rather tame. The boy was accused of sheepstealing and, rather than face the customary penalty of transportation, he hanged himself. As a suicide he was buried at a crossroads, and there the story might have ended, but strangely there have always been fresh flowers on his grave – or at least, in recent times, plastic ones. They are put there, it is assumed, by travelling gypsies, and local legend has it that during Epsom Week the flowers are in the colours of the Derby winner – but I wouldn't bet on it…

Cavenham, at the other end of the lane, offers nothing as romantic. It looks a typical estate village, neat but unexciting, and Stan I am sure would have hastened on to Icklingham across the Temple Bridge, which was once on the old London to Norwich road but is a lot quieter now.

Icklingham has had such an eventful history since Stan was there that the designer of the village sign had quite a job to pack it all in. Boadicea passed this way, and so did the Romans, so they have a place on it. The Temple Bridge is there, and Icklingham Mill, recorded in the Domesday Book. The village has two parish churches, so they both had to go on it too. And suspended in the middle is the head of Archdeacon Sudbury, whose decapitated ghost is said to haunt the area.

The sign is outside All Saints' Church, redundant now but far more interesting than St James's down the road, which was over-zealously restored by the Victorians. All Saints' still has a thatched roof, and there are more reeds inside, in the form of tussocks, forerunners of the present-day hassock. Most of the church is fourteenth century and still looks it, with a bare tiled floor (except for the tussocks), simple benches, and a splendid old ironbound chest from the same period. The church is kept locked these days, but happily the key is not far away.

The most notable event in Icklingham's recent history occurred too late to be included in the village sign, but there might be just enough space to add a bronze cheetah studded with silver. This was the prize item in the Icklingham Treasure, discovered on a local farm in the 1980s and mysteriously removed to the United States – to the considerable chagrin of the farmer, who has been trying to get it back ever since. The Treasure consisted of priceless bronzes dating back to the second century, left there by the Roman colonists long after Boadicea had come and gone. But there have also been earlier finds, from the Iron Age and beyond, and it is not too difficult to extend Icklingham's history back to the Icknield Way. Perhaps Stan should have a place on that sign too.

The modern Icknield Way Path actually passes through the farm where the Treasure was found, but don't expect to sneak off with any more, because the farmer keeps a very

Temple Bridge at Icklingham on the old London road, now just another timepath.

Icklingham's sign has two churches, the bridge, the mill, the Romans – the lot!

The 'Saxon village' at West Stow, reconstructed beside the Icknield Way.

sharp lookout. As a consolation you can positively wallow in local history if you continue into the West Stow Country Park and visit its reconstructed Saxon village. The neat wooden huts would look too sophisticated and futuristic for Stan's taste, but they do provide a reminder that a great many people passed this way and lived in these parts a very long time ago.

The next section of the Icknield Way runs through forest, but not the kind of forest that Stan would recognize, and indeed it was only planted sixty-odd years ago. When Stan was trudging along the Way this was primitive farmland, one of the outlying settlements around Thetford which were the first indication that he was nearing the end of his journey. The legacy of those early farmers was a vast sandy heath which came to be known as Breckland, inhabited almost entirely by rabbits. Lakenheath Warren, for instance, which lies in Breckland, was one of the largest and oldest warrens in England. For 600 years it was owned by the Bishops of Ely, who were thus ensured a steady supply of rabbit pies.

Today Lakenheath Warren is mostly an American air base, and the rest of Breckland is mostly forest, thanks to the arrival in 1922 of the Forestry Commission. They have created the largest lowland forest in the country, 50 000 acres, and the Icknield Way passes through a corner of it, known as the King's Forest because it was planted to commemorate George V's silver jubilee. Long lines of conifers are not to everyone's taste, but Thetford Forest offers picnic spots and nature trails and a variety of other species, much appreciated by the locals. Would it be the same, they wonder, if it was privatized? They are fairly sure of the answer.

Once out of the King's Forest the Icknield Way and the Icknield Way Path diverge, much to the irritation of some members of the Icknield Way Association who want the Path to stay on the original route to Thetford. Instead it veers off to the east to finish at Knettishall Heath Country Park, where the ingenious planners of Long Distance Paths have arranged for three of them to converge. Two of them, the Icknield Way and Peddars Way, are variations on ancient routes; the third is an unashamed invention of the 1980s, called the Angles Way, which heads off along the Waveney Valley to join another modern path, the Weavers Way.

Without a doubt there were Angles in the vicinity of Angles Way, and Norfolk's medieval weavers must have wandered near the Weavers Way, but neither route has any historical foundation. It all adds to the confusion between ancient and modern, attaching historical names to twentieth-century routes. Happily the fourth Long Distance Path in Norfolk, which links Peddars Way with Weavers Way, is called simply the Coastal Path; what a relief that nobody remembered the early invaders along that coast and called it Vikings Way…

While all the happy hikers head for Knettishall Heath, Stan the Stone Age Man almost certainly went to Thetford. To be fair once again to the Icknield Way Association, the route he took now involves private land with no public rights of way, so even the devotees have to divert a little before rejoining it at the Nuns Bridges, near the confluence of the Thet and the Little Ouse. The town that grew up there took its name from the Thet, perhaps because it sounded more progressive and lively than Little Ouseford. Since the last war Thetford has become very progressive and lively indeed, thanks to the influx of thousands of Londoners in one of the early post-war overspill schemes, and much of the old town is now quite unrecognizable.

The Nuns Bridges, however, have survived. They were built too late to help Stan, who had to splash through both rivers with his sledge, but they mark a crossing which has been used since his day, and the nuns themselves were there 800 years ago. They lived just along the Way in a monastery which they took over in 1176. The monks had been there for 150 years before that, but when the river silted up and trade dwindled, the monastery experienced the medieval equivalent of a recession, and economy cutbacks reduced them to two. In what must have been a bitter admission of defeat they packed their bags and let the women have a go – and the women ran the place very successfully until they came up against a problem much worse than a recession: Henry VIII.

The nunnery was dissolved, along with all the others, but remarkably the Conventional Church of St George, built by the nuns, survived, and it is now the headquarters of the British Trust for Ornithology, fitting successors to those wise old birds of the twelfth century.

The story of the nunnery is comparatively recent history

The Way passes through Thetford Forest – but the forest is fairly recent.

OVERLEAF *The Nuns Bridges at Thetford, where the Way forded the rivers to enter Norfolk.*

Thetford Castle Mound: was it a passport control centre on the Icknield Way?

for Thetford. The evidence of a much earlier age is just across the Nuns Bridges, a massive earthworks which is the largest in East Anglia and second only to Silbury Hill in Wiltshire, at the far end of the Ridgeway. Its origins are equally obscure. Personally I favour the local legend that, after the Devil had dug his Dyke at Newmarket, he jumped to Thetford, spun round on one foot while deciding where to dig next, and created the earthworks with his heel. Maybe his next leap took him to Silbury Hill…

The experts are sceptical about this, but for many years they could not agree on an alternative. Some said the earthworks had been built by the Celts, others favoured the Romans, or the Saxons, or the Danes. Even Oliver Cromwell got a few votes. The Normans confused the issue by building a motte and bailey castle on the same site. In the 1960s, however, excavations showed that the site had been occupied in the Iron Age, and it was decided that the ramparts date back to that era.

I like to think, however, if I have to eschew the Devil's heelmark theory, that had those excavations gone a little deeper they might have found the flint tools and axes left behind by Stan's contemporaries. After all, Thetford was a thriving agricultural and mining area in the Stone Age, and they would have been as keen to guard that ford as the Iron Age men and the Normans who came after them. Maybe this was the original passport control centre for the Icknield Way…

Once across the two rivers – and safely through customs – Stan had two or three choices of route. The experts say that the Icknield Way divided at this point; one branch headed towards Norwich, the other followed the chalk line to the Wash – the line which was followed much later by the Roman Peddars Way. In 1990 a member of the Icknield Way Association, who belonged to the pro-Thetford, anti-Knettishall Heath lobby, traced the old Icknield Way alongside the Peddars Way, until he was thwarted by the Stanford Battle Area, which has been closed to the public since the Second World War. He did note, however, that Ickburgh, on the edge of the Area, must be another Icknield Way derivation.

I prefer to believe that Stan took neither of these routes, because he had not come all this way just to enjoy a swim at Old Hunstanton or view the future site of Norwich

Cathedral. He had slogged along the Icknield Way with his sledge-load of samples to swop them for axes and knives, and he would have aimed for the flint mines we know as Grimes Graves.

The name is confusing to visitors. They are inclined to ask who Mr Grime was and why did he need so many graves. But 'graves' just meant hollows, and Grim was another name for the Anglo-Saxon god Woden, the same Grim whose name they gave to Grimsditch in Oxfordshire. When the Saxons came upon the disused mines, many centuries after they had been abandoned, they assumed that Grim had been busy with his shovel again, and Grimes Graves was the result.

So if the head flintknapper at the mines was not Mr Grime, who was he? I have a theory about this, and the nice thing about theories involving the Stone Age is that nobody can be absolutely certain they are wrong. It is based on the fact that our medieval forefathers often took their names from the jobs they did, which is why we have so many Millers and Carters and Smiths. Suppose they did the same thing in much earlier times, even in the Stone Age, when there might have been families of Shepherds, and Hunters, and Cooks?

The boss at the flint mines could have been called Knapper, of course, but Knapper hardly creates an image of get-up-and-go, and he may well have preferred a name with a little more gravitas, appropriate to his position. The job of a knapper, he may have argued, was to take each piece of flint and adapt it for new uses. He doctored, in fact, the living stone.

And thus it transpired that when Stanley completed his epic journey along the Icknield Way, having penetrated unknown territory and faced all manner of dangers and hardships, he was greeted at this remote settlement by none other than the Stone Age equivalent of Doctor Livingstone.

Or so I presume.

THE FOSSE WAY

The Long March
with Len the Roman Legionary

PREVIOUS PAGES *The Fosse Way in Somerset. The straight part is Roman, the curves came later.*

O N THE ROAD MAPS OF ENGLAND it looks as though someone has taken a rule and drawn a diagonal line from Devon to Lincolnshire. There are gaps in it here and there, where the main road has become a track or a green lane, but it is the same straight line which was drawn by the Roman road engineers in AD 47. This is the Fosse Way, perhaps the best known of the roads they left behind, because it was not just a road but a boundary, in the early days of the Roman occupation, between the conquered province of Britannia and the still unruly inhabitants of Cornwall, Wales and the North-west.

In spite of that much-quoted *'Veni, vidi, vici!'* – 'I came, I saw, I conquered!' – it has nothing whatsoever to do with Julius Caesar. He certainly came, in 55 BC and again a year later, but on the first occasion all he saw was the English coastline, because he never came ashore, and in 54 BC he only saw Kent and the countryside around London. Even that was not exactly conquered; he just rampaged around for a while, imposed a tribute on the local king – which was never paid – and went back to Gaul.

It was the Emperor Claudius who did the serious con-
quering, nearly a hundred years later. A jolly little jingle
which used to be popular in junior history lessons gives a
better idea of what happened:

> BC 55 and BC 54,
> *Julius came and did nothing much more.*
> *But Claudius came in AD 48*
> *And created Britannia, a real Roman state.*

Well, not quite. Perhaps AD 48 was selected to rhyme with 'state'. It should have read:

> *But Claudius came in AD 43*
> *And 'Veni, vidi, vici!' – yes, it was he.*

Claudius landed 40 000 men along the Kent coast, fought his way north to capture Colchester, the most important town in Britain, and in the next four years conquered all the territory as far as a line from Lincoln and Newark in the north to Bath and Axminster in the south – the line along which he built the Fosse Way.

It was a line of communication inside a buffer zone up to 30 miles wide, with military stations spaced out along it, which in later years made it a happy hunting ground for archaeologists. In fact the Fosse Way is probably the best researched and documented road in England. Nevertheless there are two features of it which still baffle the experts. Where exactly does it start at the southern end; and how did it get its name?

The name, of course, is not a Roman one. There are only two or three Roman roads in England with Roman names, such as the Via Devana which crosses the Icknield Way in Cambridgeshire, and archaeologists are very scathing about them. 'These Latin names are spurious classicisms of modern origin', wrote one, 'and though useful as labels are perhaps to be regretted as misleading.'

No, genuine Roman road names are all terribly British – or, more accurately, terribly Saxon. In the days of Edward the Confessor the four main roads of England were named as Watling Street, the Fosse Way, Hicknild Street (the updated version of the prehistoric Icknield Way) and Ermine Street. The 'Street' was the only Roman connection, coming from *via strata* (paved street), and all along the Fosse Way there are Strettons, and Stratfords, and just plain Street. But why Fosse?

The same expert who was so sour about the Via Devana merely comments: 'The uncertainty of name is a curious characteristic of British Roman roads. We do not know what names, if any, the roads bore in Roman times, and the origin of these Saxon terms for them is quite unknown.'

Really, these archaeology types give up too easily. The Fosse Way had forts along it; how about Forts Way being corrupted into Fosse Way? But my own theory is that a Saxon heard two Romans discussing how the Way was built to frustrate the rebels on the far side. Frustrate, to a Saxon ear, could well sound like Fosse Street…

Of course that expert might just possibly be wrong, and Fosse simply comes from *fossa*, the Latin word for ditch; but that rather spoils the fun.

The second riddle, over the starting point in Devon, is more tricky. On the Roman maps it starts somewhere on the estuary of the River Axe, but the experts are divided between Colyton on one side of the river, and Axmouth on the other. In Roman times the estuary was much wider and the river was much deeper, so a Roman galley could reach either.

Curiously, neither place lays claim to any Roman connection in its publicity brochures. Colyton admits it has only existed since Saxon times, and certainly its Saxon credentials are impeccable. It had a Saxon minster, the Saxon Parliament once met there, and the streets are laid out in a circular design, the classic Saxon defence pattern. But that was after the Romans had come and gone.

Axmouth is much vaguer about its origins, but it lies beneath Hawkesdown Hill, where Bronze and Iron Age relics have been found and an earthworks overlooked the estuary. If those early Britons used that side of the river, I bet the Romans did as well. So Axmouth has my vote, and if the Romans returned today, I think they would go for it too.

A Roman soldier standing in the bows of a troop-carrier galley – let's call him Len the Legionary – would be surprised to find that the mouth of the river is now narrow enough to be spanned by quite a small bridge – one of the oldest concrete bridges, incidentally, in the country, but nothing like those grim modern structures over the motorways. His galley would have no chance of getting under that, and Len would have to trans-ship to one of the little yachts which now moor in the estuary by the dozen.

His next shock would be Seaton. Seaton was created in Victorian times as a health resort, and it has changed very little since, except for the camping and caravan sites. From its appearance it seems to have no claims to any historical significance whatsoever, but one reference book does name it as the Roman ferry terminal.

A legionary's view across the Axe of a later, quainter timepath – the Seaton Tramway.

'The Fosse begins at Seaton,' it says categorically, and supports the claim by noting that a tile of the Second Legion was found there – 'which indicates that the Legion once lay there in more or less permanent quarters'. A rather sweeping deduction, I would have thought; does one tile make a garrison? I prefer to think it was dropped there by a Roman builder, on his way to Axmouth...

Seaton does have one indisputable claim to fame, however, described succinctly in its brochure as 'Britain's only open-top narrow-gauge double-decker trams in daily service'. The Seaton Tramway is to trams what the Romney Hythe & Dymchurch is to railways: a scaled-down period piece heavily reliant on fine weather for the comfort of its passengers. It trundles along the riverbank to Colyton, and Len would get a good view of it as he sailed up the Axe – not to Colyton, I maintain, but to Axmouth.

I found final confirmation in a *Reader's Digest* gazetteer. 'Axmouth', it says, 'stands at the southern end of the Fosse Way, the great Roman road which bisected England from Lincoln to Devon.' If the *Reader's Digest* says so, it must be true. And with all respect to Colyton and Seaton, Axmouth is a much prettier place; Len the Legionary would have loved it. So he and I are agreed; Axmouth is where he disembarked and set off along the Fosse Way – and that is where I began my journey too.

AFTER ALL THAT EFFORT establishing the first stage of the route, I have to confess there is not a lot more to say about it. There is no hint of a Roman road as the lane climbs inland up the wooded hills, crosses the main coast road and continues through open country to Axminster. The only village it passes through, Musbury, has two modest claims to fame, both of them rather obscure. It was the seat of the Drake family for 300 years – but not of Sir Francis himself, these were his cousins. And Ashe House, just outside the village, is said to be the birthplace of John Churchill, first Duke of Marlborough – except that the original house was burnt down in the Civil War, just before he was born, and the rebuilt house was also burnt down in 1778, so his connection with the present one is pretty tenuous. But at least Musbury can say it is on the Fosse Way – we think…

In Axminster we are on much firmer ground. Everybody knows what Axminster is famous for, and Len the Legionary would be particularly impressed by the parish church, probably the only one in England to have wall-to-wall Axminster carpeting. The industry was brought to the town by Thomas Whitty in 1775, and his factory was just by the church. When each carpet was finished the church bells were rung in celebration – or perhaps in anticipation, since in due course the church got one for itself.

The Fosse Way disappears into Axminster's one-way system, and emerges in the unmistakable straight line which leads all the way to Lincoln. At Weycroft there is a slight kink in the existing road to negotiate a railway, but you can just make out the line of the original Roman road on each side of the bridge. Weycroft is not a name that Len would recognize; in his day it was called Stratford, and very logically too, since this is where the *strata* forded the River Axe. But maybe the locals got fed up with redirecting Shakespeare's mail, and being besieged by confused tourists.

I suppose there must be a sound reason behind the choice of the new name. Wey could derive from Way, and the local farmer could have had Scottish antecedents. But try explaining that to Len the Legionary…

A few miles beyond ex-Stratford the main road turns towards Chard, but the Fosse Way continues straight along a B-road to join the main A30 at Windwhistle Hill, a name which needs no explanation. Then it passes Cricket St Thomas, which probably does. Cricket St Thomas is a thousand-acre estate, and although the name is evocative of village greens and 'Are there scones for tea?', the estate is given over to llamas and bison rather than legbreaks and bouncers. It is in fact a wildlife park, and Len might spot some familiar animals from more southern climes. It is also the headquarters of the National Heavy Horse Society, the sort which must have pulled Len's supply waggons along the Fosse Way.

From the top of Windwhistle Hill, so the local pundits say, you can see north to the British Channel and south to the sea. I had a good look and couldn't see either, but maybe Len would have had keener eyes than mine.

The Fosse Way leaves the A30 at Higher Chillington, and

The Fosse Way is now a modern main road at the aptly-named Windwhistle Hill.

The Fosse dives into a cutting near Dinnington; early trench warfare, or just erosion?

Still well hidden – and one-way traffic only for the Roman legions.

gets involved in a succession of hills and valleys which make it zig-zag about a bit in a most un-Roman fashion. When it reaches Dinnington it does something which, according to one Fosse buff, no other Roman road does, anywhere in England. It drops into a deep and narrow cutting, about 30 feet below ground level, and continues like this for a couple of miles, with the trees almost meeting overhead.

The odd thing about this is that Roman roads are always built up, not down. The Romans knew all about drainage, and they made embankments for their roads, sometimes of earth, but on their more superior roads – the ones you might call Fosse-class? – with layers of stones. The embankments could be extremely high, and might have been useful as a defence line as well as a road. They were called *aggers*, a word which, like the Fosse, might be associated with this object of irritating the locals. As well as Fosse-strating them, they agger-avated them…

Large or small, broad or narrow, the agger was an integral part of the Roman road. Yet here at Dinnington the Fosse Way plunges virtually underground, and continues in this surreptitious fashion until it reaches – yes, of course – Overstratton. Was this an area of particularly unfriendly natives, I wonder, where the Roman conquerors felt it was wise to keep their heads well down? Or did a trainee road engineer just get the plans upside down? Only Len the Legionary could tell us – and at this stage he would be too busy hoping he didn't meet another legion marching the other way. It really is a very narrow lane.

If you stay in this curious cutting you may never notice that you are passing Hinton St George, which would be a pity. It is one of my favourite villages, built in the warm golden stone that typifies the area, and well away from main roads – except, of course, the Fosse Way. Maybe that was why the Romans decided to go underground – so they didn't spoil the view.

There is another possibility which I rather prefer. They may have heard about the eerie goings-on at Hinton St George on the anniversary of the Chiselborough Fair – known in the village as Punkie Night. The menfolk failed to return from the Fair at the expected hour, and the women went in search of them, carrying hollowed-out mangolds containing candles to light their way. On Punkie Night the children make similar lanterns and carry them through the village, collecting money and singing the Punkie Song, 'It's Punkie Night tonight!'

It all sounds very reminiscent of pumpkins on Hallowe'en, but the celebration is unique to Hinton St George. It all happened long after the Romans passed that way, of course, but maybe they had a premonition that the womenfolk would be on the prowl with their punkies, and decided to stay well out of sight.

After all this excitement the Fosse Way emerges on to the main A303 road from Ilminster to Ilchester – though it does so with some difficulty, since a house and garden have been built right across it. On Petherton Bridge there used to be the effigies of what looked like two children, and the story developed that they had been drowned at that spot. On closer inspection, however, they were thought to be two grown people, broken off at the knees, and an alternative legend was created that they were the founder and his wife of the nearby chapel at Stoke-sub-Hamdon, whose effigies were said to 'repose in stone on a stone pillow'. Alas, the bridge has been rebuilt to accommodate the fast dual carriageway, and I found no trace of any effigies, either feckless or legless.

In Stoke-sub-Hamdon itself there does still exist a curious relic of the past. When the game of fives was introduced into England the only basic requirement was a large flat wall. Church towers came in very handy, and it is said the locals played fives against the tower of Montacute Church, just up the road, until a less liberal Rector had a chunk of stone dumped against it to spoil the fun. But there is still an original custom-built fives wall at Stoke-sub-Hamdon, an elegant affair with a curved top and an ornamental stone ball on each corner.

The Hamdon which Stoke is under is Hamdon Hill, and Len the Legionary may have climbed it to enjoy a picnic, because Roman pottery has been unearthed on it. But as the Fosse Way approaches Ilchester the land gets flatter, and the agger is substantially higher than the surrounding fields. Archaeologists have delved into it, and under the modern road they found a 5-inch layer of stones on top of 3 inches of flint and gravel, and some of the flints which were used to surface it. Len might have had a nostalgic march on it before it was all buried again.

Ilchester was once the county town of Somerset, but it is

The Fosse Way is halted to make way for the Ilchester bypass.

difficult to imagine it today, particularly since the bypass was built and took away much of the traffic. But for several centuries the county gaol was in the town, the sovereign's judges made regular visits, and the magistrates held their courts there. Unfortunately the magistrates decided that the town's inns were not up to their expectations and in 1846 took their courts elsewhere. The gaol had already been closed, and that was that. If the *Good Hotel Guide* had existed in 1846 the inns might have pulled their socks up, the magistrates might have stayed, and Ilchester might still be the county town. Strange how the course of history can be changed by a plate of soggy vegetables or an un-aired bed...

In Len's day there was first a military station, then a substantial town which he knew as Lindinis. Over forty decorated mosaic floors have been uncovered, and all manner of pottery and tools. It was a busy, bustling town, one of the few along the Fosse Way which is probably quieter now than when Len the Legionary passed through.

Ilchester High Street, once on the Fosse Way, is now a dead end, which Len might find confusing. He would still feel at home in the museum, however, where some of his contemporary crockery is preserved. He would also recognize the writing on a more recent relic in the Town Hall, a reminder of its more illustrious days. Ilchester possesses the oldest staff of office in England, a thirteenth-century mace. The Latin inscription on it reads: 'I am a Mark of Amity. Do not forget me (or give me away).' When I was there the mace on show was actually a replica, but the inscription had not been ignored; the original was not given away, just on loan to Taunton Museum.

If Len wandered off the Way for a mile he would be brought into the twentieth century with a jolt. Yeovilton is the home of the Fleet Air Arm Museum, which has *Concorde 002*, one of our most spectacular achievements in modern travel, and about as far from the Fosse Way as you can get.

The Way now runs through open country for 10 miles or more along the A37 main road, which makes a detour at Charlton Adam while the Fosse continues as an overgrown track and rejoins the road after half a mile. An earlier explorer records that he followed this original route, 'and that half-mile gave me a very pleasant walk along a grass-grown lane between elms and hazels, a lane that I shared with innumerable rabbits.' He would have a problem getting along it today; the rabbits have it to themselves.

The next bend in the road is at Wraxall Hill, where it zig-zags to make the steep climb, and the Romans may have done much the same. Then old and new road run parallel until they converge again on Pye Hill, and the line goes straight ahead to Beacon Hill, on the far side of Shepton Mallet. The main road leaves it after a while, and the Fosse Way continues as a minor road, then a track, then little more than a line of dots on the map. It passes through Street on the Fosse, which by now needs no explanation, and Cannards Grave, which is explained in various ways, depending on whom you happen to meet in the hostelry named after it, and how many beers they have consumed.

Mr Cannard may have been an innkeeper who murdered travellers in their beds for their money; but in that case, why is his grave commemorated and not those of his vic-tims? Or did they get their own back in the end? Another theory is that he was a smuggler who was killed for betray-ing his comrades – but what would they find to smuggle in the vicinity of Shepton Mallet? More likely he was a foot-pad or some other miscreant who was hanged at the scene of his crimes, as footpads and miscreants were wont to be. But even that version of Cannard's Grave may be, well, just a canard.

When the Fosse Way reduces to a track for the climb up Beacon Hill it is easier for the fainthearted to take the main road through Shepton Mallet, a pleasant town with one of the most unassuming fifteenth-century relics in the busi-ness. It looks more like a bus shelter than a relic, with what could be a seat under its tiled roof. Actually it is all that is left of the Shambles, the town's meat market, and the 'seat' was in fact the table on which the butcher lined up his pig's trotters and venison steaks, 500 years ago.

To reach Beacon Hill you take the Radstock road out of town and turn right along what seems a fairly innocuous lane, but it was once an ancient Way running along the top of the Mendip Hills from Wiltshire to the Bristol Channel. It was a main line of communication long before Len arrived, and the Romans made good use of it too when the imperial lead mines were established at Charterhouse, near the Cheddar Gorge. All the lead had to be transported along

From Pye Hill the Fosse makes a beeline for Beacon Hill, beyond Shepton Mallet.

OPPOSITE *The Fosse is abandoned by modern road builders beyond Brecon Hill and reverts to a green lane.*

this road, either to join the Fosse Way or to continue across it to Salisbury and beyond. Beacon Hill must have been a busy crossroads at that time, and the lead waggons must have been quite a hazard for high-speed charioteers.

It was a significant site again in the eighteenth century, when a beacon was erected on the summit of Beacon Hill – what was it called before, I wonder? – as a guide for ships at sea. The nearest sea is about 25 miles away, and I can't help thinking there must have been a simpler way of guiding mariners – particularly shortsighted ones.

The beacon has long since disappeared – not, I trust, at the cost of too many shipwrecks – and the crossroads are hardly a traffic hazard today. The Fosse Way continues as a track down the other side of the hill, while the lane just goes from nowhere in particular to Cranmore, which was also nowhere in particular (except for the people who lived there) until in recent years it became the headquarters of the privately-owned East Somerset Railway. The line used to go to Shepton Mallet, crossing the Fosse Way near Cannards Grave, so maybe the poor chap was merely hit by a train. That section of the line is now as defunct as he is, but there is enough track left at Cranmore to keep the steam buffs happy, and on Cranmore Station there is a sight to keep phone-box buffs happy too, if such a breed exists. It is the only surviving Vermilion Giant still on active service.

The Vermilion Giant, officially known as the K4, was an idea which started well, then fell away. It was a variation on the standard kiosk designed by Sir Giles Gilbert Scott in 1924. The Post Office engineers thought they could improve on Sir Giles, and enlarged the kiosk to take a letterbox and two stamp machines. But the man who had designed Liverpool Cathedral was hardly likely to slip up over a phone-box, and the engineers soon discovered the snags of their new improved formula.

Local authorities objected because the K4 was so big it blocked the pavement. Telephone users objected because when the stamp machine was being used, the noise interrupted their conversation. And stamp buyers objected because in wet weather the stamps stuck together inside the machines. Only fifty were made before the engineers cut their losses and took them out of production, their faces as red as the Vermilion Giants themselves.

The one at Cranmore was rescued by the chairman of the

railway, the wildlife artist David Shepherd, whose affection for elephants obviously extends to white ones. It was restored to its full vermilion glory, but there is a slight catch. When you put a coin in the box, you just hear Mr Shepherd's recorded voice, extolling the delights of his railway – and thanking you for your donation...

The Fosse Way track from Beacon Hill merges into the main Radstock road at Oakhill; the sight of a Fosse Cottage confirms you are back on the line again. The road makes one or two wiggles around Nettlebridge to negotiate the valley, whereas Len went straight down and up, then it straightens out in familiar style to Stratton-on-the-Fosse.

Len would find something of a novelty here, a stretch of the Fosse Way which has been 'traffic-calmed'. Little chicanes have been built into the road as it passes through the village, which would have been highly irritating for a charioteer in a hurry, but the locals are no doubt delighted, and it does enable modern drivers to admire the splendid buildings of Downside Abbey while they are waiting to get through.

Before the chicanery, if that is the word, the road was dug up for pipe-laying, and the archaeologists had another field-day. This time, under 20 inches of modern road and soil, they found a layer of cobbles about 9 inches thick. Hard going on Len's sandals, but a thorough job by the Roman engineers nonetheless.

From Stratton-on-the-Fosse the Way heads straight as ever into the built-up area between Midsomer Norton and Radstock, an area which fortunately it heads out of just as directly. It escapes from the terraced houses and the road itself to head across two deep valleys to the mining village of Clandown. Again the archaeologists got excited, because on the ridge between the valleys there is probably the best example of original untouched agger on the Fosse Way.

Even a non-expert must be impressed to see a stretch of Roman road which is almost unchanged since Len and his fellow-legionaries marched along it, some 1900 years ago. The embankment is about 3 feet high, 8 feet wide at the top and twice that width at the base. Inside, the diggers found layer after layer of stone paving, pebbles and rubble. It is more difficult to get to these days, via a bogus 'Fosseway' then up a steep footpath, but it is worth the climb if you want to feel a latter-day Len – and there is a fine view of Downside Abbey as a bonus.

Fosse Cottage, near Oakhill – a reminder that the Romans passed this way.

The Fosse Way rejoins the main road at Clandown, and they follow roughly the same line, with the road making a few wiggles to pass a reminder of another form of travel, the Titfield Thunderbolt Inn. Then the Way and the road combine again to make a bee-line for the environs of the first major stopping-place – or rather, watering-hole – on the route, the Roman religious spa of Aquae Sulis.

What is there left to say about Roman Bath? We already know more about it than the Romans knew themselves. For instance, when they found the three hot springs by a Celtic shrine to the local deity Sulis, and created their own religious complex of baths, theatre and temple, all they actually knew about the water was that it was hot, and holy. Now the experts tell us that it was originally ancient rain which fell on the Mendips about 8000 years earlier. It penetrated so deeply that it was warmed by the heat from the Earth's core and forced out again, at a constant temperature of 46.5° centigrade. In the largest spring alone it still bubbles out at the rate of a quarter of a million gallons a day, which must mean that, back in the Stone Age, you never went out in the Mendips without an umbrella.

We also know how much coinage was thrown into the Sacred Spring as offerings to the gods. I imagine no Roman would have had the nerve to fish it all out and count it. More than 12 000 coins have been recovered, spanning the entire Roman period – and not even the most inquisitive Roman could have known that, unless the last man to leave decided to have a quick tot-up before he turned out the light. Four of the coins were gold, which puts the Sacred Spring well ahead of the Trevi Fountain in the good-luck league.

The baths are still there to see, and although there is not much left of the Temple, the experts know enough about it to reconstruct it. Even the details of the altar have been discovered, down to the figures carved on the four cornerstones. And for me this is the most fascinating feature of Roman Bath, because one of those cornerstones is at the heart of an ancient mystery and a modern controversy. It was the one bearing the figures of Hercules and Apollo, and somehow it has found its way to the parish church at Compton Dando, a little village some 8 miles from Bath.

The official Roman Baths guidebook offers no explana-

Inscription in the Pump Room in York Street, Bath. It reads: 'These hot springs were used by the Romans as early as the first century. In area, in grandeur, in completeness, the baths of Aquae Sulis were unequalled. The remains of their magnificence are here disclosed.'

Part of a Roman altar from Bath on a buttress at Compton Dando; how, and why?

tions for this; it merely says the cornerstone is there, built into an external buttress of the church. I thought I detected a faint note of irritation in this rather curt statement, and when I went to Compton Dando I found I was right. In short, the Bath authorities have said in effect: 'Please can we have our cornerstone back?' – and Compton Dando has replied, very firmly, 'No, you jolly well can't.'

The village has only two claims to fame: its unusual name (corrupted from a fifteenth-century Lord of the Manor, Alexander de Alno) and its Roman cornerstone. It claims proudly that the church has the two oldest supporters of any church in the country, in the form of Hercules and Apollo, and it intends to hang on to them.

The church booklet offers two theories on how they got there. The first goes back to the twelfth century, when the Roman altar was uncovered in Bath after being buried since Saxon times. The Bishop of Bath was a very energetic chap, and a lot of church building took place in the area at that time. As the booklet puts it: 'It only needed an ecclesiastic with an eye for a bargain to whip away the stone as the Bishop's team laid it bare...'

Alternatively it may have been acquired when excavations took place at Bath in 1790. The Vicar of Compton Dando at that time may have had antiquarian leanings and managed to get hold of the cornerstone for his own church.

The argument between Bath and Compton Dando over the return of the cornerstone began in 1966 and has continued, on and off, ever since. The Spa Committee first approached the Bishop, but he said it was a matter for the parochial church council, and the council responded with a very firm 'No'. They did, however, encase the figures in glass to provide some protection from the elements. The glass is no longer there and I must say, when I visited Compton Dando, Hercules and Apollo were looking, literally, rather the worse for wear. The Spa Committee must feel the same, because recently they renewed their efforts to get them back, but Compton Dando is sticking to its guns – and its cornerstone.

'The majority opinion seems to come down firmly on the side of "what we have, we hold",' says the church booklet. 'There can never be actual proof that the stone was removed from Bath, but assuming that to be the case, as the evidence indicates, what a vast upheaval of antiquities there would be in the country if it was decided that all should be returned to their original sites!'

I am inclined to think they have a point, but I doubt that Len the Legionary would agree. I suspect he and his mates would be descending on Compton Dando before you could say Elgin Marbles…

The Fosse Way actually bypassed the original Roman city, which covered a comparatively small area of about 25 acres inside the city wall. But even in Roman times there was ribbon development, and houses filled the gap between the city and the Fosse Way, just as they do when bypasses are built today. Since then the town has extended right across the original route, so no one knows exactly where the Way crossed the River Avon, except that it was to the west of the old city. It is thought there was a fort at the crossing, and if Len had a few hours' leave, I suppose that is where he would have spent it. Bath itself, I imagine, was far too exclusive and sacred for a legionary to have a night out with the lads. So his only chance of a bath in Bath was a quick dip in the Avon.

The A4 road follows the Fosse Way alongside the river through the northern outskirts of the city, then the Way veers slightly to the left to climb the steep hill to Banner Down; a lane roughly follows its route. Today Len would be baffled by the radio mast on the summit, but the three-legged monument nearby might seem familiar to him; it does look vaguely prehistoric. Actually it is less than 150 years old, erected by the Victorians in 1858 on the spot where Somerset, Gloucestershire and Wiltshire used to meet, before bureaucracy invented the spurious county of Avon.

As he climbed the hill on his original march, Len may have glanced over his shoulder for a final view of the Roman city spread out beneath him, then he was off into open country again – now crossed by the Chippenham to Bristol road and the M4 motorway, with Colerne air base to provide aerial traffic too. A mile from the Way is Castle Combe, once named the prettiest village in England, and thus doomed for all eternity to be besieged by tourists. The bowfronted souvenir shops and olde worlde cafés in its picturesque high street are permanently obscured during the summer by anoraks and bare knees and Japanese cameras.

If you feel impelled to visit Castle Combe from the Fosse Way, do turn off that crowded street to pop into the church,

Post-Roman and pre-county of Avon: the Three Shires Stone on the Fosse Way near Bath.

because it contains one of England's ecclesiastical rarities, which most tourists miss. The font was carved in 1450 by an ingenious mason who provided a built-in stone bookrest. The guidebook calls it unique, which is always dangerous, but certainly I have seen no other like it. What a boon it must have been for parsons over the past five centuries, as they put their prayerbooks down and had both hands free to grapple with the babies; and what a fortune that mason would have made if he had put his font into mass production...

Len the Legionary would know none of this, of course. The main landmark for him would be the posting station at Nettleton Shrub, near the turn-off for Castle Combe. There is nothing to be seen of it now, but a mile further on there is the long barrow at Lugbury, which was there long before Len's day. Then comes that rather more recent creation, the M4, and the Fosse Way has to dive underneath it at Fosse Gate.

North of the M4 the Fosse becomes a track, the modern road veers right.

All the way from Bath it has been a pleasant lane, and for those who are interested in agger, there has been a lot of it about. At the M4, however, it leaves the road and becomes a track or a green lane, mostly overgrown and rather uninviting, nearly all the way to Cirencester. Those who have walked the Way in days long past have rhapsodized over this section, when it was a broad track 60 feet across, easily passable and rich in bluebells and songbirds and other rustic delights, but they would not wax so lyrical now.

However, the conservationists are fighting back, in the person of a Mr J. Rogers of Trowbridge Town Hall. Near Sherston, where the Fosse Way meets a lane and stays with it for a while, Mr Rogers erected a notice announcing that it would be closed for six months 'for repairs to surface of public footpath', known officially as Byway 37, Sherston Fosseway. The repairs were expected to take a year altogether, which is a long time to repair a footpath, so when it is finished – as indeed it may be by now – it should be restored to its former pastoral glory.

Meanwhile it is simpler to zig-zag back and forth along the lanes which cross the Fosse Way, and just stroll down the clearer sections. That means you also see some interesting villages which you would have missed on the Way. Sherston, for instance, was the home of two heroes, who lived eight centuries apart. The first was John Rattlebone, who defeated King Canute's army at the Battle of Sherston in 1016. He was much encouraged, I imagine, by the local rhyme which has been handed down over the years:

> *'Fight well, Rattlebone,*
> *Thou shalt have Sherston.'*
> *'What shall I with Sherston do*
> *Without I have all belongs thereto?'*
> *'Thou shalt have Wyck and Willesly,*
> *Easton Towne and Pinkeney…'*

It sounds like blackmail, but I hope he got them.

Rattlebone's effigy is in the church, and in the churchyard is a memorial to Sherston's other hero, George Strong. He fought in the Crimean War at the age of nineteen, and was one of the first soldiers to be awarded the Victoria Cross.

Along the road from Sherston to Malmesbury, via Easton Grey with its picturesque weir, there is a chance to walk the Fosse Way for about a mile, to where it crosses the River Avon, at this point just a modest stream. Remains of Roman foundations and tesselated pavements have been found near the crossing, and when a pipeline was laid across the river beside the existing footbridge, the remains of an ancient timber bridge were uncovered, which might just conceivably have been Roman. Only Len the Legionary could tell us for certain.

Where the Fosse Way crosses the lane from Malmesbury to Shipton Moyne it is actually metalled for a short distance, and beside it is a Water Board building which gets warm praise from an earlier rambler. 'It might be taken as a model of how to design an industrial building for the country,' he enthuses. 'It is in no way romantic and yet, though relatively new, it does not jar in the slightest.' In which case, as Water Board buildings go, it must indeed be unique.

Shipton Moyne has won an award for the county's best-kept village, but to me its most interesting feature is the name of the pub, The Cat and Custard Pot. The origin of it would be an ideal subject for *Round Britain Quiz*, where no doubt one of the experts would remember an incident in *Handley Cross*, by the Victorian writer R.S. Surtees – and what bookshelf is without it? – involving John Jorrocks,

Up hill and down dale, but the Fosse Way keeps straight on ...

Cockney grocer and hunting man. Mr Jorrocks sacked his huntsman for imbibing too freely, went hunting without him on Cat and Custard Pot Day, and still caught the fox. One side of the pub sign shows him twirling his cap in triumph, the other shows a cat with its head in a custard pot. And there the story ends.

What is not explained, however, is Cat and Custard Pot Day, an entry on the calendar which has completely escaped me. It has also escaped Dr Ebenezer Cobham Brewer, whose *Dictionary of Phrase and Fable* is my bible on such matters. He is a wealth of information on the Cat and Fiddle (trad. nursery rhyme), the Cat and Kittens (large and small pewter beer pots), and even the Cat and Mouse Act (popular name for the Prisoners Temporary Discharge for Ill-Health Act, 1913), but custard pots don't get a mention.

It is possible that Len the Legionary knew the answer, because the Romans certainly knew about custard. The first-century cook, Apicius, left a recipe for a very distinctive custard, involving not merely milk, eggs and sugar, but melted butter, wine, honey and stock – spiced with pepper, celery seed, thyme, sage and coriander. That would be quite a mixture to pour over a dish of fruit salad, but Apicius sensibly used it in a meat and vegetable casserole. Nevertheless he definitely called it custard, according to the English translation, so maybe a cat belonging to Len the Legionary caught his head in a pot of the stuff before he left home, and in a fit of nostalgia he asked for a hostelry to be named after it, just off the Fosse Way...

There are no other excitements until the Way reaches Fosse Gate, on a lane to Crudwell. At this point it looks no more than a wet wooded dip with a ditch, but some folk claim that the River Thames starts from here, and earlier visitors have got very worked up over this damp patch by the road.

Even the most devoted Wayfarer, even Len the Legionary himself, could not proceed along the Fosse Way much further, because it is blocked by Kemble Airfield. The station has been mothballed, but there is still no way through, and the Way can only be rejoined on the Tetbury-Cirencester road, at the curiously-named Jackamounts Bottom. What a wealth of unlikely legends one could devise for Mr Jackamount and his Bottom...

The road now follows the Fosse to Cirencester, past the

Thames Head Hotel, which needless to say is another claimant for the source of the Thames. It has a rather stronger case than the damp patch by the Crudwell road, because the Ordnance Survey says so too. But a great many watercourses run into each other to become the Thames, and there are as many sources as courses.

Unlike Bath, Cirencester has almost blotted out its Roman origins, except for the exhibits in its excellent Corinium Museum, but in Len's day it was the second largest city in Britain, a major military and residential centre at an important road junction. This was where the Fosse Way crossed Ermin Street, which ran from Gloucester to Silchester, and it was also the start of Akeman Street, going to St Alban's and London. How all these roads joined up has caused quite a debate among the experts, because the Fosse Way did not go straight across Ermin Street but joined it near the amphitheatre, then left it again about a mile down the road. Why did it make this apparently unnecessary sidestep?

One theory is that the Fosse Way was actually two separate roads, which were built independently and happened to meet at Cirencester. Even so, the road engineers must have known each other's activities; why veer away from each other? With their famous efficiency and their devotion to straight lines, they could hardly have missed each other by accident. I think they must have been rival contractors, who weren't on speaking terms, and avoided each other deliberately…

As Len marched into town the first thing he saw would have been the amphitheatre. He could hardly miss it, because it was one of the largest in Britain – almost a Roman Wembley Stadium. Today it is concealed behind a row of modern houses and cut off from the town by the ring road. The stone gateways and terracing, and the cobbled arena, have been grassed over, but it is still an impressive sight, and a Mecca for energetic dogs – or lazy dogs with energetic owners.

The amphitheatre is all that remains visible in Cirencester, apart from a short stretch of the town wall which is preserved in the Abbey grounds. Actually there was not as much of Cirencester to preserve as you might think from the area it covered. Much of it was unoccupied, and the Museum reckons the population was not more than 15 000. After the Romans left, it dwindled to 1000, and

Remnants of Cirencester's Roman wall; most of it provided hardcore for roads.

most of the buildings became derelict. The town prospered in medieval times through the wool trade, but in the Civil War the wooden buildings were burnt down and the remaining stone houses were later demolished and recycled for new buildings. The town walls provided excellent hardcore for roads.

So Len would not have the remotest idea where he was in Cirencester, unless he visited the Museum. Here he would find some of the splendid mosaics which were manufactured in the town, and reconstructions of Roman town house interiors. Neither, I suspect, would be very familiar to him, because legionaries only got as far as the tradesmen's entrance, but he might be intrigued, as I was, by the words carved on a piece of stone, one under the other: *ROTAS OPERA TENET AREPO SATOR*. They make a perfect acrostic, though the translation doesn't quite work: 'Arepo the sower guides the wheel carefully'.

To the average Roman this was just a clever combination of words, but to a Roman Christian it meant much more. Acrostics were used as secret codes when Christians were being persecuted, and this is assumed to be some sort of cryptic message. It is too cryptic for me, I fear, and I have no idea what Arepo was up to, but the acrostic is fascinating in its own right, as perhaps the first known example of a 'square word'.

On a more sombre note there are the tombs of two of Len's fellow soldiers, Genialis and Dannicus. They were a little before his time, because they died on active service during the very early days of the Roman occupation, before Cirencester was founded, but they would be a sobering reminder for him that there was more to being a legionary than just marching up and down the Fosse Way.

To cheer him up, I would show him one of Cirencester's more recent heirlooms, the enormous yew hedge which lines the road near the Museum, and forms the boundary of the Bathurst Estate. It is claimed to be the largest yew hedge in England, if not in Europe, and its annual clipping provides quite a tourist attraction, as well as bringing the traffic to a standstill. Athletic gardeners scramble about on ladders and scaffolding, in the horticultural equivalent of painting the Forth Bridge. If they are the same chaps who cut that vast acreage of undulating grass at the amphitheatre, they must have jobs for life.

OPPOSITE *Cirencester's amphitheatre, once a Roman Wembley Stadium, now a grassy mound.*

As Len marched off along the Fosse Way again he would probably be cursing those rival road contractors for giving him an extra couple of miles to cover on the Ermin Street sidestep but, as he climbed into the Cotswolds on what is now the A429 to Northleach, the scenery would soon be ample compensation if it looked anything like it does today. I suspect it did, because this area was selected by many rich Romans for their villas and farms. The Coln Valley, which the Fosse Way crosses about 6 miles outside Cirencester, had eight villas between the source of the river and the Thames at Lechlade (it was another of those courses for sources).

One of these villas, at Chedworth, was discovered in 1864 by a gamekeeper who was digging for a ferret and found paving and pottery instead. It is now one of the best known in the country, owned by the National Trust and documented down to the last fragment of mosaic. All the tourists turn up the valley at Fossebridge to visit it, but I also took the quiet lane on the other side of the Fosse Way, and I discovered why the Coln Valley was such a draw. Even today it is a sleepy, unspoilt little valley with a succession of sleepy, unspoilt little villages.

Colne St Dennis, Coln Rogers, Coln St Aldwyns – they are all delightful. Winson has an extra touch of charm; its village cricket team used to have the unique battlecry: 'Together Though Tired'. But it all ends abruptly at Bibury, which has undergone the same fate as Castle Combe, thanks to William Morris. 'The most beautiful village in England', he rashly wrote. It has never been the same since.

Meanwhile Len would still be slogging along the Fosse Way, straight as ever, towards another river valley, the Leach, and the town of Northleach. This was once overwhelmed by the traffic from London to South Wales but is now restored to its former peace, thanks to a bypass and the M4 motorway.

Actually in the Middle Ages Northleach was not peaceful at all; it was known throughout Europe as a wool centre, and the massive church with its 100-foot tower is a reminder of just how important it was. But there was nothing much there in Len's day, and the Fosse Way did not actually pass through it anyway.

Nor did it pass through Farmington or Cold Aston, but both little villages are only a mile off the route and worth a visit. Farmington has a much larger namesake in

The footings of Chedworth Roman villa; the house came rather later.

Connecticut, and between them they arranged a rather jolly little swap when Connecticut celebrated its 300th anniversary. The American Farmington provided a roof for the village pump, and in return a birdbath was despatched to America, made of oolite from what used to be the Fosse Quarry, just beside the Fosse Way.

Cold Aston's story is less straightforward. Originally it was just Aston; it only acquired the chilly half of its name in 1255, perhaps through some vagary in the weather, or by offending an influential visitor. In 1535 it became Aston Blank, and I can't even invent a reason for that. I did try to discover why they chose Blank, but I drew – yes, exactly.

However, some villagers preferred to be Cold rather than Blank – understandably, in my view – and for four centuries this tiny village preserved a dual identity. The Post Office called it Cold Aston, the Ordnance Survey called it Aston Blank, and on signposts it appeared as both. Eventually people got fed up with this confusing situation, and the matter was referred to higher authority. If the higher authority had been a Solomon it would surely have decreed that the village resumed its original name and became just plain Aston again (and indeed some atlases do refer to it that way) but officially it was ruled to be Cold Aston, and thus it has remained – on the whole – ever since.

Len missed all this confusion, of course, and indeed missed the villages too, but on the Fosse Way there is no avoiding what I think of as the Tourists' Trio with the Multi-barrelled Names: Bourton-on-the-Water, Stow-on-the-Wold and Moreton-in-Marsh. The first two are alongside the Way and the third lies right across it.

An earlier traveller once wrote: 'Who could resist turning aside at Bourton-on-the-Water to see the main street of the village with the little Windrush flowing along it under little arched stone footbridges, by a wide strip of grass set with poplars?'

Well, frankly, I could, largely because thousands of other people can't. The main street of the village is now clogged with cars, the little arched footbridges are festooned with sightseers, and picnickers bestrew the wide strip of what used to be grass. It is not so much Bourton-on-the-Water as Bourton-under-the-Tourist. Some enterprising brochure-writer finished it off by calling it 'The Venice of the Cotswolds': I think that Len the Legionary, who may have

Over the Cotswolds and still dead straight; the Fosse heads for Bourton-on-the-Water.

The Fosse crosses its most recent counterpart, the new section of the M40.

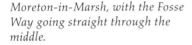

Moreton-in-Marsh, with the Fosse Way going straight through the middle.

known Venice, would have poked his eye out for that.

All that Bourton meant to Len was a bridge across the Windrush to march over, and perhaps the odd villa to march past. A Roman well and courtyard were found while digging the foundations for a bungalow, but the bungalow was built so rapidly that there was no time to uncover any more.

A little further along the Fosse Way, at Slaughter Bridge (which is not as gruesome as it sounds), another Roman road called Ryknild Street forked off to the north-west, and soon after that the Fosse also turns a few degrees to the north to make the steep climb to Stow-on-the-Wold, the highest town in the Cotswolds.

'Stow-on-the-Wold, where the wind blows cold…' Or, if you prefer: 'Stow-on-the-Wold, where the Devil caught cold…' The rhymes are recent, but no doubt the wind was pretty chilly on Len's bare knees as he reached the top of the hill. He would not have had the consolation of a warming drink at the King's Arms, as Edward VI did in 1548, nor the shelter of the church in which a thousand Royalists were imprisoned after one of Cromwell's victories. Stow St Edward, as it was originally known, only got going in the reign of Edward the Confessor – or so you would assume from the statue of King Edward in a niche on the Town Hall. The experts, however, point out that Edward the Confessor was not canonized until a hundred years after his death in 1066, and Stow was already called Stow St Edward in 1086. They reckon it was named after Edward the Martyr, who died in 978, in which case the chap in the niche is an imposter.

Whichever Edward it was, he came a long time after Len the Legionary, who left neither name nor statue. What he did leave behind, until quite recently, was a portion of the original paving of the Fosse Way, which was protected inside a railed enclosure until this century. Unfortunately it became something of a traffic hazard and was constantly being damaged, so the railings were removed and Nature allowed to take its course. Sorry about that, Len.

But at least it is downhill after Stow and only 4 miles to Moreton-in-Marsh. This is where the Fosse Way crosses a later Timepath, the stagecoach route from London to Aberystwyth, and there is more at Moreton to link with that era than with Len's. But the Romans did have a camp there when the Fosse Way was built, so it would have

offered him a rest and possibly a bed. Moreton-in-Marsh is
not, of course, marshy; the word should be March, not in
honour of Len and his fellow-marchers, but because it also
meant a boundary, and Moreton was the meeting point of
four counties.

For Len it was not only the chance of a wash and brush-
up, but also the end of the Cotswolds and the start of the
long haul through the Midlands. For the next 30 miles or so
the main road follows the straight line of the Fosse, through
good marching country but not very scenic for the more
leisurely traveller, who is inclined to put his foot down as a
result, except in Stretton on Fosse.

The main distinction of Stretton on Fosse is that it is yet
another Stretton or Stratton on the Fosse, but it also has the
merit that it does not lock its church, so I was able to read
the notice about the church repairs in 1841, for which it
received a grant from the church charity with the longest
initials in the business, the ISPEBRCC – the Incorporated
Society for Promoting the Enlargement, Building and
Repairing of Churches and Chapels. 'English Heritage' is a
lot simpler – EH?

At Halford the Fosse Way continues straight ahead as a
lane, while the main road and most of the traffic bears left to
Leamington Spa. The lane continues for the next twenty-
odd miles, going straight towards nowhere, it seems, until
you turn the page of your road map, beyond the M6 motorway, and sure enough, there in the distance is Leicester,
almost exactly in line with this lane.

For much of that 20 miles it never passes through a village, but if you have lunch in mind it is worth turning along
the Stratford upon Avon road – which Len would have recognized as a hill track – to visit the Chequers at Ettington. The
village also has a Victorian letter-box and a locked church,
and that's about it.

Each time the Fosse Way crosses a major road there are
large chevron boards, and the junction is staggered. These
are wise precautions, because this quiet lane is so straight
that drivers would be tempted to go flying straight across
the main roads. The lane is much senior in age, of course,
but that would hardly be an excuse in court.

At Chesterton Green there used to be a Roman station,
where Len could have stopped again for a breather. Today,
within sight of the road, there is a bizarre structure which

*Halford bridges, old and new,
successors to the Roman ford.*

has baffled travellers for centuries. Here's how one of them
described it:

> On the hill on my right a most
> extraordinary windmill showed. It
> looked like the lower half of a
> pillared water-tower with a
> mushroom-shaped metal top clapped
> hurriedly on it, and just under that
> the sails of the mill were pivoted –
> though there did not seem much room
> for the works between the top of the
> arches and the bottom of the roof. I
> heard afterwards that it started life
> as an observatory and only took to
> milling in later years.

He heard aright. The man responsible was Sir Edward
Peyto, whose family were Lords of the Manor for centuries.
Sir Edward held Warwick Castle against the Royalists in the
Civil War, and perhaps to celebrate his success he had this
curious edifice erected as an observatory; the sails were
indeed added later. Some say that Inigo Jones designed it,
but I doubt Mr Jones would be flattered at the suggestion.
However, Benedict Arnold must have liked it, because after
leaving his native Leamington Spa for America, he repro-
duced the design in the Old Stone Mill he built at Newport,
Rhode Island. I wonder if his neighbours assumed that all
English windmills looked that way…

A few miles further on, the Fosse Way crosses the Grand
Union Canal, then the road to Offchurch. This road is part
of another later Timepath, the drovers' road, and Offchurch
will feature in that.

At Eathorpe the direct line of the Fosse Way is blocked by
the grounds of Eathorpe Hall. The place is now deserted
except for guard dogs, or so the notice says on the gate, and
I did not fancy checking, but in the 1860s it was the home of
Samuel Shepheard, founder of the famous Shepheard's
Hotel in Cairo. Samuel had a rags-to-riches career: he was
apprenticed to a pastry cook, but ran away to sea and
became a steward on a liner. Then he got involved in a
mutiny, was put ashore in Egypt, and found himself a job in
a British hotel; in due course he built his own.

He bought Eathorpe Hall in 1860, and as there was no local demand for a luxury hotel he built a bridge instead, the one across the river which divides Eathorpe from the next village, Wappenbury; there had only been a ford before. It came in very useful when he died in 1866 and was taken across the bridge to Wappenbury for burial.

Shepheard's Hotel featured in a number of films and became well known to British officers during the Second World War, but it was burnt down in 1952. The name of Samuel Shepheard, however, is still preserved on the little bridge at Eathorpe.

I picked up the Fosse again on the other side of the village and headed for the next Stretton, this time Stretton-on-Dunsmore – and quite the most attractive Stretton on the route. While Stratton-on-the-Fosse had to cope with heavy traffic negotiating its chicanes, and Stretton on Fosse was fairly average except for that multi-initialled church charity, Stretton-on-Dunsmore lies just off the main road and is set out delightfully around its village green, with a little stream running through the centre, two good pubs beside it, and a local tradition dating back to the Saxons.

The Fosse marches on through the Midlands, as unswerving as ever.

On St Martin's Day the locals gather on a field at sunrise to pay their 'Wroth Silver' to the agent of the Duke of Buccleugh. Wroth Silver is not paid in anger, but as a form of levy. It either releases them from defending the Duke's castle if attacked, or gives them the right to drive their cattle across his land, depending on which reference book you consult. Both activities are fairly rare these days anyway, but the total involved is only 47 pence, and the villagers find it is a good investment, because the Duke stands them breakfast afterwards at the Dilkes Arms.

Back on the Fosse Way Len would miss all this jollity. Instead he would be confronted today by a roundabout and an enormous memorial. It commemorates King George V reviewing his troops before they embarked for Gallipoli in 1915. Curiously the memorial is about as far from the sea as you can get.

There is yet another Stretton to come, Stretton under Fosse, or more accurately these days, Stretton under Motorway, since it lies just below the M6. But first there is Brinklow, set on a steep hillside with its Norman mound dominating the country-side. From the top of it you can look back along the Fosse Way, disappearing southwards across the plain.

The Way becomes bendier and busier as it climbs into Brinklow, and Brinklow has become busier since Len's day too, first as a mining village for nearby Binley Colliery, now as a commuter village for Coventry and Rugby. The church, however, just beside the Fosse Way, still has reminders of its thirteenth-century past – and a collection of unlikely features which put it high in the Ecclesiastical Oddities League.

There is the Slope, for instance, a quite remarkable tilt to the floor which makes it 12 feet higher at one end than it is at the other. It gives the impression that you may need crampons to reach the altar. Even the church leaflet admits, 'this is a very curious feature'.

Then there is the Twist. The tower was built in the fifteenth century, and either the builder had a squint, or something has moved since, because at the top of its great arch there is a very pronounced twist in the stonework. The angel perched above it is trying hard not to notice. The tower also has the Hardman memorial window, a Victorian creation depicting Christ in Glory and the Last Judgement. The artist must have specialized in crowd scenes, because it is quite a challenge to count the number of faces in the stained glass. I got to a hundred, and gave up.

Out of sight in the tower is a peal of six bells, including the 'passing bell', which was rung when a person was dying, in order to scare away evil spirits which might steal the soul as it left the body, and to call for the villagers' prayers. On the bell is the suitably sombre inscription: 'My mournful sound doth warning give, that here men cannot always live.'

Which prompted me to go into the churchyard, to find one of those job-description epitaphs which gladden the hearts of all seekers after whimsy. The most famous one, I suppose, is on the grave of an engine-driver at Bromsgrove in Worcestershire: 'My engine now is cold and still, No water does my boiler fill, My coke affords its flames no more, my days of usefulness are o'er...' Then there is the watchmaker at Lydford in Devon who was 'wound up in hopes of being taken in hand by his Master and of being thoroughly cleaned, repaired and set a-going in the world to come'. There are any number of blacksmiths whose bellows have ceased to blow, but my favourite for crispness is the epitaph for a baronet which says simply: 'Good Knight'.

Brinklow has its own offering, on a tombstone in the south-east corner of the churchyard. Thomas Bolton was a

OPPOSITE *An observatory with sails; the weird windmill at Great Chesterton.*

73

deaf and dumb woodcutter who died in 1779; his epitaph, surrounded by the tools of his trade, reads:

> *He chiefly got his livelihood*
> *By faggoting and felling wood,*
> *Till Death, the conqueror of all,*
> *Gave the feller himself a fall.*

I wonder if the Romans went in for this sort of thing too. Len the Legionary, for instance, might have been given an appropriate soldier's farewell:

> *He has finished his march to eternal bliss:*
> *Halt! Well done, lad. Now: DISMISS!*

Beyond Brinklow the Fosse Way leaves the main road again and resumes its quieter, straighter route past Stretton under Fosse, over the M6, and on to its junction with that other great Roman artery, Watling Street, now the dual carriageway A5 from London to the North-west. The Romans quite reasonably assumed that, as the Fosse Way and Watling Street went from corner to corner of the country, this junction at High Cross was the exact centre of England, and High Cross has laid claim to that title ever since. This does not please Meriden, which the cartographers favour, nor Lillington, which has an oak tree reputed to mark the exact spot. My own money goes on a Birmingham suburb called Minsworth, which was literally pinpointed by a class of boys at King Edward's Grammar School. Their ingenious geography master got them to cut out forty cardboard maps of England and balance them on a drawing-pin to find their centre of gravity...

High Cross does have a monument of sorts to back up its claim. It was erected by the Earl of Denbigh and his friends in 1712, on the site of a wooden cross which had stood in the centre of the crossing. This must have been very inconvenient even for horse-drawn traffic, but I suppose nobody argued with the Earl of Denbigh. Happily Nature took a hand, and in 1791 the monument was struck by lightning, and disintegrated.

By then the Earl was beyond caring, but the remnants were gathered up and in due course were re-assembled in the garden of the High Cross Hotel. Whoever stuck them

The Fosse Way crosses Watling Street at High Cross, at the Roman centre of England.

together had no great eye for symmetry or aesthetic charm, and I have to say it was hardly worth the effort, but no doubt Len would have appreciated the gesture. It is a reminder of the crossroads' importance in the days when he marched along the Fosse Way.

At that time the area had a far greater significance than just being a crossroads or a hypothetical fulcrum. Somewhere nearby – nobody knows exactly where, though no doubt Len could have told us – the final battle was fought between the Romans and the rebel Iceni tribe from Norfolk, under their formidable Queen Boadicea. (The experts call her Boudicca these days, but if we have to give up the familiar name I prefer the Norfolk version, as immortalized by Bernard Matthews. He would call her just Boudiful…)

In AD 60 the Iceni rebelled against the Romans, destroyed Colchester, London and St Alban's, and seemed all set to chase the invaders out of Britain. But governor Paulinus got his act and his army together in the vicinity of High Cross, and when the over-confident Iceni hurled themselves at the Roman legions, they suffered a devastating defeat. Eighty thousand were said to have died in the battle, and a lot more were slaughtered later; somewhere near High Cross, in fact, were the killing fields of Roman Britain. The Romans' base camp was at Baginton, near Coventry's southern bypass, and extensive remains of the fort have been uncovered. Inside one of the reconstructed buildings you will find Len the Legionary – or at least a life-size model of him.

The High Cross junction is undramatic these days, unless you are trying to cross Watling Street in the rush-hour. The Fosse Way is only a lane on one side, and not even that on the other, just a track behind the High Cross Hotel, which eventually joins the old main road to Leicester at Sapcote.

This used to be the A46, carrying all the heavy traffic from Leicester to Coventry and the Midlands, but since the construction of the M69 motorway it has been downgraded to a B-road and now carries mostly local traffic. It is slightly eerie to drive along this broad but near-deserted road through quiet countryside, while a few miles away on each side the M69 and the M1 are carrying thousands of cars and lorries, in much the same direction. At times it is so quiet and peaceful you can almost picture Len marching along ahead.

The peacefulness soon disappears, however, when the

The High Cross monument, re-assembled and re-sited after being hit by lightning.

The Fosse Way becomes the Fosse Park Industrial Estate at Leicester – quite a shock!

OPPOSITE *A more peaceful stretch of the Fosse, with trees overhead instead of gantries.*

The reconstructed Roman fort at Baginton, base camp in the Midlands for guarding the Fosse.

Fosse Way approaches Leicester. Ahead lies the Fosse Park Industrial Estate, with its bewildering roundabouts, its overhead direction signs which you daren't look upwards to read, and its multi-lane road junctions where, inevitably, you find yourself in the wrong lane. Even sophisticated motorists can be intimidated by this road-planner's Frankenstein; Len the Legionary, I suspect, would turn round and march back to his boat. The Iceni were nothing to this…

Leicester was called Ratae by the Romans, but not surprisingly it didn't catch on. Let's face it, only Mole could live with Ratae. With one notable exception, the only reminders of Ratae are in the Museum. The exception is the Jewry Wall, a massive chunk of Roman masonry 8 feet thick, 20 feet high, and over 70 feet long, with four arched recesses. It flanked a complex which contained shops, government offices, and the largest Roman bath in England. Les was probably not allowed in the bath, but he may have reported to the office block to have his travel warrant stamped for the final stage of his march northwards, to Newark and Lincoln.

There are a couple of exhibits in the Museum he might appreciate. One is a piece of pottery on which are scratched the names of Lucius, a gladiator, and his girlfriend Lydia; the other is a boxtile on which a workman has scratched, perhaps to impress his foreman, 'Primus has made 10 tiles'. It is nice to be reminded that there were simple civilian folk among the Romans in Britain, as well as Len the Legionary and his thousands of fellow soldiers.

There is little trace of the Fosse Way in Leicester itself, and if there were, it would hardly be worth looking for it. The traffic system in the city centre is not quite as complicated as the environs of the Fosse Way Industrial Park, but I wouldn't recommend it. The suburbs are not very inviting either, though the line of the Fosse Way reappears fairly soon, and it is well established by the time it reaches Thurmaston.

This was where a Roman milestone was found, dated AD 120, the same period as the Jewry Wall. It gave the distance to Leicester as 2 miles, which means the centre of the city was a lot closer to Thurmaston in those days – or maybe the stone had been moved already. Now it has been moved again, to the Museum, and there is little else to identify the Fosse Way as it heads off along a B-road to Radcliffe on the Wreake.

finished his wife died in 1892, at the age of thirty-nine, and the church was dedicated that year in memory of them both. Then his other son was killed in the Boer War, but Robert Knowles lived on into his eighties. He was a deputy lieutenant, a magistrate and a county councillor, but I doubt that all these activities could blot out the memory of losing his family so early.

Back on the Fosse Way again, Len has not had even a whiff of a good Stilton, but refreshment awaits him ahead at the fort of Margidunum on Castle Hill, near the turnings to East Bridgford and Kneeton. The fort had an extraordinary history: burnt down, rebuilt, again demolished, again restored, then re-fortified – and all while it was still under the Romans. So what Len found when he got there depended on which year he made his march.

In the early days of the fort, when the Fosse Way was built, it covered about 7 acres, large enough to accommodate 1000 men in leather tents or dug-outs. The only luxury was a large bath-house, not the fancy sort which the aristocracy enjoyed at Bath and Leicester, but more like those you find in a football changing-room, enlarged several times.

The fort was protected by six ditches, but the locals still managed to burn the place down; maybe the redoubtable Boadicea passed this way. The Romans rebuilt it, this time providing more stone buildings. After about fifty years, though, when it was all quiet on the Fosse Way front, most of the fort was dismantled, so the Romans could indulge their passion for straight lines, and the Fosse Way was re-aligned to run straight across the site. Margidunum was reduced to a posting station, sufficient to provide Len with a beer and a sandwich, but not much good as a defence post.

That proved a problem later, when the Picts and Scots came rampaging south. A massive wall was built round the station, 9 feet thick and 20 feet high, and a remnant of that wall survived until the last century, when the remaining stones were removed to somebody's building plot.

What impresses me about Margidunum is not so much its changing fortunes as the way they have been deduced by the archaeologists, who had nothing much to go on except that chunk of wall and what they dug up on the site. They even uncovered a well, which no doubt provided Len with water for a drink and a wash. The well was lined with oak, and they found the wood still bore the marks left by the

The River Trent comes close to the Fosse Way at East Stoke, or Ad Pontem to the Romans.

sawyer. I am quite sure they could tell us if he was right- or left-handed…

When the Fosse Way was rebuilt across Margidunum, the original Way running parallel to it was abandoned, but keen agger-spotters can identify it passing through the fields beside the present main road. It is known locally as the Hump, but it is more of an almost imperceptible ridge, impossible to pick out when the lorry behind you is sitting on your rear bumper. I shall take their word for it.

Six miles further on was another Roman station, Ad Pontem, which was unusually close as Roman stations go, but Margidunum existed because the locals had already made it a good defensive position, and Ad Pontem was the handiest place to cross the Trent, which came close to the Fosse Way at that point. Today Ad Pontem is East Stoke, and consists mainly of a long high wall where the river ought to be. A track leads down to the Trent where the wall ends, and it is said the remains of a Roman bridge were found there, but these days the track is only used by the local angling club.

From here the Fosse Way runs straight into the centre of Newark, along a road which is some 2 feet higher than the houses on either side, thanks to that long-lasting Roman agger. Untroubled by the current one-way system, Len would have marched through the town along Millgate, Castlegate, Bargate and Northgate, and out the other side – quite possibly without stopping, because there is no great evidence of Roman activity in Newark. A few pieces of Roman pottery and coins have been found, and a nineteenth-century antiquarian did come up with 'Elvantona' as the Roman name for Newark, but nobody seems very convinced. 'There is no justification', says the town guide firmly.

Newark was in fact more interesting long after the Romans had gone, when the castle had been built alongside the Fosse Way at Castlegate and it became a Royalist stronghold, resisting three major sieges before being ordered to surrender by the King, who had already surrendered himself. This gave rise to the town's motto: *Dea fretus erumpe*, which Len would recognize as 'Trust in God and Sally Forth'. The English translation prompts one to wonder who Sally Forth was, and why was she so trustworthy? Newark wisely sticks to the Latin version.

Some sections of the Fosse are now tracks alongside the main road.

Lincoln's South Gate, where the Fosse Way enters the city.

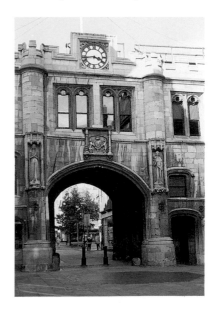

Parts of Lincoln's Roman walls survive among the modern houses.

A Roman gravestone has finished up in a church wall.

The Fosse Way leaves Newark through the maze of new roads outside the town and resumes its straight line to Lincoln along the A46. It passes through a hamlet called Brough, which in Len's day bore the much grander name of Crococolana. It sounds more Brazilian than Roman, and one visualizes the Trent infested with snapping jaws, but to Len it just meant another chance to ease his sandals.

The river was actually 2 miles away at Collingham, where there was a Roman bridge, so no doubt it was linked with the Fosse Way. The Trent has since changed its course and flows further away, but there is a reminder of its vagaries in the wall of All Saints' churchyard, a stone which marks the height of the floodwaters from 1795 onwards.

All Saints' is one of two churches in this little village, 'which might seem a questionable luxury in these days of increased costs of maintenance', as the church guide observes rather lugubriously. It explains, however, that in Saxon times Collingham was in two Manors, and each squire could only qualify as a gentleman, according to the laws of King Athelstan, if he had a church and belfry on his land. It was the Saxon equivalent of buying a title, with King Athelstan setting the pace for Lloyd George, and Collingham has been stuck with two churches ever since.

Len would not be bothered with all this; the end of his long trek is nearly in sight. Today he would see the soaring tower of Lincoln Cathedral, but at that time there were the walls of the Roman city, and the great South Gate. He marched through this and into the lower town, occupied by the service industries for the army – which were summed up pithily by one expert as 'craftsmen, traders and women'. Then through the internal south gate into the heart of Roman Lincoln, with its basilica and forum, its barracks and storehouses, its public baths and its sophisticated water and sewage systems. This was almost a Rome from Rome, a sight for sore feet, and Len, I hope, must have felt that this 200-mile slog along the Fosse Way had all been worth while.

Only remnants survive of Lindum, as the Romans called it, but there are sufficient for anyone with the right guide-book and a strong imagination to picture what Len actually saw. There are sections of the city wall, fragments of two of the gates, some granite cobblestones, a Roman gravestone, a mosaic floor, even a small section of the Fosse Way itself, preserved under a glass cover at St Mary's Guildhall. But

Lincoln's finest Roman relic is the Newport Arch, the only Roman gate-arch in England still used by traffic today.

The main arch is about the width of a chariot, the smaller one might take Len and a friend. The original Roman road lies 3 feet below the present level, but there is enough room for a car or even a sizable van. There is not, however, room for a large truck, and this was demonstrated in spectacular fashion in 1964 when a warehouse lorry smashed into the arch and caused substantial damage.

Immediately the Progressive School of Town Flatteners and Road Expanders urged that the job should be finished off. The arch had always been a traffic hazard, they said, so let's knock the rest of it down and widen the road. Mercifully they lost the day, and the City Council restored the Newport Arch, using all the original stones.

Well, not quite all, perhaps. This was the arch, after all, through which Len passed if he continued his march northwards up Ermine Street to the Humber and beyond. No doubt he would have preferred to stay in Lincoln, but I fear he was probably due for a spell of duty on Hadrian's Wall. However, he may have left something behind.

I like to think that one of those stones from the Newport Arch was never recovered after the lorry smashed into it. Somewhere in Lincoln it is let into a wall, or forms part of a garden path, or decorates a rockery. And carved on it, if we could only find it, is the simple message – in Latin, of course:

Len the Legionary was here.

Lincoln's Newport Arch, the only Roman gate-arch in England still used by road traffic.

THE RIVER OUSE

Sailing to York
with Vic the Viking

EVER SINCE AN ENTERPRISING caveman saw a log floating downstream and climbed on board for a lift, people have been using rivers for transport. First they tied logs together to form a raft, then the Peruvians thought of inflating the hides of two sealions and connected them by a wooden platform to make the first catamaran (honestly!). After that came canoes, ranging from the utility version hollowed-out treetrunk to the de luxe birchbark models made by the North American Indians. Whereupon the Peruvians, not to be outdone, made a mass-production copy using bundles of reeds, which proved so popular they still use the same design today.

As boats got bigger and better, travellers ventured out of the rivers and on to the open sea.

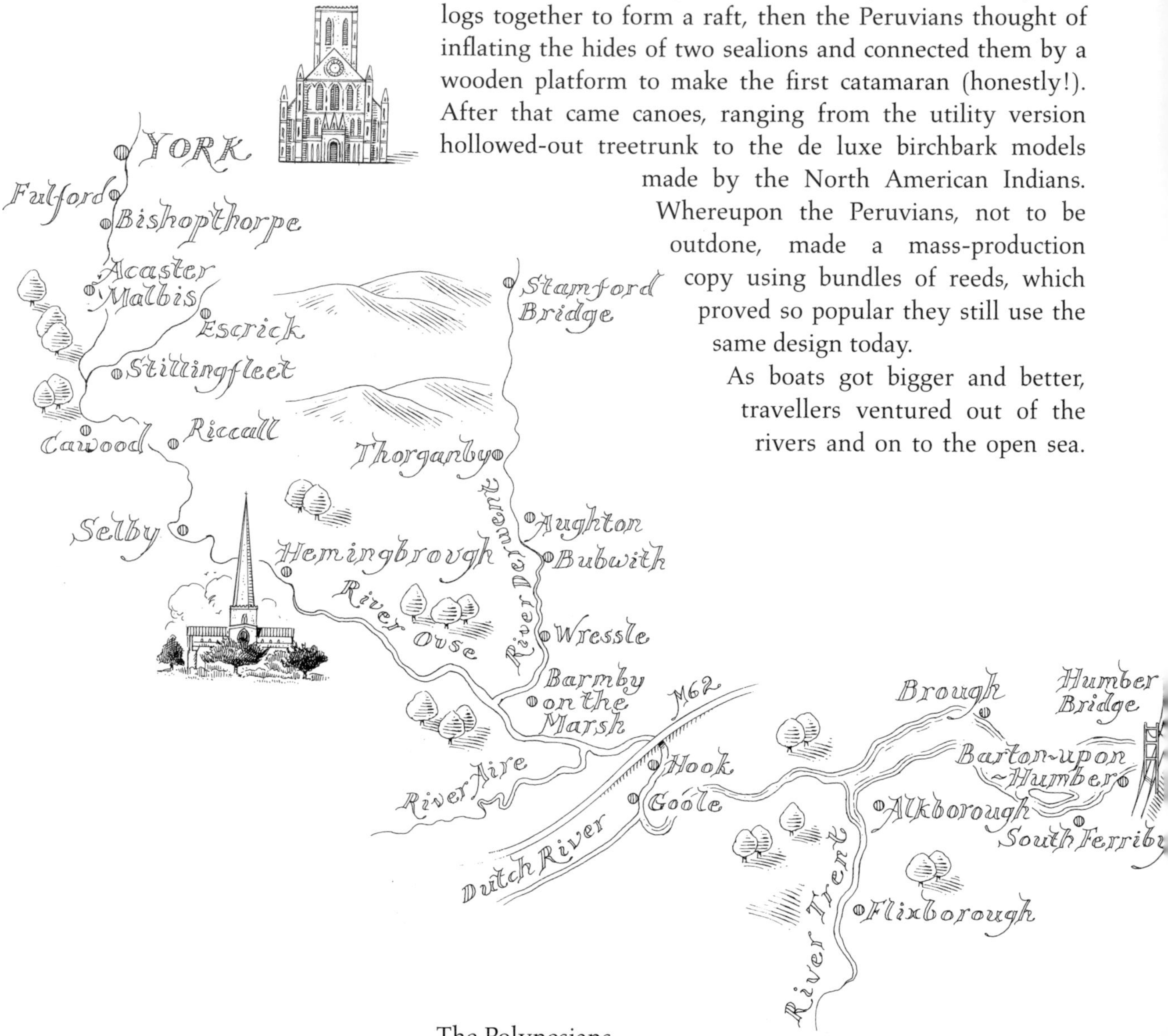

YORK
Fulford
Bishopthorpe
Acaster Malbis
Escrick
Stillingfleet
Cawood
Riccall
Stamford Bridge
Thorganby
Selby
Hemingbrough
River Derwent
Aughton
Bubwith
River Ouse
Wressle
Barmby on the Marsh
M62
River Aire
Hook
Goole
Dutch River
Brough
Humber Bridge
Barton-upon-Humber
Alkborough
South Ferriby
River Trent
Flixborough

The Polynesians in the South Pacific were building boats in 3000 BC which could carry 100 passengers for 1000 miles or more, depending how long the provisions lasted. The Egyptians and the Phoenicians were at it too, then the Greeks and Romans joined in, until the Mediterranean must have seemed like an enormous boating lake. Further north, sea-going craft began to tackle the stormier waters of the North Sea and, in the forefront, were

PREVIOUS PAGES *The River Ouse, the Viking route to York.*

the Viking longships, basically a very long rowing-boat with a sail, but capable of crossing the Atlantic 500 years before Columbus.

The more routine run for the Vikings, however, was from Norway and Denmark to Britain. With their comparatively shallow draught the longships could sail up the larger rivers, first to rape and pillage, so we are always told, then to conquer and colonize, and finally to trade. The longships were followed by the merchant ships, broader and higher and not quite so nippy, but the high sides meant they could carry a taller mast and a larger sail, which cut down on the rowing; if a longship had that amount of sail it would tilt over too far and the sea would come over the side.

Six or seven men were able to handle a merchant ship, carrying up to 5 tons of cargo. In reasonable weather and with a following wind they could cover the 1500 miles from Norway to the East Coast in a fortnight. Then, like the longships, they continued their journey up-river, to take their goods all the way to the inland markets.

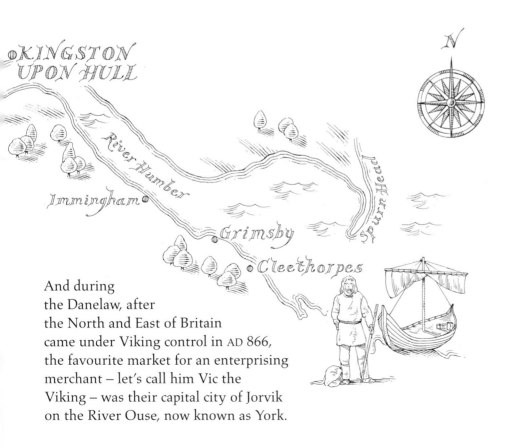

And during the Danelaw, after the North and East of Britain came under Viking control in AD 866, the favourite market for an enterprising merchant – let's call him Vic the Viking – was their capital city of Jorvik on the River Ouse, now known as York.

It is difficult to picture a Viking as a seaborne travelling salesman. The popular picture is of a ferocious character with a large beard and a horned helmet, looting, plundering, raping, pillaging, torturing, killing. You name it – if it was unpleasant enough, he did it. The names attached to some of them rather encourage this image – Erik Blood-Axe, for instance, or the more bizarre Ragnar Hairy-Breeks. But it is the writers of the Sagas who are mostly to blame; they liked to make their heroes as macho as possible, without too much regard for historical fact.

Take old Hairy-Breeks, for example. Did he have the hairy legs as well as the horns of a devil? Not a bit. He merely favoured some special suiting made from a shaggy skin which had been boiled in pitch and rolled in sand, presumably to deflect the odd sword-thrust, though the mere sight of it must have been unnerving for his enemies – let alone the smell. And there was no horned helmet; Vikings just didn't go in for that sort of thing. As that most famous of latter-day Vikings, Magnus Magnusson, once observed: 'Horns would only have been an unnecessary and potentially lethal encumbrance, and the only possible use I can imagine for them would have been as screw-on, screw-off hip flasks.'

More a head-flask than a hip-flask, perhaps, but I take his point. The myth of the horned helmets apparently began when some Bronze Age helmets were found in Denmark with long, curving horns, perhaps a ceremonial uniform. But the Bronze Age was a couple of thousand years before the Vikings, and horns like that would have been a bigger hazard for the chap alongside than for the enemy in front.

Ragnar Hairy-Breeks, shaggy-trousered but definitely horn-less, is said to have made the first attempt to capture York, but he was defeated by the Northumbrian King Aella. His hairy suit proved its worth, saving him from death in the battle, and again when Aella put him in a snake-pit. The snakes, it seemed, were quite turned off by the boiled pitch. So Aella had him stripped, and Ragnar, now Hairy-Breekless, succumbed to the snakes, but not before crying out with his last breath – as Vikings were wont to do – a final imprecation upon his slayer. In his case it was the sinister warning: 'How the piglets would grunt if they knew the plight of the boar.'

The piglets did more than grunt. According to the Saga

his three sons led a revenge attack on York, and organized it a lot better than their Dad. They rejoiced in the names of Ivar the Boneless, Ubbi the nothing-in-particular, and Halfdan of the Wide Embrace. They may sound more like all-in wrestlers than Vikings, but the fact is that a Viking called Ingmar – another form of Ivar – was one of the leaders in the historic attack of AD 866 when York was captured and the Viking occupation of North-east England began.

The history books do not mention Ingmar's bonelessness, but they do confirm that King Aella was killed, though not in quite the gruesome fashion that the Saga describes. It says the vengeful piglets 'carved the blood eagle on his back', which may sound uncomfortable rather than lethal, but in Saga terms it meant they cut his ribs from his spine, then pulled out his lungs and spread them on his back like wings. The chap who dreamed up that one must have been watching too many video nasties…

The official version is less bloodcurdling. Aella actually escaped from York when it surrendered, then led a counter-attack and died on the battlefield. The blood eagle story, it seems, was just a Saga *tour de force*.

Vikings, in fact, were as civilized as anybody else in those tough times. They had their great fighting men, of course, Erik Blood-Axe and the like, who could row their longships across the North Sea for a week or two, and still have enough breath left to jump ashore and knock the living daylights out of the locals. But somebody had to make those longships in the first place, skilled carpenters who introduced the idea of clinker-built boats, with the planks overlapping instead of flush. They had their metal craftsmen and their leatherworkers, their farmers and builders, administrators and judiciary. It was, after all, the Vikings who introduced the word 'law' into the English language. And they had their dealers and merchants, who brought furs and hides from the Arctic, spices from the Mediterranean, and wines from Europe. Many Vikings who roamed the seas were in fact traders, not raiders, and they were out to make money, not mayhem. In the ninth and tenth centuries they brought their merchant ships into the Humber estuary and sailed up the River Ouse to York, to sell their cargoes and make a bob or two for the wife and kids back home.

Such a man was Vic the Viking…

Boats still unload in York where the Vikings once moored.

York's ancient Minster, built on the site of the Viking city.

NOBODY IS QUITE SURE HOW Vic and his friends found their way across hundreds of miles of open sea, without maps or compasses or the BBC shipping forecast. They had the sun and the stars when the weather was fine, but the North Sea is not renowned for sunny days and starry nights, and much of the steering must have been done by shrewd guesswork. If Vic was the steersman, it was not just a matter of turning a wheel. He had to cope with a long paddle slung over the right-hand side at the stern – the steerboard, in fact, which later became 'starboard'. He must have needed a fair amount of muscle to keep a merchant ship on course in a heavy sea, even assuming he knew what the course was supposed to be. Yet somehow the Vikings generally made landfall where they intended, and in Vic's case it was the mouth of the Humber, where the long spit of sand and shingle called Spurn Head curls across the entrance.

Spurn Head has had its ups and downs over the centuries – literally. The sea has washed away bits of it, if not all of it, then washed it back again, and there is no guarantee that in Vic the Viking's day it existed at all, in which case he could have sailed straight into the estuary and saved the extra three miles that ships from the north have to travel today. In medieval times there was actually a port on Spurn Head called Ravenser Odd; it existed for about 150 years before disappearing in one of the Head's regular transmogrifications.

Ravenser's oddness went beyond its name, because nobody can pinpoint exactly where it was. Early mapmakers moved it about as frequently as in later years they had to move the lighthouse on Spurn Head. There were at least five of them in different positions until the last one closed in 1985, but in spite of them – or perhaps because mariners were never sure where the current one would be – there have been countless shipwrecks. Not surprisingly, Spurn Head has one of the oldest-established lifeboat stations in the country.

It also had a little railway, built for the Ministry of Defence, which was very popular with wind-sailors. They rode on a flat-topped waggon fitted with a sail, and when the wind was right they whizzed along Spurn Head at considerable speed. I trust the waggon also had a good brake, to stop them flying off the end...

Even Spurn Head has changed its shape since the Vikings arrived.

Vic the Viking would have been sorry to miss that when he sailed round – or over – Spurn Head. I am sure the idea of a longship on rails would have appealed to him. Instead he could have caught a distant glimpse of the little Viking settlements on the opposite shore of the Humber, which we now know as Cleethorpes and Grimsby – the '-by' and the '-thorpe' give the Viking connection.

Grimsby has a little Saga all to itself. The Grim in its name has nothing to do with how it looks; actually it looks a lot better than most people imagine. Grim was a Lincolnshire fisherman who found a Dane adrift in an open boat, and took him into his care. The Dane turned out to be Havlock, whose father was King of Denmark. The king had been murdered by his enemies and Havlock was pushed out to sea to perish. He was brought up by Grim the fisherman, and later regained his kingdom and repaid his benefactor with enough wealth to found Grimsby.

Cleethorpes probably dismisses this story as just another Grim fairy tale, because it cannot claim a similar Saga involving a Mr Clee; its fortunes are based more in the world of Mr Butlin. While Grimsby developed into a major port, continuing its Danish connection through the 'butter-boats' and later the butter and bacon container ferries from Denmark, Cleethorpes promoted its three miles of sands to become a family holiday resort. I doubt the visitors watching the performing dolphins in Marineland are too bothered about its link with the Vikings.

Indeed, the towns along the Humber which Vic would pass today are firmly based in the twentieth century. Immingham, for instance, has modern deep-water docks which can take ocean-going tankers, and the shore is lined with oil refineries. These blot out the memory not only of the Vikings but of a more recent event in English history, the departure of the Pilgrim Fathers from Immingham Creek in 1608.

That may not seem to tally with the school textbooks, which concentrate on the *Mayflower* setting out from Plymouth twelve years later, but this was where they first left England. They had tried to do so six months earlier, from Scotia Creek near Boston, but the ship's captain gave them away. They were arrested and sent back home, but they raised enough money to hire another boat, this time with a more trustworthy captain and from a more obscure

A more dramatic change on the south bank: the docks at Grimsby.

creek. Even so, the captain panicked when troops appeared, and set sail without the wives and families, but they caught up with their menfolk later in Holland, and in due course sailed for the New World, linking up with the *Mayflower* at Southampton. A memorial marks their earlier attempt at Scotia Creek, but nothing survives at Immingham – unless an oil refinery can be regarded as a symbol of the New World.

On the north bank of the Humber there were Viking settlements near the mouth of the Hull, which we sometimes forget was a river before there was a town, properly known as Kingston-upon-Hull. This town too has moved into the twentieth century, but not entirely of its own volition. It was bombed so extensively during the Second World War that it had to be almost entirely rebuilt. Most of the fishing fleet has been ousted by the new container ships, and the eighteenth-century dock which they sailed from has been landscaped into public gardens. Not even William Wilberforce, who spent his early years in Hull before setting off to abolish slavery, would recognize the town today, let alone Vic the Viking.

In any case, Vic would probably be more interested in what he was about to sail under, rather than what he was sailing past. Just up-river from Hull is that marvel of the new age of travel – or the Department of Transport's most spectacular white elephant, as some regard it – the Humber Bridge.

I have no doubt the bridge is very handy if you commute to Hull from across the river, and certainly I have no complaints about it myself. When I drive from Norfolk to Yorkshire it is sometimes pleasant to meander through the Lincolnshire Wolds rather than belt up the Great North Road, even though the bridge toll seems to go up every year. But cross-river commuters and Wolds wanderers are comparatively rare breeds, and the heavy traffic from the south keeps to the trunk roads and the motorways. The Humber Bridge is not quite the longest suspension bridge in the world – the Japanese have built one 1000 feet longer – but foot for foot, it must surely be the quietest.

Never mind; it has at least one devoted admirer. The playwright Alan Plater has called it 'the best and biggest and most beautiful damn bridge in the whole world'. Mr Plater, incidentally, comes from Hull.

The Humber Bridge, a modern marvel spanning the old Viking route.

At the southern end of the bridge is Barton-upon-Humber, which was once a bigger port than Hull. These days its main claim to fame is just being at the southern end of the Humber Bridge…

Once Vic got beyond it he would see very little to interest him on either bank these days; some of it must look even more desolate now than when the Vikings were around. The chalk and limestone quarries at South Ferriby, for instance, are now derelict, and the remains of the lighters which used to ply there can be seen sticking out of the mud at low tide. They were sunk there to prevent further erosion, though it is difficult for a visitor to understand why they bothered. The bell-buoy that tolls continuously in the estuary to warn ships away from Read's Island sounds as if it is permanently in mourning for a dead coastline.

When Vic first passed this way there was much more activity. Ermine Street, the great Roman road from London and Lincoln, reached the Humber somewhere between Read's Island and Winteringham, and a ferry crossed the river to what is now the village of Brough. This was the route taken by Len the Legionary, of Fosse Way fame, if he was sent on from Lincoln to Hadrian's Wall. It seems likely that the road and the ferry continued in use after the Romans left, and Vic may have had to watch out for the ferryboats as he sailed his merchant ship up-river.

Ahead of him was the upper reach of the Humber, leading into the confluence of the Ouse and the Trent. On a hill which overlooks the meeting place of the three great rivers stands Alkborough, where the remains of a Roman camp may still have been visible. This has always been a notable vantage point, and today from the top of the church tower you should be able to see Lincoln Cathedral to the south and Beverley Minster to the north. Hawk-eyed observers have even claimed to see York Minster, but perhaps they improved their vision with a pinch of salt.

For me, however, Alkborough is not as notable for its views as for its mazes. Vic the Viking must have known about mazes, because they go back to the Greek legend of the minotaur imprisoned in the labyrinth; I always thought of it when I heard the Royal Scots Guards playing 'A Maze in Greece'. The first Alkborough maze, according to most experts, was carved into the turf by monks from a nearby monastery in medieval times, but I see no reason why the

The junction of the Humber and the Trent, a Viking crossroad.

Roman soldiers who occupied the camp did not carve out the original design, to while away the time between guard duties. If Vic moored nearby for a breather, he might well have come across it too.

The fact that it still exists is largely due to a maze enthusiast called J. Goulton-Constable, a former squire of Alkborough who died in 1922. He not only preserved the turf maze but reproduced it in the floor of the church porch and in a stained-glass window. A fourth replica appears on his tombstone in the churchyard. The Royal Scots Guards could well dedicate one of their performances to him.

The turf maze is known as Julian's Bower, though the Julian connection is rather obscure. It might refer to Julius, the son of a Trojan called Aeneas who settled near Rome and introduced the maze games that were popular in Troy; some mazes are still called Troy Town or the City of Troy. But there is also the legend of St Julian, who opened a hospice for travellers which became known as Julian's Bower, and because mazes have often been associated with travelling life's tortuous path, there might be a connection – albeit just as tortuous – between Julian and the maze. It seems to me that 'Vic the Viking's Bower' would make just as much sense…

It was at this junction of the rivers that the first Viking raiders had to decide whether to head northwards up the Ouse or towards the Midlands along the Trent. Those who chose the Trent were under the leadership of a character whose name, I am assured, was Snot. He it was who founded the city of Snottingham; it was only later that they discreetly dropped the 'S'. In fairness I should say that there is a quite different explanation which has nothing to do with Vikings; you can believe it – or Snot.

Vic the Viking, I assume, did not think a lot of Snot, and sailed up the Ouse instead. That meant he missed the Saxon monastery just outside Flixborough, a few miles up the Trent. It was built in the seventh century and was certainly still there in his day. Plenty of other Vikings knew it – probably Snot's lot. It was surrounded by Viking settlements: Lonigsby, Coleby, Thealby, Normanby – always that distinctive '-by'.

The monastery was there long before them, but it did not last long after them. In fact, it may well have been submerged by sand while they were still around, and it was not rediscovered until a few years ago, when quarrying began

Alkborough's turf maze; the Vikings might still recognize it.

and Saxon burials were found. More digging produced a complete ground plan of the monastery, with fourteen timbered halls connected by metalled pathways. Among the relics was a ring inscribed with the first half of the alphabet, and the experts say this may have been an aide-memoire for prayers said in alphabetical order. Its owner presumably had memorized the prayers, but needed a crib to remember the alphabet.

Vic's contemporaries may well have done business at the monastery. Fragments were found of German and French pottery and foreign-made glass, which could have been sold to the monks by the Viking traders. There were also coins from the Frisian Islands, which extend along the Danish coast. I wonder if that means the Danish Vikings would only give change in their own local currency…

Vic, of course, missed out on all this. He was sailing up the Ouse, much narrower than the Humber and rather more scenic. Until now it has been difficult to keep a close watch on his progress without acquiring a boat, but from here it is possible to stay close to the river by car. A lane joins the Ouse at Ousefleet, after passing through Adlingfleet, with Faxfleet and Yokefleet on the opposite bank. It continues to Swinefleet. 'Fleet' not only means a lot of ships or a lot of speed, it can be a creek or inlet, and in earlier days there were no doubt plenty of inlets along the Ouse. A great many dykes and drains have been dug since then to reclaim the marshland, and the original riverbank has altered. The countryside gets more like the Fens or the Netherlands, and at the entrance to Goole is the largest dyke of all, the so-called Dutch River, which really does have a Fen connection. It was the work of Cornelius Vermuyden, the Dutchman who widened and straightened the other River Ouse, and drained the Fens.

The Dutch River links the Yorkshire Ouse with the River Don, and drains the Hatfield Chase marshes. Vic would have sailed past a boggy wilderness, instead of the rich farmland that exists today. There is a great contrast, too, between the Dutch River and the Ouse. The first runs straight as a die for 6 miles before linking up with the Don and the Aire and Calder Canal; at Goole the Ouse twists and turns into an S-bend.

Vic is 50 miles from the sea now, but if he could see Goole today he would hardly think so. It has been a busy

A latter-day Viking merchant heads upriver for Goole.

port since the canal was opened in 1826, first exporting coal and textiles, now handling 2 million tons of mixed cargoes a year, carried by 2000 vessels. They are the successors to Vic the Viking, and he would be much impressed.

He might be less impressed by Goole itself. Most of it was built in the last century, in a style best described as Victorian artisan. Its main architectural claim to fame is one of its two water towers, which at one time was said to be the biggest in England, holding three-quarters of a million gallons. One wonders why they ever needed the second one.

It is not perhaps the ideal town in which to linger, unless you have business there, but if your arrival at the swing bridge on the main road coincides with a boat, you may have no option. The delay can be irritating, but I was amply compensated when I saw the name of the boat that was holding us up. Vic has not been forgotten in Goole: it was called *The Viking*.

I suspect he has been forgotten, though, in Hook, just beyond Goole. Although it lies within a curve of the Ouse – hence, perhaps, its name – the river is virtually out of sight unless you go in search of it down a side road. A house called Moorings gives a hint of its presence, but I doubt Vic would take advantage of it. Hook is all rather anonymous, though the Blacksmith's Arms does try to preserve a village pub atmosphere, and the landlady's enormous Yorkshire puddings with onions and gravy are the real thing.

If Vic continued round that bend in the Ouse today he would be confronted by his second impressive bridge, carrying the M62 motorway across the river. Beyond it is a more modest swing bridge on the old main road. Then he would be off into open country again at last, and by road the next place to pick him up is at Barmby on the Marsh, an isolated village at the end of a long lane across the marshes. This is where the River Derwent runs into the Ouse, and the rural atmosphere is rather spoilt by the giant cooling towers at Long Drax, and the very businesslike barrage across the Derwent. Neither would mean much to Vic the Viking, but to the Electricity Generating Board and the Water Authority they mean quite a lot.

The Ouse is still tidal at this point, and the Derwent barrage was built in the 1970s, partly as a flood defence but mainly to prevent the tide washing into the Derwent. If it did, the good folk of Hull and the surrounding countryside

ABOVE *Goole's swing bridge; it is still used by a boat called* The Viking.

OPPOSITE *The Dutch River, a later timepath created by Vermuyden to drain the marshes.*

An ancient waterway brought up to date; the river barrage across the Derwent.

Impressive if unpicturesque: cooling towers loom over the Ouse at Long Drax.

could find themselves drinking some very salty water. I gather it is an expensive operation, keeping the sea out of the taps. The barrage alone cost £4 000 000 and at the extraction plant upstream, with its pipe lines and massive reservoir tanks, they have been pumping in another £20 000 000 on improvement works – as well as all that water.

The barrage would effectively prevent Vic the Viking from sailing up the Derwent, but he was probably not keen to do so anyway because trade would have been pretty thin. Although the Derwent is 60 miles long, Malton is the only town of any size along its entire length, and Malton is considerably further away than York. However, it does have some villages worth a visit, if Vic fancied a detour today.

Wressle, for instance, not only has an intriguing name – do the villagers call themselves Wresslers? – but also the only surviving castle of any note in the old East Riding. The castle indeed has survived longer than the Ridings, which disappeared when Humberside was created, to the eternal regret of every Yorkshireman and woman. Part of the castle was knocked down after the Civil War, and more of it was burnt down in 1796, but its two towers and the main hall remain. If you care to risk the climb up one of the stair turrets on top of the towers you will be rewarded, so I am told, by being able to see no fewer than thirty churches. I am afraid I prefer to see them at ground level.

One of these churches is at Bubwith, further up the Derwent, and what you cannot see from the stair turret are the helmet and the wooden sword inside the church, which used to be carried at the funerals of Lords of the Manor. The next church is at Aughton, and from the turret it must sometimes seem to be on an island, when the floodwaters of the Derwent get as far as the churchyard.

Aughton is an isolated little village at the end of a cul-de-sac, but a notable family once lived there. Inside the church – again invisible from the turret – is a portrait brass of Sir Richard Aske, dated 1460. Sir Richard himself is not prominent in the history books, but his descendant, Sir Robert Aske, actually made history in 1536. He led an uprising against King Henry VIII in protest against the dissolution of the monasteries.

Sir Robert mustered 30 000 men on Skipton Moor and led a march to London in what became known in history as the Pilgrimage of Grace. In Henry's view, however, this was not a pilgrimage, just a straightforward rebellion, and he dealt with it in his customary fashion. The march was broken up, a great many people were imprisoned, and Sir Robert himself was executed at York eight months later.

A farmhouse now stands on the site of his manor house near the church, but the link between the Aske family and the village still exists. A later Robert Aske was made a baronet in 1922, and the baronetcy passed to his son Conan, who had a distinguished military career before being ordained in 1970. Although he made his home in Worcestershire, his full title is recorded as the Rev. Sir Conan Aske, Bt., of Aughton, East Riding of Yorkshire. None of your 'Humberside' nonsense for the Askes…

Although Vic the Viking never came this way, other Vikings did. On the opposite bank from Aughton is the Norse village of Thorganby – the 'Thor' would give the game away even without the familiar '-by'. It looks a very English village now, with a Georgian manorhouse, a farmhouse with a dovecote, and a seventeenth-century pub with beams and log fires – and a tasty line in the house speciality, 'poacher's broth'. Nevertheless, it has a significant Viking connection. The Viking army may have marched through it on the way to their crushing defeat in 1066, which effectively ended their involvement in English history.

But I am getting ahead of myself, and of Vic, who is still sailing peacefully up the Ouse, leaving the Derwent behind him. By road the next place to catch up with him is Hemingbrough, now bypassed by the A163 to Selby, and snoozing placidly between the main road and the river.

Hemingbrough church is undoubtedly one of those visible from the stair turrets at Wressle castle. Indeed you could hardly miss it. The tower is only 60 feet high, but the spire rises for another 120 feet, a landmark for many miles across the flat and featureless Plain of York. The church itself is big in proportion, established as a collegiate church by Prior Washington of Durham in the fifteenth century. The Prior must have had either a sense of humour or a sense of his own importance, because around the top of the tower are carvings of washing tubs or tuns, a pictorial pun on his name.

The woodcarvers responsible for the bench-ends in the church had a bit of fun, too. There is a jester complete with cap and bells among the more orthodox dragons and the

A more traditional landmark: the lofty spire of Hemingbrough church.

occasional monkey. But the main item of interest is the solitary misericord in the choir stalls. The experts have dated it around 1200, which would make it the oldest bottom-rest in England.

It would still not be old enough, of course, for Vic to take advantage of it. There would be no church and no spire, just the flat watermeadows which still separate the village from the river. One lane runs across them, called Landing Road, but like the Moorings at Hook, there would not be much temptation for Vic to land. Selby, which by its name was another Viking settlement, is only four miles ahead.

Actually there is no trace of the Vikings in the town or the local histories. Perhaps it is significant that the first Abbot of Selby, Benedict of Auxerre, referred to it as 'Selebaie' when he described how he was told in a vision to found an abbey there. Is Selby just the Anglicized version or was it the other way round? In 1069, according to legend, he sailed up the Ouse until three swans appeared on the water in front of him. He took this to mean that he had arrived at the chosen site, though I am not quite sure why. The vision referred to Selebaie, not Swanbaie; shouldn't they have been seals?

Anyway, Benedict planted a cross and built a hut where the abbey was to be built – and makes no mention of any Vikings having been there already. The only people he had to worry about were the Norman governor and King William, as the land was royal property. He handled them so persuasively that he was given the land and made Abbot.

The Abbey has dominated Selby ever since, but it is not the town's most familiar feature – not to motorists, anyway. If Vic sailed up to Selby today, the first thing to catch his eye would be the bridge; and up until 1991 the second thing he saw would be the queues of cars waiting to get across it. It was a tollbridge, privately owned and operated, and a cause of constant delays – not only when it was open for river traffic, but even more so at peak times when the toll collectors could not keep up with the vehicles wanting to cross.

The original bridge was built in 1792, and at the time it was welcomed with delight by the 8743 people who were counted using the ferry in a month – let alone the 3263 horses, the 127 oxen and the 2248 sheep. This traffic census was enough to convince the authorities that a bridge was

Selby, once a Viking settlement, now a busy market town.

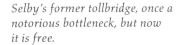

Selby's former tollbridge, once a notorious bottleneck, but now it is free.

needed, and private individuals raised £10 000 to build it, headed by the Lord of the Manor, Lord Edward Petre. He owned the ferry, as it happened, and he may have felt that if you can't beat 'em, join 'em. More likely, he knew a good investment when he saw one.

Tolls were fixed at two shillings for coaches, a penny for a cow and a halfpenny for pedestrians. Remembering the number of people and animals crossing the river in a month, it is obvious that Lord Edward was on to a good thing. For the first century of its existence everyone was delighted with the Selby tollbridge – except, I suppose, the ferrymen. But then a love-hate relationship began to develop between the bridge and the increasing number of people who used it – no longer in stagecoaches or herding cows, but driving cars and vans and lorries.

The first meetings to discuss getting the bridge into public ownership and end the tolls took place in 1891, and they continued, off and on, for the next hundred years. During that period there were two world wars, men reached the moon, we got nuclear power, *Concorde*, and the microwave oven; but at Selby bridge the queues just continued to grow.

It did change hands in 1901, but only to another private company. It was also rebuilt in 1970, but the tolls continued. Then in 1989 there was a taste of freedom. The swing bridge at Cawood, four miles up-river, had to be closed for repairs, and North Yorkshire County Council, realizing the extra traffic that would use Selby bridge and the chaos that would result, formed a consortium of local councils and business-people to 'buy out' the tolls for three months, at a cost of about £6000 a week.

For three months the bridge-users had never had it so good. I am sure that several of them just drove back and forth across the bridge for the sheer hell of it. Inspired, goaded, egged on, galvanized – call it what you will – the authorities agreed that Selby tollbridge had reached, as it were, its Sel-by date. They came up with a package involving about £500 000 of taxpayers', ratepayers' and business people's money to buy the bridge and eliminate the tolls.

On 19 September 1991, the chairman of the County Council drove across the bridge in a coach-and-four, dressed in period costume, to hand over the final toll of a Georgian shilling and two sixpences. The last paying foot-passenger, a nine-year-old from the local primary school, paid the final

The Norman columns in Selby Abbey, still a long way off their Sel-by date …

Away from the tourists, Selby's flour and cattlefeed mills line the riverbank.

halfpenny, and the tollkeeper, in this case a member of the Percy family whose company had owned the bridge for ninety years, handed over the deed of gift in return. Selby tollbridge became just another bridge.

There continue to be delays, of course, because shipping still has priority over road traffic and the bridge has to be swung open for the successors of Vic the Viking. But this is not very frequent, and Selby is no longer the biggest bottleneck in Yorkshire.

Most of the river traffic comes from the flour and cattlefeed mills which line the bank up-river. It is an unlovely area, and Vic would be glad to get past it and set off again into the peaceful Yorkshire countryside. But it was not all that peaceful for the Vikings who sailed up the river after him in 1066, the army which disembarked at the next riverside village of Riccall for the sequence of events which led to the Battle of Stamford Bridge.

Riccall is an unassuming place, with a nice old Norman church and not much else. It hardly looks like the base camp of an invading army, but this was where 200 Viking longships (or perhaps 500 or 1000, the estimates vary) were hauled ashore while King Harald of Norway set off with his men to recapture the city of York.

The Vikings had lost control of Yorkshire when Erik Blood-Axe, the last of the Scandinavian kings of York, failed to live up to his name and was ignominiously expelled. It became part of a united England, ruled by a Saxon earl, but there was still a large Viking population, and back home in Norway they kept an eye on how things were going.

They were gratified to see that under Earl Tostig things were not going at all well. For ten years he rampaged around Yorkshire, indulging in just as much rape and pillage as any Viking, until the locals got fed up with it and turfed him out as well. This was rather embarrassing for the King of England, because Tostig happened to be his brother. It would have helped if Tostig had cleared out and stayed out, but instead he lurked across the Channel in Flanders, planning revenge.

It was a good moment for King Harald to get in on the act, and he promised support for Tostig. Much encouraged, Tostig sailed up the Humber to make a comeback, but again the locals chased him off, and as he was retreating out of the estuary, the King of England turned up with his fleet and chased him off towards Scotland. Confusingly, his name was Harold too, but Harold-with-an-o.

That should have been the end of Tostig, but Harald-with-an-a was ready to join in now, and he brought 200 longships (or 500 or 1000) to link up with the remnants of Tostig's forces. Again they sailed up the Humber and this time reached Riccall, where they disembarked to march on York. Meanwhile, Harold-with-an-o was back in the south, worrying about a possible invasion from Normandy; it was all getting extremely complicated.

Tostig and Harald-with-an-a were intercepted at Fulford, a mile or so outside York, but this time the defenders were thoroughly trounced. They marched into York in triumph, acquired provisions and hostages, and then – rather oddly – marched out again, back to their ships. News of this reached Harold-with-an-o, and he had to decide between waiting for the Normans or dealing with the Vikings. The Vikings got priority, and he made a dramatic forced march up to Yorkshire, arriving at Tadcaster only four days after the Battle of Fulford.

Harald-with-an-a had meanwhile decided to go to Stamford Bridge on the River Derwent. Some historians say he had arranged to collect more tributes there, others suggest he had heard that Harold-with-an-o was on his way and thought that would be a good place to take him on. Or maybe he was an early Chelsea supporter and just fancied the name. Whatever the reason, he and Tostig left the longships at Riccall for a second time, and marched across country to Stamford Bridge. This was when the residents of Thorganby probably had the chance to wave an odd Viking flag as he went by.

The Battle of Stamford Bridge was an epic encounter, with some 60 000 men involved on each side. Harold-with-an-o proved the better general, and so many Vikings were killed that when the survivors struggled back to Riccall, there were only enough to man twenty-four longships out of the original 200 (or 500 or 1000). But it was a Viking who proved the greatest hero of Stamford Bridge, a giant Norwegian in the Arnie Schwarzenegger mould, who held the bridge singlehanded as his comrades retreated, against all attempts to dislodge him. Finally a sneaky Saxon rowed a boat under the bridge and thrust a spear upwards between the timbers, dealing him a fatal blow where it hurt most. It

The riverbank at Riccall, where the Viking army landed – and hastily departed.

OPPOSITE *Cawood's swing bridge is modern, but Cawood itself is older than the Vikings.*

was the end also for Harald-with-an-a, killed by an arrow (an occupational hazard for kings with that sort of name), and for Tostig, who died at the hands of his brother, Harold-with-an-o.

The painful incident on the bridge gave rise to a curious tradition which was maintained at Stamford Bridge until the last century. At an annual feast in September, on the anniversary of the battle, the locals made tub-shaped pies, in memory of the supposedly tub-shaped boat used by the sneaky Saxon. I doubt that Arnie the Viking would appreciate the thought.

The bridge itself is supposed to have survived until 1727, when a stone bridge replaced it, but as recently as a hundred years ago, when the waters of the Derwent were particularly low, the stone piers of the original bridge were laid bare. About the same time, a Norwegian spear was found in the river, and the fields by the bridge are still known as the Battle Flats. Stamford Bridge was, in fact, the Pons Belli of Yorkshire, the site of the last great Saxon victory, so the last word should go to the victor, Harold-with-an-o. It is said that when he was asked what terms he would offer if Harald-with-an-a surrendered he replied: 'Six feet of English earth – or, if he is a giant, seven.'

I hope he made the most of his moment of glory. A few days later, word reached him in York that William of Normandy had landed in Kent. 'Ho hum, another day, another battle,' said Harold, or words to that effect, and set off again for the south. The rest, as they say, is history…

Back at Riccall there was no hint of all this impending mayhem as Vic the Viking continued his journey up the Ouse. Perhaps it was as well he could not foresee the fate of those who were to come after him. In any case he would have been too busy negotiating the sharp bend in the river just above Riccall, before it straightened out again towards Kelfield and Cawood.

Cawood was a settlement long before Vic arrived. Prehistoric travellers forded the river where the swing bridge operates now, a Bronze Age ring has been found there, as have the remains of a Roman villa. But it was the Viking period which saw the beginning of its entry in the history books with the foundation of the 'Castle', as it is known locally, one part of which still stands today.

It was not the Vikings, however, who built it. The

The monument in Cawood church to George Mountain, Archbishop of York – for a fortnight.

Cawood church may contain a Mountain, but it stands on little more than a molehill.

subsidize apprentices. There is a handsome monument to the Archbishop in Cawood church.

Cawood Castle-cum-Palace went downhill after that. During the Civil War it changed hands between Royalists and Parliamentarians a number of times, not as a palace but as a prison, and what was left of the building from the fighting was wrecked by the prisoners. The Archbishops based themselves at Bishopthorpe (why not Archbishopthorpe, I wonder?) and Cawood's days of glory were over. Now the village sits, rather uneasily, on one of the richest seams of coal in Britain, part of the Selby coalfield, hoping the miners don't get too enthusiastic down below.

All this was a long way into the future when Vic the Viking passed by. For him, Cawood was merely a stopping-place with perhaps an earlier church on the rising ground by the river, where the present church stands now. This is the highest point in the area; a benchmark on the church tower records that it is all of 29 feet 3 inches above sea level. The plain here is indeed very flat and very low, and the nearby villages are easily visible across the fields.

Stillingfleet, for instance, is up a tributary of the Ouse, 3 miles from Cawood, and if Vic were sailing past today he might well pay a nostalgic visit to the parish church. On the great south door the ironwork has been identified as Viking in character, and there is even a representation of a Viking longship with little figures in it. In the churchyard there is a later reminder of the river traffic on the Ouse. It is a memorial to ten carol singers and a parish clerk who drowned in the river after visiting neighbouring villages on Boxing Day, 1833 – or, since carol singing generally finishes on Christmas Eve, perhaps they had just enjoyed a long and convivial Christmas. They are buried there in a communal grave.

Vic could hardly sail up that tributary today; it is little more than a stream. He might have done so, however, in Viking times, because even in the twentieth century the floods can be deep enough for a Viking ship. A plaque on the bridge across the stream recalls that in March, 1947, the depth of water reached 21 feet. At that rate, Vic could have sailed even further up the stream to Escrick, remembered in the history books as the home of Sir Thomas Knyvet, who discovered barrels of gunpowder in the House of Commons cellars in 1605. Guy Fawkes himself is said to have been born and brought up in Bishopthorpe, which is only a few miles away. One wonders how the Knyvet and Fawkes families got on...

Back on the Ouse, Vic the Viking is on his final lap to York. The river makes a wide loop at Naburn, where a chain ferry operated across the river to Acaster Malbis until about forty years ago. To cross the river now you need to hitch a lift on one of the yachts from the Yorkshire Ouse Sailing Club, which is based at Naburn. Its clubhouse used to be the blacksmith's shop.

Acaster was the site of one of the Roman forts which were said to line the river every 2 miles from York to the Humber. If that were the case, then the next one would have been at Bishopthorpe, and the remains of both these forts, and possibly others as well, could still have been standing as Vic the Viking sailed by. Judging by its name there was certainly a Viking settlement at Bishopthorpe, along with Copmanthorpe and Middlethorpe adjoining it. Two of its streets, Coney Street (Konung meant a king) and Goodramgate, have Viking origins, and Vic might have felt quite at home as he neared the end of his voyage. He was too early to have seen the Archbishop's residence, which is now the star attraction for the cruise boats that sail down the river from York, but he would not have been too bothered; Jorvik was only 3 miles ahead.

Nothing is left of the town which Vic saw as he sailed up the Ouse. Most of its buildings were made of wood and have long since disappeared. 'Alas, poor Jorvik,' as you would expect me to say, and indeed we do know it well, because there have been such extensive digs in the city in recent years that a fairly complete picture has been built up of life in Jorvik and along the waterfront in the days of Vic the Viking.

We know that he would have sailed past the junction with the River Foss – which became unrecognizable when the Normans damned the Foss to flood the ditches round their new castle. It is likely that he tied up at Skeldergate, just below the Ouse Bridge; there was a bridge in Viking times and, as now, this was the main waterfront area. Skeldergate is just one of the road names that have survived: Coppergate, Fishergate, and so on.

We know that in the centre of the city, where if you look upwards today you will see a frilly-skirted American Indian,

The Bishop's Palace at Bishopthorpe; the Vikings would be impressed.

The new A64 road bridge is quite impressive too.

The Ouse Bridge in York – and yes, beyond it that's the Viking Hotel …

a horned red devil, and on the clock in Coney Street (there is the Viking connection again) a little admiral taking a sighting with his sextant, there were single-storey houses of wattle and daub with thatched roofs, set in plots of land divided by wattlework fences; workshops and market stalls, craftsmen working in metal and leather, cloth weavers and bone carvers, and of course the coopers, or cupmakers, of Coppergate. Along the waterfront there were merchant ships unloading their cargoes in barrels and baskets, and Vic preparing for his first night ashore…

But there is no need to try and describe all this. The Jorvik Viking Centre has done it much better. It has created its own version of a Timepath, a 'Timecar' which carries you back through a thousand years into a reconstructed Coppergate, complete with sounds and smells – and Vic the Viking himself.

No, he is not one of the anonymous figures which inhabit this newly created Viking scene, though they do include three seamen unloading their ship, who look very like him. But I am convinced that the Viking Centre has not only re-created Viking Coppergate, it has re-created Vic the Viking himself.

In 1986 a relatively undamaged skull was dug up during excavations in Fishergate, an area near the river. It belonged to a slightly-built male Viking, about thirty years old. Nobody did much about it for five years, until the medical physics department at University College Hospital tried out their new laser-scanning technique on it. The scanner is normally used to forecast what facial surgery will look like when the scars heal, but in the case of the Viking skull it created a three-dimensional graphic. Then another scan was taken of a doctor at the hospital, of similar age and build. All sorts of data were fed into a computer along with the scans, and up came the image of how the skull must have looked when it was covered by skin and tissue.

From this image a head was modelled which was an exact replica of how the thirty-year-old Viking looked when he was alive. A sculptor used the computer data to recreate the body that went with the skull. They dressed it in Viking clothes, sat it down beside a basket of fish, gave it a knife in one hand and a fish to gut in the other, and announced they had re-created 'Eymund the Fisherman'. But I wonder…

No doubt they assumed he was a fisherman because the skull was found in Fishergate. But other folk frequented the fish market besides fishermen – somebody had to buy the fish, after all – and I am convinced that one of the customers was a certain merchant seaman who had just sailed into Jorvik, unloaded his cargo, and had gone to Fishergate to buy a nice herring for his tea.

I have no idea why he dropped dead there – but then nobody knows why 'Eymund' did either. The same fate could have befallen either of them: a sudden heart attack, a poisoned mussel, even a fishbone stuck in the throat. We know the whole population of Jorvik suffered from gut worms, some of them a foot or more long; this may have been a worm too far. It seems to me that, whatever the cause, there is no more reason to believe that he was a fisherman called Eymund than that he was a seaman called Vic.

What clinches it for me, though, is that the nice people at the Jorvik Centre obviously agree. 'We have re-created your Vic', they all say. Most people think they are saying Jorvik, but I know better, and I am sure you do too.

So be it. Take away the fishknife and the fish, give him a rope to knot, or a sail to mend, and after ten centuries – meet Vic the Viking…

York's Stonegate: the name is a reminder that, long ago, the Vikings were here.

THE
CORPSE TRAIL

*Down Swaledale
with Paul the Bearer*

PREVIOUS PAGES *Swaledale in North Yorkshire – a magnificent setting for a macabre trail.*

GETTING ABOUT in rural Britain in the Middle Ages must have been a very tedious exercise. When Robert Louis Stevenson wrote, 'I travel not to go anywhere, but to go. I travel for travel's sake', he didn't have to bounce about in an ox-cart on a rutted road, assuming he even had the luxury of a road. In many remote areas there were just tracks over the hills and fells, most of them too narrow for a cart, some of them too tricky even to ride a horse. This was the domain of the packhorse, the only means of transporting goods for any distance in the isolated areas of the Lake District and the Yorkshire Dales.

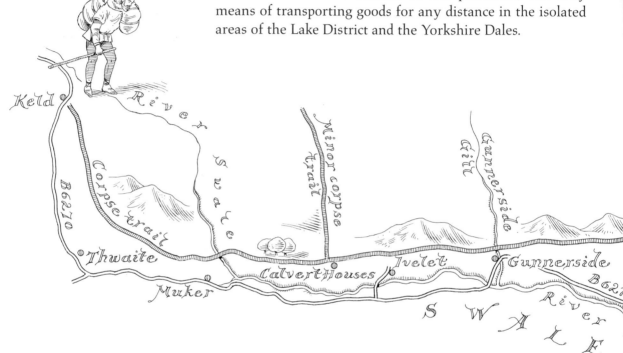

That era has left behind some obvious reminders, like the Packhorse Inns dotted around Yorkshire and Derbyshire, and all those packhorse bridges, with the parapets just far enough apart for a single file of horses, and low enough to be cleared by the panniers. And there are less obvious links – like Mick Jagger.

The most popular breed of packhorse was actually a pony, a short sturdy animal from Germany called Jaegar. It became anglicized to Jagger, and the packmen who wandered the fells and dales with their ponies acquired the name as well. It is more than likely that Mick Jagger's family is descended from these medieval rolling stones…

The packtrains used to have twenty or thirty of these Jaegar ponies. Their panniers were loaded, not with upmarket woolies but with salt, and coal, and lead. The one at the front had bells on its harness to guide the others if a mist came down, and also, I am assured, to warn packtrains coming the other way. I am not sure why this should be useful, since packhorses don't travel at the sort of speed which could cause a fatal head-on collision, and on most of these tracks there was no room to get out of the way even if you knew something was coming. The first test of a packman, I suspect, was to be able to make your packtrain go backwards.

There were a number of specialized packhorse trails where the loads were not for barter but for burial, and these loads were carried, not always by ponies but by people. These were the corpse trails, routes taken across the hills by funeral parties from the remote homes of the deceased to the nearest consecrated ground, sometimes involving many miles of tortuous paths and, in winter, appalling conditions.

The most famous of these, and I am afraid the most bogus, is the Lyke Wake Walk across the North Yorkshire moors from Osmotherley to Ravenscar, a distance of 40 miles from the most westerly to the most easterly extremity of the Cleveland Hills. It sounds genuine enough. 'Lyke' means corpse, as in the lych-gate of a church, and 'wake' of course is the vigil over the body; 'walk' just rounds it off. It is given an extra flavour of authenticity by the Cleveland Lyke Wake Dirge, an ancient lament in such broad dialect that it is almost incomprehensible to a southerner, and I suspect that some Yorkshire folk have to concentrate to make it out. Here's a sample:

> *If ivver thoo gav o' thy siller an' gowd,*
> *Ivvery neet an' all,*
> *on t'Brig o Dreead thoo'll finnd footho'd,*
> *An' Christ tak up thy saul.*
> *But if siller an' gowd thoo never gav neean,*
> *Ivvery neet an' all,*
> *Thoo'll doon, doon tum'le towards Hell Fleeames,*
> *And Christ tak up thy saul...*

Which means, I think, 'If you've been generous then you're OK, but if not, you've had it – every night and all.'

As well as the Bridge of Dread, the Dirge features Whinny Moor: 'When thoo frae hence away art passed... Ti Whinny Moor thoo cums at last', which reflects the old Yorkshire belief that the souls of the departed had to cross the moor. It was a throwback to the Bronze Age practice of burning bodies and burying them on the high points of the moors, where the burial barrows can still be seen. But that's about it, so far as the authenticity of the Lyke Wake Walk is concerned. If you think about it, why should bodies be carried across the moor for 40 miles when there were churchyards within a few miles of both Osmotherley and Ravenscar? Even if the family insisted on a moorland hike, Rosedale Abbey was halfway along the route, so why not stop there?

No, I am afraid the Walk dates back less than forty years. An enthusiastic walker called Bill Cowley devised it in 1955, after realizing it was possible to cross the Cleveland Hills over uninterrupted open moors, and issued a challenge to anyone who could complete the walk in twenty-four hours. He did it himself for a start, and in the years that followed, the Lyke Wake Walk became so popular that these days there is a Lyke Wake Club whose members call themselves Dirgers, ranging from an eighty-one-year-old cleric to two twelve-year-old boys. All of them have made the crossing; several have done it both ways. There seems no limit to the urge to dirge.

One group actually made the crossing carrying a coffin, but that is the nearest that the Lyke Wake Walk has come to a corpse trail. Mr Cowley himself has exploded that myth. In a guidebook he wrote for dirgers, he wrote: 'There is no suggestion that corpses were carried over the Lyke Wake Walk, and the connection between Walk and Dirge is merely that members of the first party to do the Walk, like many who have done it since, finding themselves in the middle of Wheeldale Moor at 3 a.m., felt a great sympathy with all the souls who had to do such a crossing, and a real affection for the poetry of the Dirge.'

The genuine corpse trails were in fact much shorter. Even in the wilds of the North Country, it was rarely necessary to walk 40 miles to find a church, even in medieval times. The first corpse trail I came across was in the Lake District, in the unlikely vicinity of the Ravenglass and Eskdale Railway. Both the original railway and the trail terminated at Boot, an improbable name for an attractive little Eskdale village. The trail started at Wasdale Head, on the far side of Scafell, and ended in the graveyard of St Catherine's Church at Boot.

The distance is only 6 miles as the crow files, but as the funeral cortège struggled across the open moor it must have seemed a lot further. Sometimes the body was dragged by the mourners on a sledge, sometimes it was strapped on a packhorse. The packhorse sounds the better bet, but on one unfortunate occasion the horse became scared and bolted, disappearing into the mountain mist with the body still on its back.

To add to the general discomfiture, when the mother of the deceased was told the news back in Wasdale, she never recovered from the shock. A day or two later, her body was taken along the same route, on the back of another horse. This time the procession found itself in a terrible snowstorm and, sure enough, that horse bolted too. The son's body was recovered in due course by a search-party, but the other horse and its load were never seen again. Well, not quite. They do say that a ghostly horse has been spotted on a stormy night plodding along the corpse trail, bearing a ghostly body (if that is feasible) on its back. One hopes it is heading in the right direction, to Boot…

My favourite corpse trail, however – and I hope that doesn't sound too morbid – is in Swaledale, not only because this is probably the loveliest dale in North Yorkshire but because it has many more stories to tell than just one lurid legend. The routes taken by these trails were specifically planned to avoid places of habitation, in case the spirit of the dead was tempted to return, and indeed the trail from Wasdale is about as far from habitation as you can get. But in Swaledale the villages are never far away, and as the journey from the top of the dale to Grinton churchyard took a couple of days, it was quite reasonable for a member of the funeral cortège – let's call him Paul the Bearer – to stop along the way for rest and refreshment. It made a more interesting excursion for Paul – and for those who are coming after him…

NOBODY KNOWS WHEN the first corpse was carried along the Swaledale corpse trail. Grinton church was founded by the monks of Bridlington 900 years ago but its period of greatest importance was during the Middle Ages when its parish was one of the largest in England, 20 miles long and covering 50 000 acres, as far as the Cumbrian border. Anyone who died in the dale had to be carried down to Grinton, if the burial was to be in consecrated ground. Most of them were taken along the corpse trail, some 12 miles from one end of the dale to the other. It provided the principal route for the bodies – the trunk road, as it were – but there were also subsidiary trails which joined it at various points, coming down from the little communities on the hills.

Grinton church's monopoly of burials ended in 1580, when a chapel of ease was built at Muker, halfway down the dale. From then on the corpse trail was cut in two; funeral processions from the upper dale only went as far as Muker. Paul the Bearer had no such luck in the pre-1580s; he had to cover the full 12 miles, carrying the body shoulder-high on a stretcher, inside a wicker container. On the return journey, unencumbered, he probably only took a few hours, but the standard time for a funeral procession was two days and a night.

The mourners would assemble, as they often do today, at the home of the bereaved, and biscuits were handed round before they set off. But instead of a short drive to a nearby church, these Swaledale mourners faced the long hike down the dale. It must have been a daunting prospect – two days scrambling along narrow and probably slippery hillside tracks, with the River Swale having to be forded twice, but the good news was that the deceased's family arranged food and accommodation en route, so at least they didn't have to carry two days' haversack rations. All they had to carry, in fact, was the corpse, and four of the younger and fitter mourners were designated as bearers. One of them, on this occasion, was Paul.

The main assembly point for the corpse trail in Upper Swaledale was the little village of Keld. These days they need go no further, because there is a churchyard in the village, albeit a Nonconformist one. Groups still assemble in Keld for the walk down into the dale, but these walkers are carrying cameras rather than corpses. The village is a great centre for walking, set close to the Pennine Way and the coast-to-coast walk that crosses it, in addition to the corpse trail itself, and a youth hostel helps to increase the seasonal congestion in the village street.

Not that there is much else to do in Keld except walk out of it. Even that devoted Yorkshire Dale walker, Mike Harding, was a little depressed by his unsuccessful efforts to buy some milk. 'The youth hostel was closed, the only shop was disguised as a garage and had no window, a local Quaker family had helped to close the only pub in the village in the 1950s, and a farmer I asked said he had none. As the Ancient Mariner might have said: "Cows, cows, everywhere, Yet ne'er a drop to drink…"'

Well, Keld was pretty quiet while I was there too, out of season. The only concession to tourism was the box at the entrance to some wasteground which passed as a car park, inviting me to contribute 50 pence – and park as long as I liked. I suppose the day may come when Keld has parking meters and even a milk bar, but I suspect Mr Harding would prefer to go thirsty. Keld is still recognizable as an old lead-mining village, and I hope will remain so, if only to preserve the memory of Neddy Dick.

There are many tales about Neddy Dick, not all of them entirely believable, but each involves his peculiar musical

Keld's Victorian churchyard looks out on the start of the medieval corpse trail.

talents. His principal instrument was the harmonium, but this came to be the basis for more exotic forms of music-making. He acquired a collection of bells, some say from old grandfather clocks, and he played these with one hand while accompanying himself on the harmonium with the other. Then he switched from bells to stones, having discovered that when he dropped one, it made a vaguely musical noise. He collected stones of various sizes and constructed a sort of stone xylophone, which he took on tour in a horse and cart and enlivened many a Swaledale soirée with his 'rock band' – Mike Harding's phrase, not mine. I am sure Paul the Bearer would have appreciated his company during his overnight stop on the corpse trail.

Neddy Dick has long since gone, alas, and so has his stone xylophone, last seen in a state of disintegration in some-body's wash-house, but the corpse trail, far older than either of them, lives on, and is easy to follow out of Keld, along-side the Swale. Keld means 'a place by the river', and this is where the Swale really becomes a river, as several streams join forces to go rushing off down the dale. Some say it is the fastest-running river in Britain – one of those useful claims which cannot be proved or disproved – it certainly rushes over some spectacular waterfalls just below the village.

Kisden Force is the most dramatic, set in a deep wooded gorge near the point where the corpse trail veers away from the river to go round the far side of Kisden Hill, towering 600 feet above. The Pennine Way, however, continues paral-lel to the river, passing the delightfully-named Crackpot Hall on the far bank. The Hall is just a ruin now, and I could not decide whether it had been the home of a local eccentric or merely had trouble with its chimneys. It transpires, how-ever, that this 'crackpot' comes from old Norse – the Vikings got into these parts too – and means 'pothole of the crows'. There are a lot of potholes in Swaledale, also a lot of crows, and the Vikings must have seen a link between the two. There is actually a village further down the dale called Crackpot, which must look splendid on headed notepaper.

This definition gives 'crackpot' a whole new dimension in colourful inventive. Without it, calling somebody a crackpot is just gently insulting, but when you are actually saying, 'You are a pothole of the crows' – what a put-down!

Meanwhile, on the other side of Kisden Hill, Paul is carrying his burden down the corpse trail, probably not

OPPOSITE *The Swale, the 'fastest-running river in Britain' – here at its fastest.*

BELOW *Kisden Force, a spectacular stopping-place along the trail.*

TOP *The old school at Muker, once with two famous pupils, now a craft shop and tea-room.*

ABOVE *The plaque on Muker school in memory of the Keartons.*

appreciating the magnificent scenery around him, though later walkers have waxed ecstatic about the views down the dale. 'A wonderland', wrote one. 'Breathtaking', wrote another. 'The finest scenery along the entire length of the Pennine Way.' What can I add? It's really rather good.

The Pennine Way and the corpse trail meet up again at Kisden Farm, on the lower slopes of Kisden Hill, then the Pennine Way heads off towards Thwaite on the main road, while Paul avoids the village and continues down the dale towards Muker. He is not missing much because Thwaite, like Keld, is just a cluster of houses where the principal occupation seems to be watching the walkers go by but, like Keld again, it has produced its own celebrity. A pair of them, in fact, not quite in the same unique mould as Neddy Dick, but outstanding in their own field.

Richard and Cherry Kearton – two brothers, in spite of that misleading Christian name – were the sons of a Victorian gamekeeper who went to the village school at Muker. They both developed talents as naturalists, and a London publisher who came to Swaledale for a shoot was so impressed by Richard that he gave him a job in his office. Cherry soon followed his brother to London, and while Richard became a noted writer and lecturer, Cherry went in for wildlife photography. They collaborated on several books, and became nationally known.

In the days before the telephoto lens, big-game photography was even more hazardous than it is today, but it also presented problems in taking pictures of animals which were not wild, just shy. One of the brothers' subterfuges was to hide inside a stuffed cow – Cherry, presumably, was the front legs, so he could take the photographs. They described their embarrassment on occasions when the stuffed cow was blown over by the wind, or worse still, when it was spotted by a bull. But the books they produced revolutionized the study of wildlife and popularized natural history at a time when it was thought rather effete.

In his later years Cherry Kearton made films and broadcasts for the BBC – and, tragically, it was outside Broadcasting House in London that he was killed in an air raid in 1940. There is a plaque in memory of the Keartons on Muker schoolhouse, now a craft shop and tea room. In Thwaite their name is also immortalized over the teacups, at the Kearton Guest House.

Paul the Bearer would know nothing of the Keartons, nor of natural history, but he would be familiar with a natural phenomenon which still exists near Thwaite, by the road that climbs out of Swaledale and heads over the moors to Hawes. He may even have known it by the same name, the Buttertubs, because these deep limestone potholes were used, it is said, by farmers who had failed to sell their butter at market. They hung the butter down the holes on the end of a rope, keeping it in cold storage in fact, until the next market day. I only hope there were no crows connected with these potholes, or they would probably have finished off the butter; it really would have been a crackpot idea. As it was, there might have been the odd butter-thief around who hauled it up again as soon as the farmer was out of sight. But even today it can be dangerous to go too close to the Buttertubs; frost and water are working away on the limestone all the time. Maybe a farmer just hoped to find the thief down the pothole, alongside the butter.

The Buttertubs, limestone potholes where farmers kept their butter in cold storage.

Paul the Bearer, now near Muker, is tackling another natural hazard. The funeral party has to ford the Swale here to follow the easier north bank down the dale. Before doing so, however, he and the cortège make a detour into Muker for a little sustenance at the Queen's Head. Even after the church was built at Muker and there was no more through traffic on the corpse trail, the Queen's Head still provided food and drink for funeral parties, and the practice continued until the beginning of this century. The mourners drank out of decorated 'funeral mugs', which were hung from the kitchen ceiling between funerals. The Queen's Head became a private house after the First World War, and the mugs have long since gone, but the building is still recognizable, with its inn-like courtyard.

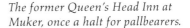

The former Queen's Head Inn at Muker, once a halt for pallbearers.

It stands close by Muker church, which took away half of Grinton's funeral trade in 1580. It has been so comprehensively 'restored' a couple of times that it is difficult to picture it with a thatched roof, with its floor covered with rushes, and no pews, just benches along the sides so that the aged and infirm could 'go to the wall'. In the eighteenth century slates replaced the thatch, a three-decker pulpit and pews were installed (some of the pews with their backs to the pulpit, which allowed a little shut-eye during the sermon), and a wood platform was erected for the musicians – bass fiddle, violin, clarinet and harmonium.

A post-corpse trail notice in Muker church, setting out the rules for the village hearse.

The present Rampsholme Bridge near Muker; pallbearers had to wade across.

The Victorians readjusted all this, but they did preserve the board which sets out the charges for the hearse which the parish bought in 1836, and which superceded Paul the Bearer and his colleagues. Actually they were not made entirely redundant, because the hearse stopped at the school, and the coffin was carried from there to the church. The hearse was not a very grand vehicle, basically a wooden box on four wheels, with black plumes round the box and leather round the wheels to quieten them. The charge was sixpence for funerals within Muker itself, and sixpence a mile outside. Paul would have appreciated that mileage rate for his 12-mile trek along the corpse trail.

What I appreciated at Muker church was one of the tombstones in the churchyard. One often finds quaint little epitaphs in country churchyards which are endearing in their simplicity, but there is nothing simple about the epitaph to Edward and Ann Broderick, written by 'the son Luke':

> *I want the world to know*
> *That I know;*
> *That there is no fame;*
> *That all life is co-equal;*
> *That deficiency in intellect is the why*
> *Of deficiency in action.*
> *That everything is right;*
> *That every atom vibrates*
> *At its proper time according to the true results*
> *Of the forces that went before.*

I wonder what Paul the Bearer – or even Einstein – would make of that…

Actually the Broderick family would not have been too popular with Paul and his fellow bearers, quite apart from their obscure taste in epitaphs. One Broderick directed that his body should be buried on the hills above Muker. He died in mid-winter at Hawes, in the next dale, so first his remains had to be carried over Buttertubs Pass in a blizzard as far as Muker. There the curate announced that he had been forbidden by his bishop to conduct a funeral service on unconsecrated ground – and the bearers no doubt hoped the family would give up the idea and go to the churchyard instead. The Brodericks, however, did not give up that easily; the cortège climbed up the hill, and the dead man's brother read the service. I think that rated more than sixpence a mile...

Having emptied his funeral mug once or twice at the Queen's Head, Paul is back on duty on the corpse trail. To ford the river the wicker basket is transferred to a pony – the river is too fast and deep for pallbearers to keep their footing with a load on their shoulders. But once across, it is back on their shoulders again, until the next pause at Calvert Houses. These are just a small group of buildings – 'a shrunken hamlet', as one writer puts it, and you can't get a smaller community than that – but in Paul's day there was a beer tavern called the Traveller's Rest, where I suspect he dropped in for another pint.

Calvert Houses, where two corpse trails met.

At Calvert Houses a subsidiary corpse trail joined the main one, coming down from the north side of Upper Swaledale. It circled Rogan's Seat which, at 2200 feet, is the highest point in the area, and whoever Rogan was, he could hardly have needed a seat more than the pallbearers by the time they reached the Traveller's Rest. No doubt they and Paul exchange commiserations and a round or two, if their arrivals coincide.

Then Paul continues along the corpse trail to Ivelet, and here we know he takes another rest, because beside Ivelet Bridge is a 'corpse-stone', where the bodies were placed while the bearers took a breather. Some sceptics say the corpse-stone only got its name because it happens to be shaped like a coffin, but it is surely much too handy a size, in much too pleasant a spot, for Paul not to make use of it.

The bridge itself, a graceful single span with a semicircular arch, did not exist in Paul's day, though it looks as if it should. It was built with the help of a bequest of £5 from a Mr Swale, who did not die until 1687. His family, incidentally, lived in Swaledale for 600 years, from 1138 to 1733, starting with Alured de Swale, nephew of Walter de Gaunt, who was a kinsman of William the Conqueror. That may only interest you if your name is Swale and you fancy your chances as heir to the throne, but I wonder if this is something of a record for a Yorkshire Dale. Were there Wensleys in Wensleydale for six centuries? Or Wharfes in Wharfedale? Nidders in Niddersdale? And what about the sons and Aires of Airedale...?

The 'corpse-stone' by Ivelet Bridge; pallbearers would put down their load to have a breather.

By this time Paul must be well on his way along the corpse trail to Gunnerside, now as sleepy a village as the

The seventeenth-century Ivelet Bridge, built too late for the medieval pallbearers.

others but once the centre of the Swaledale leadmining industry. Lead has been mined in Swaledale and Arkengarthdale (ah, how many Arkengarths?) from the days when Romans used it for waterpipes and roofs. After they left, the locals carried on, and it is recorded that in AD 672, Swaledale miners met merchants in Catterick to negotiate a price for their lead, so the mines must have been doing well without the Roman know-how.

Then the monasteries took over, shrewd operators who exploited the mines and made nice profits for the Abbots of Fountains and Rievaulx, and the Prior of Bridlington. Private operators built the industry up to a peak in the late eighteenth century, but by the late nineteenth it was petering out, and the last mine closed in 1910. In Swaledale the population slumped from 7000 to 2000 as the miners and their families moved away in search of work. Most of Gunnerside migrated to Lancashire, leaving behind a Methodist church large enough to take 500 people, and on the slopes of Gunnerside Gill the crumbling ruins of mine buildings, kilns and crushing mills. Arkengarthdale, which joins Swaledale further down the corpse trail, is a much starker landscape of old workings, crumbling chimneys and roofless cottages, but Gunnerside Gill looks desolate enough.

The miners would be hard at it when Paul goes by, making money for the monasteries until Henry VIII put in his notorious take-over bid. But Gunnerside was not a recognized stop on the corpse trail – it was too well-populated an area – so he doesn't have another break until he reaches the little hamlet of Blades, high above the river. This was the regular overnight stop for funeral parties – or rather, for the corpses. They were left in the 'dead-house', a sort of medieval mortuary, while the cortège headed down the hill to Feetham on the main road, to spend the night at the Punchbowl Inn.

The dead-house is in ruins now, but the Punchbowl is very much alive, a convivial hostelry with an excellent line in bar lunches. It has been much altered since Paul's day, but you can still make out the line of the original roof gables, and one of the internal doors is an elaborate studded affair which Paul would recognize as the front door that he passed through on his way to the bar.

The Punchbowl was no doubt as convivial then as it is now, and I can quite believe the story of the funeral parties

The ruins of the 'dead-house' where corpses were left overnight ...

who happened to meet there, having left their wicker baskets in the dead-house up the hill. After a heavy night they tottered up to Blades next morning, picked up their burdens, and set off along the corpse trail. It was only when the bodies were taken out of the wicker baskets to be interred that they found they had been carrying the wrong ones...

Paul, I trust, spends a more meditative night at the Punchbowl, and sets off next morning refreshed for the final lap of the journey. The corpse trail continues along the hillside, some hundreds of feet above the river to avoid the marshier areas below. Before reaching Healaugh, however, the cortège must decide whether to cross the river here and continue to Grinton on the far side, or remain on the north bank and cross at Grinton itself. It depends, I imagine, on the time of year, the state of the river, and the bogginess of the banks.

I expect that Paul, given the option, would cross the river here, to avoid going too close to the market town of Reeth, straight ahead. The opposite bank has had few inhabitants since the local tribe, the Brigantes, dug out a massive earthwork to defend Swaledale against the Romans. It covers 2 acres and the rampart is 16 feet high, so it took a lot of Brigantes and a lot of digging, and it has lasted a very long time. It is known as Maiden's Castle, perhaps because the Brigantes were led by a woman called Cartimandua, a sort of Boadicea of the North.

According to a reputable history book she divorced her husband Venutius in AD 69. Divorced? Then, more believably, she co-habited with his armour-bearer. She also led a tribal revolt against the Romans, much as Boadicea had done in East Anglia nine years before, but maybe the knives on her chariot-wheels were not as sharp – or the armour-bearer was too demanding – and she never got very far.

Maiden Castle has been deserted for centuries, and that is the way Paul would like it, but I hope some problem with the river crossing keeps him on the north bank, because Reeth is not only interesting in its own right, it is also the gateway to Arkengarthdale, which is very interesting indeed.

Reeth, like Gunnerside, was an important mining centre, but it was a knitting centre too. What Swaledale produced in considerable quantity was not only lead but the famous Swaledale sheep, and while the men were digging, the

TOP ...*while the pallbearers spent a meditative night at the Punchbowl Inn.*

ABOVE *The original front door of the Punchbowl, now transferred inside.*

women were knitting. Actually the men knitted too, during their rest periods, so that instead of taking forty winks they were said to take 'six needles' – which would have a sinister connotation in these drug-conscious days but was very innocent then. Knitting may seem rather cissy for a burly leadminer, but try saying that to a burly leadminer…

The other famous feature of Reeth is its band. Brass bands have been very strong in Swaledale, and every village of any note, one might say, had its own band and bandroom. Some of them were very modest – the bandroom, that is, not the band. Modesty is not usually associated with brass bandsmen. At Muker the room only held sixteen people, or twelve with instruments. The volume of noise on rehearsal nights in such a confined space was impressive, but the neighbours didn't seem to mind. In fact, on one occasion I am told that one of them rushed into the bandroom, not to complain, but to cry: 'That was champion, lads. Come outside and listen for yourselves.' On second thoughts, perhaps it was just a subtle way of stopping them…

Reeth had one of the most successful bands in Swaledale, which reached the national finals in 1973 under its leader and bandmaster, the Rev. Edward Tindall. The local paper got very excited about it, and produced the memorable headline: 'Band with Hopes of Glory'. Alas, the hopes did not materialize, due to a succession of mishaps which even the bandmaster's divine connections failed to avert.

First, the accommodation in London was double-booked, and nobody got to bed before midnight. Second, they were drawn to play sixth, which gave them no time for practice beforehand. Third, the euphonium player could not get to London at all, and his stand-in was so nervous he fluffed his notes. And fourth, the principal cornet player had to attend a family funeral and, although he did arrive at the contest in time, he had no breath left to blow his cornet.

The adjudicator observed that 'whilst the instrumentalists were of high quality, they appeared to lack pre-contest practice', which was quite true. The Band with Hopes of Glory returned without a trophy – but they got a hero's welcome anyway.

The road from Reeth up Arkengarthdale was one of the first in the dales to be turnpiked, because of its importance to the leadmining industry, and the whole history of the dale revolves around the mines. But it has other fascinating

OPPOSITE *Stone walls, along the corpse trail.*

Tan Hill Inn – the highest inn in England, built originally for the benefit of the miners.

The Old Powderhouse in CB, the village named after mineowner Charles Bathurst.

features, too. Where else, for instance, can you find two neighbouring hamlets called Booze and Whaw?

I would like to think that 'Whaw!' was a natural follow-up to Booze, but I am sure the locals are fed up with that sort of comment. 'Booze' is either derived from 'the house by the river', or it is a contraction of 'bull house', depending on which defensive argument you prefer. Either way, I have to confirm that there is not a pub in sight.

There is one, however, at the top of Arkengarthdale, and a very famous pub too. The Tan Hill Inn features in all the record books as the highest pub in England, 1732 feet above sea level. I have to confess that, if it were not for this curious distinction and it was situated in any other location, I would not look twice at the Tan Hill Inn. It is an unremarkable building, as plain and featureless as the countryside around it, with nothing that one looks for in a quaint old English pub – except a very large car park. But in fact the Inn has quite a story to tell in its own right.

As far back as the thirteenth century, Tan Hill was the centre of the local coalmining industry, and the inn was built to provide refreshment for the miners who lived in 'bothies' on Tan Hill during the week, and returned to their families in Swaledale at weekends. The carters who took away the coal no doubt had a glass or two there as well, and there are still memories of a Victorian coal-dealer called Elhamah, who led a team of coal-laden donkeys around the isolated farmsteads, helping to keep the home fires burning. He was noted for blowing a horn to announce the arrival of his coal caravans, just as delivery men and women sound their horns today.

However, the main customers for Tan Hill coal were the Arkengarthdale leadmines, and in the seventeenth century these were acquired by a Dr Bathurst. It was his grandson Charles who gave his name – or rather, his initials – to the company which owned the mines, and to the community which grew up around them. So here is another curious feature of Arkengarthdale, a hamlet known only by initials. The local hostelry is called the CB Hotel, and in a field nearby is an octagonal building with its roof still intact called the Old Powderhouse CB.

The hotel and the powderhouse are about all that survive intact of the old CB empire. For the rest, there is little but derelict workings and vast acres of spoil heaps, their conical shapes and grey anonymity making parts of the dale look like a moonscape. Many years ago I suppose Arkengarthdale was as green and pleasant as Swaledale itself; now Charles Bathurst's initials just stand for Completely Barren…

There was mining on the moors above Grinton too, the village where Paul's odyssey is about to end. About a mile away is the Grinton Smelt Mill, still in one piece but used these days for other purposes. But Grinton itself has managed to regain its unspoilt rural character, and the only obvious connection with Arkengarthdale and its desolation is the Arkle Beck, which joins the Swale at Grinton, flowing nearly as fast as its namesake used to run.

The corpse trail approaches Grinton church – and journey's end.

Paul and his party either ford the river near the present road bridge or, if they crossed earlier, they would come along the track that runs along the opposite bank, between the river and the churchyard. Above them soars the high roof and tower of St Andrew's, sometimes called the Cathedral of the Dales, and one of three ecclesiastical buildings which dominated this area of Swaledale. A few miles away at Marrick and Ellerton were a Benedictine priory and a Cistercian priory, on opposite sides of the river but accessible to one another by stepping stones. It would have been more fun if one priory had monks and the other nuns, but they were both all-female. Only the ruined tower of the Cistercian priory survives, but the other is still used as a residential youth centre.

The twelfth-century Marrick Priory, now a field study centre.

Grinton church has continued to function as a church throughout all this, and various features of it are just as Paul the Bearer would remember them. The grooves around the door were there in his day, caused by swords and arrows being sharpened on the stones. So was the fourteenth-century font cover, which replaced the original Norman one. He could have looked through the squint, the little window for lepers to watch the service without mixing with the congregation. And he could have admired – at a distance, perhaps – the chained Bible which has rested on the same stand for 600 years.

Outside in the churchyard he would feel at home too. I could not identify any graves from his era, but the scene must be much the same. Here he lowers his stretcher for the last time, and the body is taken out of its wicker basket and buried in a linen shroud.

A century or so later, that would have been illegal. In

An alternative route for the pallbearers – but they had to keep below 40 …

The end of the corpse trail, Grinton churchyard.

order to encourage the woollen industry, the Government passed an Act decreeing that all burials must be in cloth or clothing made entirely of wool. Most people preferred the traditional approach, and at Grinton a local leadminer was fined £5 – a substantial sum for a seventeenth-century miner – for burying his daughter in linen. This method of drumming up business for an ailing industry never caught on, otherwise in the last century, when leadmining started to decline, they might have insisted that every body was buried with a pigot of lead, and these days it would be a hundredweight of coal…

As Paul the Bearer leaves the churchyard after the burial and prepares for the long walk home, he would see Blackburn Hall, which in his day was the Vicarage and still stands near the church. What he would also see today is a phenomenon all too familiar to us at most churches, but unknown to him – an appeal notice for the church restoration fund. In his day the monks or the Lord of the Manor looked after that sort of thing.

Grinton, however, is fortunate in having a famous patron for its roof appeal. The Swaledale scenery became familiar to millions of viewers through the television series *All Creatures Great and Small*. The cast spent a lot of time in the dale and, not surprisingly, developed a considerable affection for it. As a result Robert Hardy, who played the irascible senior vet, agreed to launch the appeal and be its patron in 1991. When I was there two years later the appeal had raised £90 000 and was still going strong. 'All things bright and beautiful' must be a particularly popular hymn at Grinton church.

Paul the Bearer would be glad to know that such efforts are being made to preserve the church at the end of the corpse trail. I would have liked to find some reminder of him there, and I rather hoped that he would have left the chained bible open at one of the pages in the New Testament where St Paul is on his travels, and is welcomed as the bearer of good tidings. In some bibles the sentence does not quite finish at the end of the page, and there is just a welcome for 'Paul the bearer…'

No such luck, I'm afraid. But let's retrace our steps to the corpse-stone at Ivelet Bridge. The stone has been greatly worn over the centuries by all those wicker coffins, then by wind and weather, and as a result various lines and patterns have become ingrained in the surface. If you look very closely, you may see one pattern which looks uncommonly like the initial 'P'. It was left behind, I am quite sure, by Paul the Bearer – with perhaps a little help – much later – from his friends…

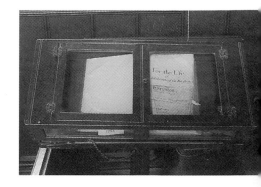

The chained Bible in Grinton church – an early anti-theft device.

THE WELSH ROAD

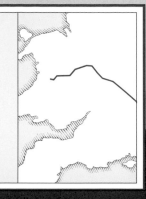

---
*The Cattle Route to London
with Dai the Drover*

'YE ROAST BEEF OF OLDE ENGLAND' has a splendid traditional ring about it. When Dr Johnson sat down to dinner with his friends Garrick and Sheridan and Sir Joshua Reynolds – and, of course, the ubiquitous Boswell – the table would not be complete without a substantial joint of it in pride of place. But alas, the myth has to be exploded.

Ye Roast Beef of Olde England
almost certainly came from Scotland or Wales,
brought to London on the hoof along the old drovers' roads.

In Wales the thought of Olde England being credited with producing Welsh beef must have been particularly irksome. Every year, by the end of the eighteenth century, 9000 cattle swam across the Menai Strait from Anglesey to set off along the drove roads to London. Another 20 000 came from Cardiganshire; 30 000 passed through Herefordshire alone. And having waved their cattle goodbye, the Welsh farmers returned to their staple diet of barley bread and potatoes, with the occasional herring as a treat. A 1794 report notes that 'malt liquor and meat are not within their reach', which is particularly poignant. One can always manage, after all, without meat…

In those days, incidentally, the term 'cattle' could mean sheep as well, and a great many Welsh mountain ewes were driven along the drove roads to London – so the Welsh farmers and their families went without mutton as well as beef. But to save confusion, the cattle I am talking about are the sort that go 'moo' rather than 'baa'.

The drovers must have been a very mixed bunch. Contemporary descriptions of them are so contradictory that they obviously had everyone guessing. Some depict

PREVIOUS PAGES The Long Mynd, on the drovers' route from Wales to London.

them as models of honesty and integrity; others condemn them as rogues. Like the cattlemen of the Wild West, who fulfilled much the same function, there were doubtless good guys and bad guys; it was just difficult to spot them because they all wore black hats.

Even among their fellow Welshmen they were not always esteemed. A nineteenth-century bard called Thomas Edwards composed the unkind epitaph:

The old drover sleeps,
his term completed,
Throughout his wasted
life he cheated.
His world is now a
narrow bed –
Fie, let him cheat
there instead.

Englishmen found them particularly unbearable, probably because they couldn't understand a word they said. The combination of a party of Welsh drovers and a couple of hundred cattle heading straight for you could be quite an unnerving sight. This is how one Englishman described it in the *Farmers' Magazine*:

> *Imagine some hundreds of bullocks like an immense forest of horns, propelled hurriedly towards you amid the hideous and uproarious shouting of a set of semi-barbarous drovers who value a restive bullock far beyond the life of a human being, driving their mad and noisy herds over every person they meet, if not fortunate enough to get out of the way...*

Actually the average speed of a drove was 2 miles an hour, so not too many Englishmen got trampled underfoot, but certainly it was as well for farmers to keep their own cattle off the road as the drove went by; once they were mixed up with the Welsh ones, there was little chance of retrieving them.

On the other hand, droving was a job which not only required stamina and skill, but also honesty and integrity. Until the first drovers' bank was founded – by a drover – in 1799, farmers just had to trust the men who took their cattle to England because they received nothing for them until the drovers got back, and even then they had to trust them to pay the right amount. In addition, drovers were often asked to take large sums of money with them to deliver to relations or businesses in London; they were the only people who regularly travelled these long distances from the remoter corners of Wales.

Quite apart from disappearing with the money themselves, the drovers faced the constant risk of being robbed by footpads, or swindled by dishonest innkeepers, or plied with too much liquor by con-men who stole their cattle as well. But ever since Tudor times a drover had to be licensed, and to get a licence he had to be over thirty, married, and a householder. This is not to say that every middle-aged man with a wife and a house is necessarily honest, but it did weed out the vagrants and the juvenile offenders, and on the whole the system seemed to work. Drovers were certainly shrewd, and mostly sober.

Some of them, in fact, rose to notable positions in Wales. David Jones, who founded the Black Ox Bank at Llandovery for the benefit of drovers, later became High Sheriff of Carmarthenshire. Another drover, Evan Davies, achieved the same office in Radnorshire, and one farmer-drover, Benjamin Evans of Pembrokeshire, became a pastor. That hardly tallies with the 'semi-barbarous' image in the *Farmers' Magazine*.

Some, like Pastor Evans, combined farming with droving, and took their own cattle to England, along with those of their neighbours and friends. Although they had to be licensed they could use casual labour to help with the drove – which perhaps is how the troublemakers crept in. In that case it was easy to spot the goodies and the baddies; the drover rode a pony, the hired man walked.

It was the responsibility of the man in charge of the group – let's call him Dai the Drover – to work out the best route, preferably avoiding turnpikes, which could be expensive, and flooded rivers, which could be fatal. He would have to plan the overnight stopping places, an inn or a friendly farmhouse where the cattle – and the hired hands – could sleep in a nearby 'stance' or fenced field. The charge for the cattle was generally a halfpenny per head per night, hence the 'halfpenny fields' which are still found along the old drove roads. The men, presumably, slept in the hedges for nothing.

If a farmer was prepared to accommodate the drovers he planted three conifers in a prominent position, to attract passing trade. Conifers do grow fast, but it hardly seems a practical system if he was starting from scratch. A simple 'Pull-in for Drovers' sign at the side of the road might have got quicker results.

After about a fortnight on the road, when the drove reached the Home Counties, the drover would have to decide whether to head straight for Smithfield Market, or sell the beasts at Barnet Fair, just outside London. If it had been a gruelling journey he might give the cattle some grazing time to fatten up; certainly it was more profitable at times to sell the cattle in the lush grazing areas of Northamptonshire or Buckinghamshire, if the drove had come down the main northern route from Wales to London, still known as the Welsh Road.

But those decisions are in the future. It is now just one minute after midnight on a Monday morning in the 1790s,

The Kerry Hills, where the drovers assembled to set off for Smithfield.

the moment drovers have to wait for because they cannot travel on a Sunday. Up in the Welsh Hills Dai the Drover is getting the cattle on the move with the Welsh equivalent of 'Hiyo Silver!' The actual words are 'Haiprw Ho!' or even 'How how tarw!' but to English ears – and to the cattle – it is just one hell of a yell. It means that another consignment of Ye Roast Beef of Olde England is on the way…

Dai the Drover is based in what is now Powys, and he has collected some of the cattle from the market at Llanidloes. In his day it was a great centre for buying and selling cattle, so much so that by 1852 they had to issue a special proclamation in the town, declaring that farmers and dealers must stop their animals wandering the streets unattended. That was when the flannel industry had developed, and the town authorities reckoned there was more profit to be made from cloth than cattle. For Dai, however, there is no problem; the cattle still have the right of way, and he has built up a drove of some 200 head for the journey.

One of the old droving maps shows a route from Llanidloes to Llandinam, along what is now the A470, which continues through Newton and Welshpool to Shrewsbury. Dai, however, turns off at Llandinam to take another route over the open hills, no doubt to avoid a few tolls. The start of it is marked by Little London Farm, a name which usually indicates a connection with the drovers. There are assorted London Streets, London Ends and Little Londons all along the Welsh Road, christened by the drovers, one assumes, as a reminder of where they were going, or where they had just been. Dai would think of all these Londons as Llundain, but the Ordnance Survey rules otherwise.

It has been an easy route along the river valley to Llandinam, but now Dai and his drove are climbing steadily. This is no problem for the cattle, which are small and nimble – so small, in fact, that the English refer to them disrespectfully as Welsh runts, but it means they can climb like goats. They also have a goat's capacity for eating almost anything. During the winter, so the story goes, they will feed happily on the ropes that tie up the bales of hay, and leave the hay itself to the cissies.

So they are quite happy to turn off the road and head for the hills, with a little encouragement from Dai's corgis. These little dogs were as popular with drovers as they are now with royalty, because they are so low-slung that they could snap at the heels of the cattle then duck under the backward kicks.

On two of the hills above Llandinam are the two extremes in hill-top decoration. One has a prehistoric barrow which Dai the Drover knows as the Giant's Grave; the other has a radio mast, which he doesn't know at all, but perhaps in centuries to come, when its purpose is completely forgotten, it will be known as the Giant's Flagpole.

It dominates the countryside, as radio masts are wont to do, and Dai would be glad to turn his back on it and head for the uncluttered Kerry Hills, where the Kerry Ridgeway was once walked by the Iron Age folk who dug the Giant's Grave, long before it became a drove road. They dug more graves here too, twin barrows known as the Two Tumps, and this is where Dai is heading for, a popular gathering point for the Monmouthshire drovers.

On the way to the Two Tumps he crosses the road at Knighton, and here is another reminder of the droving days, a farm called the Cider House. Cider may not be immediately associated with Welsh drovers, but long before Dai's time the cidermakers of Herefordshire sent their salesmen across the border with a cartful of samples. They found a welcome in the hillsides, and in due course cider houses appeared along many of the drovers' routes. The one on the Knighton road is not perhaps the most picturesque these days – the present buildings were erected by someone with a taste for black corrugated iron – but Dai would have welcomed a refreshing glass or two before climbing to the Two Tumps.

On the way, the drove has to negotiate another relic of the Giant's Grave era, a substantial dyke which was part of the fortifications guarding a hilltop settlement on the Ridgeway. Then there are no more interruptions for a couple of miles, until he reaches the lane that leads off the Ridgeway to another favourite assembly point for the drovers, the Anchor Inn, right on the border between England and Wales.

There is nothing nautical about the Anchor; it just happens to be in the hamlet of that name. These days it is not very inn-like either because it must have been closed for years, and although the sales brochure refers to 'many interesting features' it looks singularly featureless from the road. It is described as a former coaching inn, and I suppose the occasional coach may have climbed to this obscure outpost in the hills, but its real place in history is as a rallying point for the drovers, before they left Wales behind and set off to join the Welsh Road to London.

I looked hard for the stance which the cattle must have used. I gather that stances were so well fertilized by drove after drove that, even a century or more later, the grass is still that much greener. At the Anchor Inn, though, I could see no hint of this. Maybe the stance has been lost under the 'terraced beer gardens and gravel parking area' mentioned in the brochure, but it was difficult to identify the gardens or the gravel, let alone a stance. One feature, however, has not changed. The brochure extols the panoramic views, and certainly they are splendid, in every direction. I doubt that Dai enjoyed them as much as I did, with a couple of hundred cattle to worry about, but indeed all along the Kerry Ridgeway the scenery is quite stunning.

Fortunately it is still possible to follow it for quite a way, even by car, and the Forestry Commission have kindly provided picnic tables where the views are finest. The tables would not have lasted long with Dai's cattle around, but the Ridgeway is quieter these days. Only walkers can follow it after that, but by doubling round some lanes it is possible to rejoin it further on, and follow it back to where it crosses Offa's Dyke.

There was a time-gap of almost exactly a thousand years between King Offa digging his Dyke to keep the Welsh out of his territory, and Dai the Drover taking his cattle across it, but even today, two hundred years after that, the Dyke has survived for long stretches as a formidable obstacle. Romantics may grieve that such an historic barrier was breached, not by force of arms but by the English desire for fresh beef.

There is little to hint these days that Dai passed this way, unless it is a hedgerow which may have helped to enclose a stance while he had a break for lunch. But it seems unlikely, because only a few miles ahead is Bishop's Castle, where there is a more probable stance behind the Castle Hotel, and where a road called Welsh Street confirms that Dai came through the town.

OPPOSITE *Heading for the Welsh border and into Shropshire.*

BELOW *Offa's Dyke, constructed to keep out the Welsh, but no problem for the drovers.*

Other strangers came this way too. A tombstone in the churchyard marks what was called locally the Slave's Grave: 'Here lies the body of I.D., a native of Africa, who died in this town, September 9th, 1801.' That was only seven years later, and I like to picture I.D. watching with some astonishment as Dai the Drover brings his 200 head of cattle along Welsh Street. I doubt that he drives them down the High Street, which is so steep that the drove could become a stampede. It could also knock away the supports from the town's celebrated House on Crutches, with disastrous results.

Bishop's Castle may sound more like a chess move than a town, but the name has a logical explanation. An Anglo-Saxon landowner with the expressive name of Egwin Shakehead was a victim, as you might gather, of the palsy, until he was miraculously cured at the shrine of St Ethelbert in Hereford. As a result the grateful Egwin – now renamed, I assume, Egwin Steadyhead – bequeathed his manor to the Bishops of Hereford, who built a castle on the estate to establish their presence. It was on the site of the present bowling green behind the Castle Hotel, an area which may also have been favoured by Dai the Drover's cattle.

Thanks to the influence of the bishops, the settlement around the castle achieved a status out of all proportion to its size. For a long time it was the smallest borough in England, and a 'rotten borough' at that, returning two Members of Parliament until the rules were changed in 1832.

When the townsfolk weren't voting they were playing fives. Church towers were often used as fives walls when the game was first introduced to England, and the church at Bishop's Castle is one of the few which still has the evidence. There is a red-painted line on the tower which marked the edge of the playing area.

After a night in town Dai heads for the high ground again, this time the Long Mynd, which is another economical toll-free zone. The route there takes him close to Lydbury North, and if he is a sporting man who prefers a more bloodthirsty spectacle than fives, there is the cockpit on the Walcot estate where it is said the Walcot family gambled away their inheritance. The octagonal building still stands there, in rather a sorry state these days, but no doubt the local cocks hope it stays that way.

The drove climbs on to the Long Mynd at Plowden and follows the ancient track along the ridge known as the Port

Way. This was generally the name given to Roman roads which led to the sea, but the Long Mynd is almost as far from the sea as you can get, and anyway there is a Roman road running parallel to it along the foot of the Long Mynd. But whatever its origin, the Port Way is still much as Dai would remember it, thanks to the ministrations of the National Trust. Parts of it have been gentrified to help the ramblers, but it is mostly a natural track through heather and bracken, with the breathtaking views on either side which are such a feature of Dai's route so far – though he might be unnerved by the huge silent birds that swoop around the skies, based on the local gliding club.

The Long Mynd is 10 miles long, and Dai takes full advantage of the turnpike-free track before descending on to the main Shrewsbury road at Leebotwood, where the route today returns abruptly to the twentieth century. Leebotwood has not been improved by the increased traffic on the road, but the thatched Pound Inn does try to be a reminder of the old droving days. I doubt that Dai lingers here anyway; he has another high ridge in his sights, Wenlock Edge, and the drove heads across country to join it at Longville-in-the-Dale.

On the way he passes close to Cardington, a name usually associated with the doomed airship, the R101, but that was based at Cardington in Bedfordshire. This Cardington is very different, a quiet little village tucked away in the hills, where they have concentrated on curious chimneys rather than airships. The unromantically-named Barracks, for instance, actually a private house, has very tall narrow brick ones, while Plaish Hall goes in for very ornate Tudor chimney-stacks to cope with the output from the vast fireplaces. The Hall is the only claim to fame of this Cardington; it was built by Judge William Leighton, Chief Justice of North Wales under James I. His effigy lies on its side in the church, head resting comfortably on hand, dreaming perhaps of bigger and better chimneys.

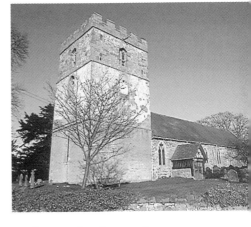

Cardington church, near the drovers' route, where a Welsh judge is buried.

Unlike the Long Mynd, Wenlock Edge has not been left to its own devices. A road runs along the top of the ridge from Longville to Much Wenlock, and inevitably there is a Wenlock Edge Inn near its most scenic point. However, the view across the valley – beyond the 'Beware of Cliffs' sign – is as spectacular as Dai would remember it. And it is near the Wenlock Edge Inn that Dai has to make the first major

145

Bridgnorth, one of the drovers' routes across the Severn.

Drovers paid a halfpenny per animal for overnight grazing; now it's an airport.

decision about his route.

Nobody knows the exact details of the roads the drovers took, but at this point Dai has to decide between two alternatives. The first is to turn off the ridge and go down through the flatter countryside to Bridgnorth, then continue for another 10 miles to an overnight stop at Halfpenny Green. The name is about the only reminder that this was one of the traditional stopovers for drovers, where they paid a halfpenny a head to park their cattle overnight. These days they park aircraft at Halfpenny Green Airport, and the fee, I suspect, is rather higher.

From Halfpenny Green the drover's road vanishes into the southern fringe of the vast conurbation which now surrounds Birmingham. It could well be buried beneath the new M42 motorway, emerging to join the Welsh Road somewhere near Hampton-in-Arden. It is not a route that Dai would relish today, and nor do I.

Instead, I think he would much prefer to take the other alternative, and continue along the top of Wenlock Edge; he has always shown an inclination for keeping to the high ground. This route also avoids any big towns like Bridgnorth, and even these days it is mostly through open countryside until it reaches the northern outskirts of Birmingham.

The only town it passes through is Much Wenlock, where the old timbered Guildhall still displays a notice forbidding waggoners to drive along certain streets on market days with loaded or unloaded carts, unless they are carrying goods for market. There is no mention of driving cattle through the streets, but this must have been unpopular too, and Dai probably took his drove past Wenlock Priory instead, on the outskirts of town. And now he has another decision to make: where to cross the River Severn.

The best-known crossing-place in this area is Ironbridge, and the bridge itself had been in place for twenty years when Dai the Drover came to this area. But Ironbridge was already part of the Industrial Revolution, and there must have been all manner of turnpikes and tolls to pay, which would not appeal to Dai. In addition, the Severn flows through a deep gorge at Ironbridge, so he could not cheat and swim the cattle across. Instead, I think he would have plumped for Coalport, 4 miles downstream and, in spite of its name, right on the fringe of the industrial sprawl, well away from the vast smelting works at its near-namesake, Coalbrookdale.

The bridge at Coalport looks like a miniature version of Ironbridge, but it was built more than forty years later, too late for Dai the Drover. Beside it is the Woodbridge Inn, which indicates there was an earlier wooden one, but in any case the river is more accessible here, and Dai probably swims his cattle across to save more money. A breed which can swim the Menai Strait would not have too much trouble with the Severn.

He could not avoid the factory area altogether. The Coalport China Company was in full production at that time, and some of its buildings and kilns by the river survive, as part of the Ironbridge Gorge open-air museum, but the surroundings are still attractive, and the 10-miles-an-hour speed restriction on the bridge, plus a weight restriction and a narrow winding approach from each side, ensures that the heavy traffic still keeps away.

Beyond Coalport, Dai heads into open country again to join one of the main drovers' routes from North Wales to London, at Tong. These days Tong is largely regarded as just another junction on the M54 motorway, but to me it means two examples of eccentric English architecture, the church tower and the pyramid aviary. The tower is square at the bottom and octagonal at the top, with a miniature stone spire thrown in. The aviary had pigeons in the four upper floors, including the little conical one at the top, and poultry down below. It has occurred to me that it might be fun to combine the two structures, since the aviary is shaped more like a church steeple than a pyramid. It would certainly look more impressive on the church tower than that odd little spire…

There is a direct drovers' route from Tong to Wolverhampton and Wednesbury, but undoubtedly more tolls are involved, and Dai prefers to make a wider sweep along another recognized route, through open country north of the M54. As it approaches the Birmingham conurbation we can only start guessing at the precise route he takes, but there are one or two pointers which survive among the urban sprawl. The Rising Sun at Brownhills was a drovers' inn, and there is a Welshman's Hill at Aldridge. The route disappears at Sutton Coldfield, but comes up for air at Coleshill, which may still look vaguely familiar to Dai

Wenlock Edge, little changed since the drovers passed this way.

One of the main obstacles on the route from Wales – the River Severn.

even today – certainly more so than anything he has seen in the last 20 miles.

Coleshill has been there a long time, and the River Cole which flows past it has been there much longer. Unfortunately there is nothing very picturesque about the area these days; even Hams Hall, which sounds promising, turns out to be a redundant power station.

Dai's route becomes clearer now, though hardly more attractive. It is a dual carriageway which crosses the M6 motorway at a point where the view is dominated by a hill, which did not exist in his day. It is in fact a landfill site, where the rubbish creates enough methane gas to generate sufficient electricity for a town the size of Warwick. I am also told the rubbish does not smell and does not blow about the place when the wind gets up, but I did not linger long enough to check.

Coleshill is now close to Birmingham's environs, but drovers might still recognize it.

The Welsh Road, as it is now called, crosses the main Coventry road at Stonebridge, a name which is more romantic than it looks, and logically it should follow the dual carriageway to the George in the Tree Inn at Berkswell, another notable rendezvous for drovers. That would also take it close to Hampton in Arden, where the alternative route from Wenlock Edge, round the southern outskirts of Birmingham, would have joined it. However, the experts say that Dai's route detoured in the other direction to pass through Meriden, and indeed a great many people have made the same detour since, to say they have been to the centre of England. I doubt that Dai the Drover would be too bothered about that, particularly as he was Welsh. Perhaps there was a toll he wanted to dodge on the direct route.

The George in the Tree appears to have moved its location as well as altered its appearance since Dai was there. The village centre of Berkswell is a mile away, off the main road and still distinctly rural. Its main feature is the stocks, which curiously has five holes for the miscreants' legs. Unimaginative folk say this is merely because the wood around the sixth hole rotted away, but I prefer the theory that it was designed for a trio of troublemakers, one of whom only had one leg…

The George in the Tree stands on the busy main road, part of a postwar development which calls itself Balsall Common. It is quite possible, however, that the inn came within the old parish boundary of Berkswell, and it is recorded as such in the reference books. There is no hint today, alas, of its droving connections. It has become a Beefeater Inn, built in standard Brewery Tudor with all the accoutrements of a modern roadhouse. Only the name survives.

Although there has been ribbon development at Balsall Common, the ribbons on each side of the main road are well back from the road itself. I cherish the thought that this is out of respect to the old drove road which passed along this route, and which needed a width of about 20 feet from hedge to hedge for the cattle to go through. More logically, I suspect, the houses were built away from the road to avoid the noise and the dirt; but Dai the Drover would appreciate the result anyway.

The next major landmark on the Welsh Road is Kenilworth Castle, and you cannot find a more distinctive landmark than that. As a prime example of one of the ruins that Cromwell knocked about a bit, Kenilworth Castle takes the cannonball. It has been called the grandest fortress ruin in England, which sounds to me a rather dubious distinction – rather like calling the *Titanic* the grandest wreck in the Atlantic – but you can see what they mean. Even on a fine day it looms gloomily over the landscape, and if Dai was riding by with his cattle on a wild and windswept evening, even his sturdy Welsh frame might have experienced the odd shiver.

Before it was 'dismantled' – the euphemistic Cromwellian phrase for knocking the daylights out of it – Kenilworth Castle passed through so many distinguished hands that estate agents would have sold their souls to have it on their books. The de Clinton family, Henry III, Simon de Montfort, John of Gaunt, Henry IV – they all had the castle at various times. But it was Robert Dudley, Earl of Leicester, who put it into the *Michelin Guide* bracket, converting the old apartments and adding new ones, building the Long Barn and the Great Gatehouse, and generally creating a castle fit for a queen. The queen was suitably impressed, and frequently sampled the specialities of the house…

The most spectacular event was a party which lasted eighteen days and cost £1000 a day, probably enough to feed the rest of Kenilworth for a year. If Cromwell had come along on the nineteenth day to knock the place down, I doubt that anyone would have noticed.

OVERLEAF *Kenilworth Castle, perhaps the most famous historic landmark on the Welsh Road.*

These days the town leads a strange double life, with some of the delightful old buildings still preserved near the castle, but a new main street which could be any shopping centre from Wolverhampton to Watford, and some equally uninspired housing to go with it. The battered ruins of the castle look utterly magnificent by comparison.

Dai and his cattle ford the Avon at Chesford Bridge, leaving behind several cattle-shoes which are still being found today. It may be odd to think of cattle with shoes on, but for these long journeys the shoes were as essential to a bullock as horse-shoes are to a horse. As cattle have cloven hooves an ordinary horse-shoe would not fit, so either it was split in half, or twin arcs of metal were custom-made to fit on each side of the cleft in the hoof.

Shoeing a bullock was not the same genteel process which horses undergo at a smithy. Welsh runts, I gather, are reluctant to lift each foot on demand, and the only way to shoe them was the way they rope cattle in the Wild West, with a lasso. The loop dropped down over the animal's legs and then tightened to trip it over. A fair amount of muscle was required to bring down a Welsh runt, small though they were, and the chap who felled them had to be, well, quite a feller.

Judging by the number of shoes found at Chesford Bridge and elsewhere along the drove roads, Welsh cattle were quite good at getting their own back, by de-shoeing themselves en route. I am sure the chaps who had put them on in the first place, being sensible fellers, did not provide the equivalent of a 500-mile warranty, so each lost shoe meant a profit for the nearest smithy on the road, and an extra bill for Dai. The going rate for cattle-shoeing was between tenpence and a shilling a beast, and I suspect that, even if only one shoe needed replacing, in the tradition of modern car repair work the smith insisted on replacing all four...

Assuming that his cattle are running on all four shoes, Dai continues to Cubbington on the outskirts of Leamington Spa, where a 'Welsh Road' sign is still a reminder of his passing. Ahead there is another name which will remind him of home, the village of Offchurch, named after the creator of Offa's Dyke, and some say the King's last resting-place.

The original Offa's church at Offchurch was built in the eighth century, and the present one still contains pieces of a stone coffin, which tradition says was occupied by the remains of Offa himself. Another tradition, equally unconfirmed, says the pockmarks in the tower were caused by Cromwell's bullets. Perhaps they had a few left over to celebrate after 'dismantling' Kenilworth Castle.

The church has an unusually long connection with one family, the Knightleys. It began when Edmond Knightley was granted the village by Henry VIII, and a Knightley was there when Dai brought his cattle through the village. The link only ended in 1911 with the death of Jane, Countess of Aylesford, in 1911; the oak panelling in her memory behind the altar unfortunately covers up some of the more ancient features of the church. But two other features struck me — one of them quite literally.

The entrance to the church is through a little door set into the main one, but I did not realize this until I turned the handle and stepped purposefully forward, assuming the whole door was opening. The little one is only about five feet high, and I am over six; the resultant impact, I am told, was very funny indeed.

The second feature is funny-peculiar rather than funny-ho-ho. A seventeenth-century memorial tablet on one wall has a skull at the top, which is quite common, and a cherub in a full-bottomed wig at the bottom, which isn't. I consulted the church guidebook for enlightenment. 'The purpose of this macabre object,' it says, 'is nowhere recorded.' I can only assume that the deceased was either a judge with an angelic nature, or a small boy much advanced for his years.

Once through Offchurch, Dai drives his cattle across an earlier Timepath, the Fosse Way; the two eras are linked by the nearby Welsh Road Farm. Then the Welsh Road crosses the canal, and here again the name is preserved; the lock near the bridge is called the Welsh Road Lock. In fact, the further Dai penetrates into this part of the Midlands, the more reminders there seem to be.

Southam, the next little town on the route, has a Welsh Road, and it also has more old inns than a place of its size seems to warrant, another indication that thirsty drovers passed this way. At one of these inns, the Craven Arms, there is a relic of another Timepath era. During renovations a receptacle for letters was found, dating back to the days before Anthony Trollope, who had a day job as a Post Office

Offchurch, where the drovers followed in the path of King Offa.

surveyor, introduced the pillar-box. Letters had to be left at coaching inns to be picked up by the London stage. Several old coins were found in the box, which seems a little odd; why did people post coins in a letter-box? Perhaps it was a tip for the coachman, which he never discovered, or maybe the customers of the Craven Arms, late in the evening, mistook it for one of those charity boxes which no bar can be without. One of the donations may even have come from Dai the Drover.

In the last century Southam was selected for two quite different social experiments, which took place on the same site and are commemorated by the same memorial. The first Provident Dispensary was opened there in 1823, an early forerunner of the National Health Service, where medicines and medical advice were dispensed to the poor. The idea was copied in the Midlands but never caught on elsewhere; it was another century and a quarter before free prescriptions reappeared.

When the dispensary was demolished the site was turned into garden allotments 'for the early instruction of boys in the management of land' – another pioneering project which, in fact, attracted a visit from the Speaker of the House of Commons, but again it didn't last. All that remains is the multi-purpose memorial, a sort of overgrown bird-bath, which bears an inscription about the Provident Dispensary on one side, and a reference to the allotments, and the Speaker's visit, on another.

On the way out of Southam along the Welsh Road, Dai the Drover would today pass Farthingfields, a name which might make him think he had found some half-price grazing land for his cattle. A road called Drover's Way would confuse him further. Farthingfields is actually a new housing estate which takes its name from a coin that was minted in Southam in 1666, but the developers remembered the town's other historical connection too, hence the Drover's Way on the estate.

Undistracted by any twentieth-century imitations, Dai keeps to the original route, a typically wide-verged drovers' road which crosses the Oxford Canal and leads to Priors Hardwick. The road skirts the village, but there is one of those obvious connections with the drovers, a lane called London End. There is also a less obvious one, a pond which is known locally as the cowpool. That may seem a fairly

Southam Mint, once licensed to make money, now just licensed.

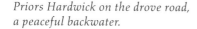

Priors Hardwick on the drove road, a peaceful backwater.

average English name for a rural watering-hole, but it is the 'pool' which experts say is the give-away. Usually in this part of the Midlands a pond would be known as a pit, so this should be a cowpit; but the Welsh word for a pond is 'pwll', which sounds like 'pool', and thus, so they say, there is a link with the drovers. Well, it's a worth a try…

Apart from its droving connections, genuine or contrived, Priors Hardwick has a long history of its own. It is the lone survivor in an area of deserted medieval villages; Hodnell, Watergate and Wills Pastures have all disappeared. Wills Pastures is an evocative name if you live in Norfolk, because a favourite saying about the weather is to note what it's doing 'over Will's mother's house'. Maybe we could get an early warning from the Midlands of what is in store for East Anglia by checking on the weather over Wills Pastures.

The reminders of the drovers come thick and fast now, as Dai heads steadily south-east into Buckinghamshire. At Upper Boddington, where again the road avoids the village itself, the village again has a London End – in fact two, one at each side. At Aston le Walls there is another Welsh Road sign, and at Culworth the old maps show that this is the junction of two major drove roads, the Welsh Road and Banbury Lane. If Dai decides to sell some of his cattle at Northampton Fair, this is where he would turn off.

Banbury Lane existed long before the drovers made use of it. In the Iron Age it linked a camp at Bunsbury Hill, near Northampton, with another one at Tadmarton, on the far side of Banbury, and it continued to the Rollright Stones, which come a respectable third behind Stonehenge and Avebury in the Famous Prehistoric Stones League. Our early ancestors must have tramped through Culworth to indulge in the mysterious ceremonies at the Stones, and no doubt to take back strange stories about them to their families.

The drovers from South Wales who used Banbury Lane long afterwards must have had their own theories about the Stones, and maybe they started the one about the local king who was told by a witch that if he climbed the hill on which they then stood, and could see the nearby village of Long Compton, he would be king of all England. It sounded like a doddle, but the witch must have been an undercover agent for the king's enemies, because when he reached the summit with his men a heavy mist surrounded him and blotted out

A narrow lane with wide verges – the typical drove road.

Culworth was once the junction of two busy drove roads; it is much quieter now.

155

the view. The witch then administered the coup de grâce and turned them all into stone. One group of the Rollright Stones is called the Whispering Knights, and I can imagine what they whispered. 'I say, look what's happening to the king. I wonder – a-a-a-aaahh...'

As recently as the First World War, Banbury Lane remained little more than a grassy track, with hedges wide enough apart to accommodate any belated cattle drovers. Now it has graduated into quite a busy B-road linking Banbury and Northampton, but fortunately it leaves the original route to bypass Culworth, so the village must be a lot quieter now than when it was being criss-crossed by herds of Welsh cattle. It had other excitements too; only a few years before Dai passed through, a group of local cut-throats known as the Culworth Gang was executed after terrorizing the neighbourhood. Their exploits are still recorded in the village pub.

Dai is not tempted by Banbury Lane and continues down the Welsh Road to Sulgrave. It broadens out as it enters the village, and it is not too difficult to picture Dai and his men driving the cattle down the street in a great cloud of dust, like a scene from an old Western, and with just as much noise and clatter. It was the noise, in fact, which most impressed one eye-witness of a cattle drove:

> *The noise consisted of the shouting of the drovers, combined I suppose with a certain amount of noise from the cattle. But it was the men's voices that chiefly attracted attention. It was something out of the common, neither shouting, calling, crying, singing, hallo-ing or anything else, but a noise of itself, apparently made to carry, and capable of arresting the countryside. The horsemen and two of the cattle acted as leaders to the rest, and the men kept calling and shouting the whole time...*

It makes *High Noon* seem pretty tame.

With all that shouting, Dai and his men must have worked up quite a thirst, and there used to be the Magpie

Inn, now a farmhouse, which they liked to patronize. These days the village pub is the Star, shrewdly placed down a side road near Sulgrave's main attraction, Sulgrave Manor, the home of George Washington's ancestors and a Mecca for American tourists.

The Star went through the same metamorphosis as the Magpie, in reverse. It started as a farmhouse and only became a pub about 150 years ago, too late for Dai to have a drink there. If he did so today he would be able to catch up on the more dramatic events of recent history. The walls are decorated with front pages of the *Daily Telegraph*, announcing the outbreak of the last war, the death of Churchill, Kennedy's assassination, and so on, while a blackboard beside the menu gives a list of 'On this Day' anniversaries, which would have enlightened him further. I noted that my visit coincided with Burt Lancaster's birthday, and something unpleasant happening to the Suffragettes. Something unpleasant had also happened to one of the customers; sitting by the fire in the bar was a skeleton in a plaid scarf...

The Americans, I am sure, love all this, but they love Sulgrave Manor more. It is endowed by the Colonial Dames of America, its trustees include the American Ambassador in London and, of course, the American flag flies in the garden. The origin of that flag can be found inside the church, where many of the Washingtons are buried. A window above the Washington Pew depicts the family's coat of arms, which features the mullets and bars which became the Stars and Stripes.

The Welsh Road continues through Helmdon and Syresham, where reminders of the droving days are sparse, though the crenellated Castle Farm that lies between them may stir memories for Dai of the border castles back home. But Buckingham now lies a few miles ahead, and he has other things on his mind; this is where another decision must be made.

He has been on the road now for ten days or more, and there must be a temptation to dispose of the cattle at Buckingham, where they would be fattened for the London market, and he could head back home. If he continued, he could either go through Leighton Buzzard and Dunstable to sell the cattle at Barnet Fair, or keep to the Welsh Road and head straight for London and Smithfield Market.

Both these routes are now busy main roads all the way

from Buckingham, and the towns they pass through have retained few memories of the drovers. The final stage of the Welsh Road, through Beaconsfield, Gerrards Cross and Uxbridge, also joins the stagecoach route which is the next Timepath. I am sure that Dai is bearing all this in mind for my future convenience when he decides on a more interesting destination, beyond Buckingham.

The centre of Buckingham itself still looks like a traditional market town, with a nice old bridge over the river, and even a nice old gaol with ivy growing up the walls – though no doubt in the eighteenth century it was unpleasant enough inside. But the steep narrow streets are not geared for cattle, and Dai stays out of town. Instead he continues for a mile or so along the Aylesbury road to spend the night at a famous drovers' house, the New Inn at Padbury.

Stories have been handed down to the present generation about the drovers at the New Inn. In 1925 an eighty-eight-year-old woman who lived there as a child told how dealers arrived ahead of the droves to book accommodation for the men and beasts, and how her uncle, the landlord, was delighted to have them, not only for the custom but for the excellent manure that was left on his field. She recalled, however, that before the men were allowed in the house, her aunt took up the carpets in the bedroom and threw the curtains over the bed. Welsh drovers, it seems, were not entirely house-trained.

That did not apply, I am sure, to two well-known drover-dealers with repetitive names who also patronized the New Inn, Roderick Roderick and Rees Rees. Mr Roderick passed that way en route for Leighton Buzzard, and Mr Rees actually bought a farm at Padbury to fatten any cattle he had failed to sell along the Welsh Road.

With all this droving background, I was quite looking forward to visiting the New Inn, but it is now a very ordinary-looking establishment with a white stucco front, and petrol pumps in the car park. There was no sign of the much-manured field of yesteryear; cars are replenished at the New Inn instead of cattle, and they do not leave such a useful deposit behind.

Dai spends his final night with the cattle at Padbury, then continues along the Welsh Road to Winslow, where it divides. One route goes to Leighton Buzzard and Barnet Fair, the other to Aylesbury and Smithfield. Winslow itself

ABOVE *Sulgrave Manor, home of the Washingtons, complete with Stars and Stripes.*

OPPOSITE *The rich Buckingham pastures where the sovereign's cattle were fattened.*

has an obscure link with our old friend King Offa; he may have stayed here in AD 752 while he was supervising the building of St Alban's Abbey. One is inclined to forget that he went in for building abbeys as well as digging dykes. The little town's most famous son in more recent times was the Baptist minister John Keach, who propounded the disturbing suggestion in 1695 that children should be allowed to play with their toys on Sundays. This radical idea earned him a fine of £20 and a day in the pillory.

Dai takes his cattle through the market square, not far from John Keach's chapel, and out of the town again along the Aylesbury road. He is not, however, going as far as Aylesbury. His destination is Whitchurch, now little more than a village but once an important town and borough, and set amidst the most famous grazing grounds in Buckinghamshire. They are probably best known today through a painting by Rex Whistler for a famous Shell poster, but in Dai's day this was where prize cattle were raised for top people. At one time, on a vast field covering 300 acres, all the cattle and sheep were reserved exclusively for the Royal Household. The pastures were so nutritious that the Welsh cattle which were fattened on them derived an extra-special succulence. And this is where Dai the Drover comes in.

Dai is an intelligent fellow, or we would not have followed him all this way. He knows the excellence of these pastures, the high prices that are fetched by the cattle which graze on them, and hence the good prices that local farmers are prepared to pay for the right kind of cattle to fatten. Dai reckons he has the right kind of cattle – and he knows a local farmer, John Westcar, who lives at Creslow, on the outskirts of Whitchurch, where the richest pastures – and the richest pickings – lie.

If he could have foreseen what John Westcar was going to do, some twenty years later, he might have thought twice about dealing with him. Westcar had the bright idea of sending his cattle to Smithfield via the Grand Union Canal – thus putting the first nail in the cattle drovers' coffin. The coming of the railways finally hammered down the lid. By the 1860s the drovers were reduced to making short local journeys between markets and farms; those who could not give up the life on the road sometimes joined travelling circuses to look after the horses. The last man to drive cattle

OPPOSITE *A reminder of Buckingham's important status in the days of the drovers.*

The drovers have gone – but cattle still graze alongside the drove roads.

any distance in Wales took 100 bullocks from Aberystwyth to Hereford in 1870; the drove roads to London were used for the last time in 1900, when a flock of mountain ewes was driven from Cardiganshire to Harrow-on-the-Hill.

As for John Westcar himself, he became very rich and very respected – except among drovers. There is a bas-relief of him in the church, which one critic says 'contrasts incongruously' with a nearby fifteenth-century painting of St Margaret of Antioch. Unfortunately I could not judge for myself; Whitchurch is one of those parishes which have presumably surrendered to the vandals and keep their churches locked, to the disappointment of bona fide visitors.

I am assured, however, that he cuts an impressive figure, an old gentleman of eighty-four escorted by a cow and a sheep. He lived long enough, in fact, to see the coming of the first railways, which completed the demise of the drovers that he had begun. His inscription reads:

> *Unblemished let me live, or die unknown;*
> *O grant an honest fame, or grant me none.*

The reason for his fame, honest or – in drovers' eyes – misplaced, is probably long forgotten, and those green pastures at Creslow are now dominated by the masts of a communications station. But the locality has not lost its link with the royal larders; a Friesian herd at nearby North Marston now supplies the milk for Windsor Castle.

All this was still in the future, however, when Dai the Drover meets John Westcar at Whitchurch, and strikes a satisfactory bargain over the cattle. They would have been worth about £4 a head in Wales, and at Smithfield they would fetch as much as £12. Even if he sells them to John Westcar at a figure only midway between, he still receives about £1600 for the drove – in cash.

And this, I fear, is when Dai takes the wrong decision at last. It is perhaps understandable. He has been on the road for nearly a fortnight, and he has a long journey back. The drove has been successfully completed, he has made a decent profit, the money is in his pocket. Instead of starting back straight away, he decides to have a night out in Aylesbury, 5 miles away. And thus, one might say, the Dai is cast...

We shall never know what happened to Dai the Drover, but with that amount of cash in his possession one can guess. He could have been attacked by footpads on the way, or struck down in a back street of the town, or even murdered in his bed at the inn where he stayed. The only clue we have is at St Mary's parish church, Aylesbury.

There are some fine memorials in St Mary's. The one in memory of Sir Henry Lee's wife and their three children, for instance, is a magnificent affair which Sir Henry decreed should always have fresh crimson flowers on the little altar at which his wife's effigy kneels. Four hundred years later his wishes have not been forgotten; the crimson flowers are always there.

But there is no memorial to Dai. The church register does not even mention him by name. It just records that in 1794 'a Welshman was buried in the Welsh language'.

It is a sad end to Dai's journey, if indeed it was Dai. Whoever it was, I am glad that he was given a good Welsh send-off in this English church, presumably by his fellow drovers, and I like to think that a part of him made the journey back along the Welsh Road, up on to Wenlock Edge and over the Long Mynd, and deep into the Kerry Hills, back among the black cattle that can still be found on the Welsh mountains. Dai may not have any other memorial but they are reminders for us, now that the drovers have gone.

Earlier I quoted an unkind farewell to a Welsh drover. Here is a kinder one, for Dai:

> 'Nol blino 'n triglo pob tref,
> Teg edrych tuag adref.

It means:

> After being tired of passing through every town,
> It is fair to look towards home.

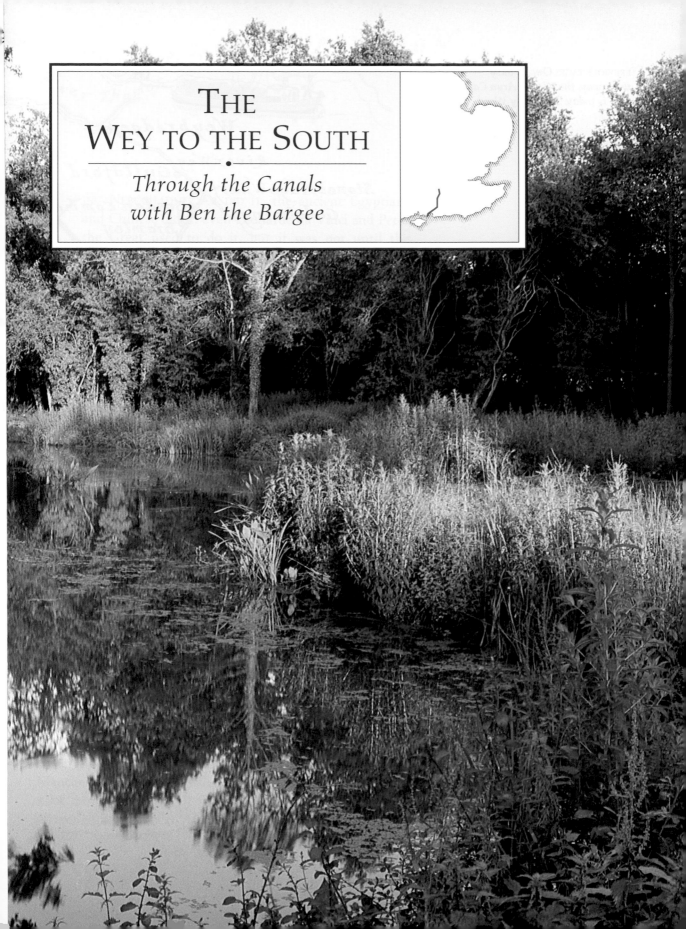

THE
WEY TO THE SOUTH

*Through the Canals
with Ben the Bargee*

Brindley went on to design and build the canal system which connects the Mersey, the Trent, the Severn and the Thames, and in the next twenty years the industrial Midlands had a comprehensive network linking it with London and the North. Britain as a whole had an extra 3000 miles of navigable waterways.

But not all of them survived. With the coming of the railways, the canal bubble burst. Goods trains are a lot faster than barges, and they carry a lot more. Some canals did manage to stay in business, but others were only used by pleasure craft, and a considerable number were abandoned. Today there is not only a network of canals, but a network of empty canal-beds.

Many of the casualties were in the south of England, at that time a non-industrial area with not much potential for heavy traffic anyway – and the railways soon grabbed what there was. Few of the canal companies ever made much of a profit, even in their heyday. By the 1870s they were rapidly collapsing – and in due course the canal banks, the locks and the wharves collapsed too. It was a hundred years before an interest in canals revived, not to build new ones but to restore the old. One notable example has been the Wey & Arun Canal, part of a former waterway which has been dubbed, romantically, 'London's Lost Route to the Sea'. It was left to become derelict in 1871.

At the beginning of the nineteenth century, one of the greatest canal enthusiasts in the south of England was George O'Brien Wyndham, third Earl of Egremont – millionaire, landowner, and entrepreneur. He succeeded to the title when he was eleven, and lost no time in celebrating; by the time he got married he had kept several mistresses and produced ten children. But his second love was canals, and it was he who inspired the ambitious – and as it turned out, sadly unpropitious – project to create a continuous waterway from London to Portsmouth. Napoleon was causing problems at the time, and an inland route avoiding the English Channel seemed a jolly good idea.

The River Wey was already navigable, so barges could sail up the Thames from the Port of London, turn left at Weybridge and get as far as Godalming. They were only 20 miles from the River Arun at Newbridge, which was navigable southwards to Arundel, Littlehampton and the sea.

Various schemes were proposed and discarded before

Lord Egremont launched his plan to connect the two rivers in 1810. By that time he was already involved in the waterway business; he was sole proprietor of the company which made the River Rother navigable between Midhurst and its junction with the Arun, and a canal branched off it to link up, conveniently, with his estate at Petworth. Now he wanted to get on with the route from London to the Solent – which would be handy, of course, for carrying his own estate produce too.

It took him three years to push the Wey & Arun Canal Bill through Parliament, and another three to build it. The canal was opened in 1816, running for 18 miles through the Surrey and Sussex countryside, from Shalford on the River Wey to Newbridge, near Billingshurst, on the Arun.

Even before it was finished, his Lordship was at work on the next stage, to link the Arun with Chichester Harbour, and thence to Portsmouth. He was principal shareholder in the company which applied in 1815 to build the Portsmouth & Arun Canal, running from Ford, which is on the Arun between Arundel and Littlehampton, to the Harbour, with an arm leading into Chichester itself; the city, confusingly, is a few miles from the harbour named after it. From the harbour the barges would be towed along a dredged channel past Hayling Island to Portsea, where they entered a 2-mile canal to Portsmouth. It all sounded great…

The section between Chichester and the harbour was built as a ship canal, 50 feet wide and 8 feet deep, large enough to take ships of 100 tons. It was opened in 1822, and a year later came the opening of the last link in the route from London, the section between the Chichester arm and the Arun.

Three days before the opening, in May 1823, a barge left the Port of London laden with some 20 tons of assorted groceries. It spent the first night at Weybridge, then continued through Guildford to tie up at Stonebridge Wharf, at the entrance to the Wey & Arun Canal. Up to that point, the two men manning the barge had assumed that the groceries were destined for Arundel, which was the normal end of the line. But at Stonebridge the bargemaster sent word to the senior man – let's call him Ben the Bargee – that they had a new destination. When they arrived at Arundel in two days' time they would keep on going; they were to be the first through barge on London's new route to the sea…

Narrowboats still use Stonebridge Wharf, but there is no way through to the Wey & Arun.

STONEBRIDGE WHARF IS ONLY A couple of miles up-river from Guildford, but it has fared very differently. Guildford was already a busy town, and it has become so much busier that motorists hardly even notice the river as they negotiate the one-way system over the bridges. Happily the Yvonne Arnaud Theatre has been sited on the lock island, giving a new focal point on the river. Stonebridge Wharf, on the other hand, has virtually disappeared since the Wey & Arun closed. Holiday craft use the site as a mooring, summer caravans park on the other bank, a modern office block soars behind it. Only the wharfingers' cottages further along the bank, now owned by the National Trust, and the black-painted wooden stone-house for gunpowder have been preserved.

Gunpowder seems an unlikely cargo for a quiet rural waterway, but Stonebridge was the loading point for the Chilworth powder mills, and barges carried it through Guildford to the London arsenals. Not surprisingly, the good folk of Guildford were not too happy about this, and they made it illegal for gunpowder barges to moor within half a mile of the town.

Not every boatman observed this rule, and there was nearly a disaster when one tied up overnight near the High Street bridge, which was conveniently close to his home. That night a fire broke out in a timber yard about 50 yards downstream, and when firemen arrived it had reached the water's edge. Imagine their surprise, one might say, when they found a barge with 20 tons of gunpowder on board, moored close by. Fortunately they were able to rouse the boatman and get it moved before Guildford was blown off the map.

That was in 1862, however, nearly forty years after Ben ties up at Stonebridge, and his load of groceries is rather less lethal. Having received his new instructions, Ben and his mate – whose name should be Bill to complete a familiar combination but, to avoid confusion, let's call him Bob – set off to the canal entrance, Ben at the tiller, Bob leading the horse. And today, that is as far as they would get. The entrance is under the main road that runs by the river, and what used to be a canal-sized arch is now just a small square culvert. So goodbye Ben, and goodbye Bob…

Fortunately the arch is still open in 1823, and beyond the road there is open countryside where houses now line the

Wharfinger Cottages near Stonebridge Wharf, now National Trust properties.

bank, their lawns not only running down to the canal but continuing on the other side, linked by wooden footbridges. This must be a daunting sight to a canal restorer; there is no way, I suspect, that these householders would enjoy having pleasure boats sailing through their gardens…

For Ben and Bob, however, there are no problems, and they are off on the first leg of their canal odyssey. Their next encounter with a road is at Gosden, where the bridge has multiplied curiously since their day. When the Guildford–Horsham railway was built alongside the canal, a longer bridge was needed to take the road over them both. Instead of starting afresh, a bigger bridge was grafted on to the side of the old one, like an outsize Siamese twin. These days there is nothing underneath except a footpath and a line of indentations in the grass; the railway was abandoned too.

On Gosden Common Ben comes to the first aqueduct on the route. It is not exactly on the majestic scale of a James Brindley or a Thomas Telford aqueduct – it just negotiates a modest stream. The remains of it are hardly recognizable as an aqueduct at all.

Ahead, the village of Bramley lies on the canal – literally; it has now disappeared completely under new housing development. But for Ben the Bargee there is just a scattering of cottages alongside the canal, and one of them is Wharf Cottage, the home of James Stanton – coal and timber merchant, bargemaster, and superintendent of the Wey & Arun Canal for nearly forty years.

Stanton was a shrewd businessman. His pay as superintendent was never more than a sovereign a week – the directors hardly seemed to rate it as a full-time job, thus displaying the sort of business acumen which eventually helped the company to collapse. But Stanton developed his own enterprises so successfully that, in later years, his son William was able to make a bid to buy the ailing company. He was probably fortunate that the bid failed.

James Stanton is understandably too busy to chat with Ben and Bob – unlike his son who became a well-known figure in later years, standing on the wharf in his high top-hat and smock, chatting to the few boatmen who still came that way. William took over his father's prosperous coal and timber business, and also became one of the biggest barge operators on the canal. Even when the canal company eventually

The entrance to the Wey & Arun Canal – a square hole under the road.

went into liquidation, he still ran his barges from London to his wharf at Bramley, until sections of the neglected waterway became too silted up or overgrown to get them through – whereupon the old chap went into the pleasure-boat business and hired out skiffs instead. He really did rather well out of the Wey & Arun – one of the few people who did – and he must have been sad to see it go.

He would be even sadder to see how the developers have now blotted it out altogether. I am told that the lock cottage is still there somewhere, 'but it needs an astute eye to spot it', and I fear mine was not astute enough. What I can visualize, however, is a shadowy bearded figure in a tall top-hat and smock, standing among the modern houses where the canal used to be, still waiting for the next barge to come by...

Ben leaves Bramley behind and continues into open country again. Here the scene would be more familiar to him today, as he comes to the first evidence that the canal restorers are in action. First a stretch at Birtley was cleared by local anglers, then a major breach in the bank was repaired, a causeway blocking the channel was removed, and various other works were carried out by a group whose efforts are more apparent from now on, the Wey & Arun Canal Trust. It was formed in 1970, almost exactly a hundred years after the canal closed; it has a long way to go, but Birtley is the start.

That particular stretch is away from the road, but any passing motorist on the lane from Bramley to Wonersh can see the canal as it used to be in Ben's day, at Run Common. Ben would not have much of a run there now; the old road bridge has been lowered, the wharf has vanished, and there is no sign of the 'winding hole', the basin where he could turn his barge if he changed his mind about Chichester. But the Trust has cleared and dredged the canal, and there is water in it again.

So one can picture Ben as he leaves the road behind and the barge continues out of sight to Rowley Lock, one of twenty-two locks on the Wey & Arun, and the first that he would find functioning today. It brings the canal up to its summit level – not a spectacular climb by canal standards but it has involved seven locks to do it. There is a level run for 5 miles now, across the county border into Sussex, but these days there are other obstacles to negotiate.

OPPOSITE *A problem for the canal restorers: footbridges link private gardens at Shalford.*

A warning and a wilderness on one side of the bridge at Dunsfold …

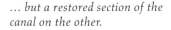

… but a restored section of the canal on the other.

The obvious one is the Elmbridge road. Looking over the road bridge, it seems unlikely that anything could pass under it again – particularly as the canal bed on one side has become a builder's yard – but the first law of restoration reads: 'There are no engineering obstacles that cannot reasonably be overcome with modern engineering facilities' – so Elm Bridge, watch out…

Ben has no such problem, of course, as he sails under the bridge and pauses at the wharf. There is no trace of the wharf today; instead, Ben would see the imposing entrance to 'Elmbridge New Village' – actually a group of retirement homes.

The canal passes within a mile of Cranleigh, along a restored stretch which Ben would recognize. He would also recognize Fast Bridge, which used to carry the road over the canal and has now been restored. Today the bridge beside Fast Bridge is much faster, on the main road to Guildford, and the little culvert underneath it would give Ben quite a jolt. Maybe the Trust has a 'modern engineering facility' to put back the clock…

Farnhurst Bridge, the next on the canal, has been restored too, though it goes to nowhere in particular. But the Compasses Bridge, just ahead, goes to somewhere very particular – and it is particular about who uses it too. This is one of the entrances to Dunsfold airfield, now occupied by British Aerospace. The canal runs along its perimeter, close enough for the guard at the gate to keep an eye on the volunteers from the Canal Trust who are clearing it.

It is the other side of the canal, though, which is of more interest to Ben. A few yards down the road from the Compasses Bridge is the Three Compasses Inn, the scene of great high jinks and jollity seven years earlier, when the Earl of Egremont and his friends, the Mayor of Guildford and his Corporation, and the leading shareholders of the canal company prepared themselves with a glass or two of hot punch before embarking on the inaugural voyage to Guildford. There to cheer them off were most of the village and about 200 navigators, as navvies preferred to be called, who had dug the canal. Having done their duty, they returned to the Compasses to tackle a roasted ox and 200 gallons of beer.

Meanwhile Lord Egremont and his guests made their majestic progress up the canal in four decorated barges, followed by eight undecorated ones carrying coal and timber; this was not entirely a pleasure trip. A couple of bands accompanied the party, causing a few stampedes among the local cows and sheep, and at Guildford an ecstatic welcome awaited.

'The sunshine, the music, the numerous assembly of spectators, and the merry peal of bells of Guildford, Shalford and Godalming, all heard at this time, gave an effect to the scene which could not be contemplated but with the most lively and pleasing emotions,' enthused the local paper. Actually the canal company had cheated a bit; 'the merry peal of the bells' had been booked and paid for well in advance.

The Three Compasses, scene of the launch party for the inaugural voyage on the canal.

There was a procession through the streets to the White Hart, where the 130 guests managed to demolish a substantial dinner and fifty bottles of port. Lord Egremont was flanked by Lord Grantley and Lord Onslow, and at some stage of the evening, such was the conviviality of the occasion, their Lordships burst into song. *The Times* correspondent, who had no doubt been at the port too, was equally carried away. 'And thus has opened under the happiest and most promising auspices, a canal of 18 miles in length through a beautiful and picturesque country, to which it is as ornamental as it promises to be beneficial.'

Alas, alas…

Today, looking towards Guildford from the Compasses Bridge, it is not difficult to appreciate all this exultation; it is in water again and does indeed look usable as well as ornamental. But from the other side of the bridge, the canal presents a more realistic picture: overgrown, weedy, blocked by branches and debris, and generally pretty depressing. The Canal Trust is tackling this section, but the contrast does epitomize, on the one hand the early promise of the Wey & Arun, and on the other its unhappy end.

Ben and Bob, taking their barge under the bridge in 1823, only know the good news; the bad news comes many years later. They have a jug or two themselves at the Compasses and resume their journey. At the next road-crossing the canal enters Sidney Wood, quite a contrast to the open country they have passed through so far. If it had not been for a local landowner, Sir Harry Goring, they would still be out in the sunshine, but Sir Harry objected to the more direct route because it would have disturbed his pheasants.

The former lockhouse in Sidney Wood, now much extended and privately occupied.

The Onslow Arms at Loxwood, once a canalside inn, but the canal is now blocked.

OPPOSITE *Brewhurst Lock has survived well over the years, but still needs further work.*

The detour through the wood added a mile and a half to the length of the canal and £15 000 to the cost, but the pheasants were left in peace – until October 1st…

The wood may look picturesque, but for Ben and Bob it means a lot of hard work. This is where the canal starts to drop 90 feet in 2 miles, and the barge has to negotiate nine locks in the process. In the middle of the wood they pass the Lock House, which incorporates the main workshop of the canal company, and they have a word with John Cole, who lived there for thirty years, building and repairing lock-gates and other equipment as well as supervising the locks.

Today Lock House still stands, but it is much altered and privately occupied. The canal is derelict and the locks have virtually disappeared, but the wood itself is owned by the Forestry Commission, and from the bridle paths one can see how much work lies ahead for the Canal Trust. Ben and Bob have a very comfortable time by comparison.

Things improve, however, once the canal leaves the wood. Ben takes his barge through Devil's Hole Lock, and while the lock itself is still a devil of a hole, the bridge has been rebuilt through a youth employment training scheme. When the canal reaches Loxwood, however, it needs more than a training scheme to restore the road bridge to its original hump-back. It is now flat, to speed up the considerable traffic on the road to Worthing. On one side of it the canal has become a footpath; on the other, behind the Onslow Arms, it was used for years as a bottle dump.

Loxwood itself has changed, too, since the canal days, when it was virtually run by a sect call the Cokelers, whose religious fervour was matched by their business skills. Their real name was the Dependent Brethren, and nobody seems quite sure where 'Cokeler' came from; I am assured that, although they were teetotal, they had no particular affinity for cocoa. Their founder, John Sirgood, arrived from London in 1850, pushing a handcart containing his worldly goods, including – when she got tired – his wife. He converted many of the villages to his rather puritanical beliefs, and his chapel became the main centre of worship. The Cokelers also set up a remarkable village supermarket, known as the Combination Stores, which incorporated a butcher's, a bakery and, in later years, a petrol station and a taxi service.

Although there was a certain resentment at first, at this take-over of the village's spiritual and domestic needs,

Ben now comes in sight of a much more imposing castle than Burpham's modest mound. As he passes Arundel Park the towers of Arundel Castle come into view – though not quite so many towers as he would see today, because the fifteenth Duke of Norfolk decided to add a couple more. In fact, the original medieval castle was so knocked about and neglected, then restored, extended and altered, that its early occupants would hardly recognize it; Arundel Castle now epitomizes the Victorian idea of what a medieval castle should be. But the Norfolks seem to like it, and the public visit it in their thousands, so the first Norman Earl of Arundel, William d'Albini, can be satisfied with the way his investment has turned out.

One feature of the castle which has survived unchanged is Morglay the Magnificent. Morglay is not a person but a sword. It is kept in the secure surroundings of the Armoury though, as it is nearly 6 feet long, it can hardly be smuggled out in a handbag. The story goes that Morglay belonged to a giant called Bevis, whose idea of a paddle was to walk across the Solent from Southampton to Cowes. He decided to be buried in the vicinity of Arundel Castle, and selected his resting-place by hurling Morglay from the battlements. It landed half-a-mile away, giving the locals quite a turn, and the mound which marks where it fell is still known as Bevis's Grave.

The air is free of flying weaponry when Ben ties up at Arundel wharf. In the past this has been the end of the run for him and Bob. They would unload their cargo and doubt-less go off to enjoy a pint or two to celebrate at the Norfolk Arms, where in earlier years the leading lights of the Arun Navigation Company held their committee meetings. Curiously, since it was on his doorstep, the Duke of Norfolk was not involved until three years after the company was formed; he was obviously not in the Egremont league where canals were concerned. But he did get bitten by the bug after a while, and he was one of Lord Egremont's biggest support-ers when he planned the Portsmouth & Arun Canal – which now lies ahead for Ben and Bob, a few miles further down the river at Ford.

This is new territory for them, and they have to be wary of the tide as the river gets closer to Littlehampton Harbour and the sea. Ships of 200 tons come up this stretch of the river, and for two men with a barge this must be like taking

OPPOSITE This muddy creek was where the Portsmouth & Arun Canal linked up with the Arun.

a tandem on to a motorway. As they round the bend of the river at Ford, by the Ship & Anchor Inn, they must be relieved to see the lock which marks the entrance to the new canal.

They would not be so relieved to see it now. A group of battered houseboats are high and dry on the mud outside the gates, which look impossible to budge. This is a rather seedy corner of the boatyard which now surrounds the modernized Ship & Anchor, and the river itself is dominated by the railway bridge which helped to put the canal out of business.

Through the lock and into the canal for the first time, Ben finds an astonishing armada assembling for the inaugural procession next morning. Several other barges with assorted cargoes are already there, lined up behind an imposing decorated pleasure barge at the front of the queue. This is the first pleasure craft that Ben has ever seen on the canals; amateur boatmen are firmly discouraged because of their propensity for leaving lock gates open and draining large stretches of water. But this boat is not exactly being operated by amateurs; it belongs – inevitably – to the Earl of Egremont.

Other barges have been smartened up to carry local dignitaries, and behind are the working barges, symbols of what the canal is all about. Some carry chalk fertilizer for farmers along the route; four others, like Ben, have groceries and goods for Chichester. He discovers, however, that his is the only barge to come all the way from London – a distinction which, I trust, earns him a few jugs of beer that evening at the Ship & Anchor...

The morning of 26 May 1823 is bright and sunny, and Ben and Bob get their first taste of glory as the crowds assemble along the bank. The main interest, of course, is in the barge at the front, but when word spreads that they are completing the first through run from London to Chichester they get special attention. Someone even ties a coloured ribbon on the horse.

Lord Egremont arrives early to welcome his guests. He is a distinguished figure, into his seventies by now but looking none the worse for the romantic exertions of his earlier years. With him is his friend and fellow director, the Duke of Norfolk. According to the London *Morning Post*, the Duke of Norfolk had his own pleasure barge, but the *Sussex Weekly Advertiser* does not mention it and, in my experience, it is the local paper that gets it right. The news actually took nine days to reach the London papers, by which time memories had probably faded anyway.

Next came the barges of the Mayors of Guildford and Arundel, 'who were numerously accompanied by gentlemen from their respective neighbourhoods' – nothing like a good freebie to bring out the numerous gentlemen. Behind them are six more barges of assorted gentry, also game for any sort of celebration – 'gay parties of Ladies and Gentlemen', as the *Advertiser* describes them. And bringing up the rear are the working barges, headed by Ben and Bob and their beribboned horse.

A canal footbridge at Yapton marooned in the middle of a housing estate.

The assembly time is eleven o'clock, but it is another half-hour before all the guests have found the right boat and they set off along the new canal – or, as the *Advertiser* more poetically puts it, 'the flotilla began to glide upon its bosom'. An extra barge has discreetly interposed itself ahead of his Lordship's, carrying an entire brass band, and another has joined the gay Ladies and Gentlemen. It is a splendid if slightly incongruous scene, a noisy, colourful water pageant set in the heart of normally peaceful farmland.

'The loveliness of the day heightened the rich and varied charms of the highly cultivated country through which the aquatic procession passed,' coos the *Advertiser*.

'The procession glided through a country possessing every beauty which high cultivation interspersed with occasional plantations could give it,' vouchsafes the *Post*. For once, local and national Press agree.

At Yapton the barges pass the turning basin and the canal office, and sail under a bridge crowded with cheering villagers. Today the turning basin has disappeared underneath a recreation ground, the canal office is occupied by a firm of estate agents, and the bridge arches bizarrely above the gardens of a new housing estate; the only other reminder is a turning off the main street through the village which is called Canal Road.

Yapton canal office is now an estate agent's – and the basin is a recreation ground.

The barges continue along the new canal past Barnham, where more villagers turn out to welcome them, but today Barnham does not even boast a Canal Road. Indeed, no trace of the canal remains, apart from a vague line through the fields in some places, and the remnants of an old bridge in another. The Portsmouth & Arun is now barren.

At Hunston this all changes. This is the junction where

the much wider arm from Chichester comes in, and the main canal broadens out too from here to Chichester Harbour, to form a ship canal between Chichester and the sea – albeit with a right-angle bend in the middle. Today this 4-mile passage survives, but at the junction a house and garden sit across the line of the canal where Lord Egremont's procession arrived from Ford.

It is met at the junction by an 80-ton schooner and five sloops which have sailed up from the harbour, and the whole cavalcade heads up the Chichester arm to the town basin – 'amidst the firing of cannon and the cheers of an immense body of spectators who had assembled to greet their arrival.'

Lord Egremont and about seventy of his friends go off to the Swan Inn for an early dinner. The townsfolk hold a fair, complete with donkey races, diving for oranges and 'jumping in the sack' – a phrase which the *Sussex Weekly Advertiser* might hesitate to use today. As for Ben and Bob, they get a special mention in the *Morning Post*: 'The arrival of the barge at Ford from London in three days has proved the practicability of transporting goods from the metropolis to Portsmouth in four, as a barge can conveniently navigate from Ford to Portsmouth in one day.'

Ben leaves that final Portsmouth lap to Lord Egremont to complete next day, not in a barge but a steam vessel towing two barges behind, through Chichester Harbour to the Portsea Canal and Portsmouth – to be greeted by more crowds, more cannon, and another dinner. Ben, meanwhile, has to wait at Chichester for a cargo to take back to London – and that, I fear, may be a long wait. This is one of the snags with the Portsmouth & Arun Canal; even before the railway came, it was difficult to find return cargoes. The only regular shipment was a monthly load of bullion from Portsmouth, which involved four armed guards living on board, and that was rather beyond the capacity of Ben's barge.

During the twelve months after that jolly inaugural procession, the canal carried only a twelfth of the traffic that was expected; in the next four years it dwindled to a few hundred tons. Things rallied for a while under an energetic manager, but by 1840 he had to admit defeat. The ship canal between Chichester and the harbour continued to function into the next century, but the canal between Hunston and Ford fell into disuse, less than twenty years after it was

The Richmond Arms at Chichester Basin, built at the same time as the canal.

OPPOSITE *Chichester Basin, terminus for the ship canal.*

BELOW *Still much as Turner painted it; the view towards Chichester from Hunston Bridge.*

opened; the Portsea section of the canal had already been closed. The Portsmouth & Arun Canal was the last stretch to be completed, and the first to be lost, on London's lost route to the sea.

Lord Egremont did not live to see it happen; he died in 1837. But he did see the writing on the wall; he had already given up his shares in the company. It was only a matter of time before the rest of his dream collapsed.

Cargoes could still come up the Arun from Little-hampton, but why bother when the coastal route was quicker and cheaper, with no locks to negotiate and no tolls to pay – and any threat from across the Channel had long since passed. Local traffic kept things going for a while, until it was hived off by the railways. The Wey & Arun closed in 1871, the Arun Navigation was formally abandoned in 1896. Ironically the Guildford–Horsham railway, which played a large part in putting the canal out of business, was itself closed in 1965.

The Chichester Ship Canal fared rather better. It saw its last commercial boat in 1906, and it was abandoned for many years, but in 1957 the County Council took it over and, in co-operation with the Chichester Canal Society, it has restored about half its length for fishing and boating. The view today from Hunston bridge, looking along the Chichester arm towards the cathedral on the skyline, is much as Turner painted it in 1829. But the bridge itself is a modern one, replacing the Poyntz swing bridge (named after a relative of Lord Egremont, of course) which is now pre-served on the bank further along the canal.

Chichester basin looks much as it used to, except for the lack of barges; the new bypass bridge would be too low for them anyway. The Richmond Arms, built at the same time as the basin, looks much the same too. Some of the old warehouses still stand but the biggest warehouse by the basin is very new and very incongruous; it turns out to be the postal sorting office.

The other end at Chichester Harbour looks very differ-ent. The canal itself is full of weeds, and it is reduced to a culvert under the main road. A concrete dam now regulates the water at the lock called Manhood End (named after the Manhood Peninsula, not in memory of failing powers), and houseboats are moored on the final stretch. The massive Salterns Lock, which links the canal with the harbour, is still

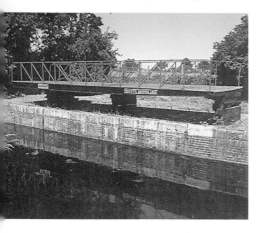

This swing bridge was originally at Hunston; it swings no longer.

operational but the former inn beside it – named, inevitably, the Egremont Arms – is now a private house. Alongside the canal is a vast marina, a striking contrast to the basin at Chichester. It is packed with millions of pounds-worth of yachts and cruisers – a sight to dazzle, bewilder, and fill with envy the likes of Ben the Bargee.

And what of Ben himself?

Well, the last barge to make the through journey from London to Chichester, called the *Trout*, had been making the run regularly for years – even, perhaps, since 1823. In 1835, for instance, it is known to have carried 13 tons of cattle up to Smithfield, which must have been quite an experience for the boatman, let alone the cattle. On its final run, in September 1840, it was laden with 6 tons of groceries for the good folk of Chichester – the same cargo that was carried on that inaugural voyage, seventeen years before.

That may be a coincidence but I hope there was a nostalgic welcome for the *Trout* as it arrived at Chichester basin, and I hope a few beers were lined up in the Richmond Arms. Because I am quite sure, if there is any justice, the man at the tiller was Ben the Bargee…

The canal at Chichester Harbour – given over to houseboats and water lilies.

THE MAILCOACH RUN

Riding The Aberystwyth
with Bill the Blunderbuss

I T MUST HAVE FEATURED on almost as many Christmas cards as the robin – a coach-and-four bowling through a snow-covered countryside or arriving at a snow-covered inn, driven by a snow-covered coachman with a snow-covered guard at the rear, blowing his snow-covered horn. Perched on the roof, a collection of characters straight out of the *Pickwick Papers*, top-hatted, portly, enormously jolly – and covered in snow…

The scene epitomizes not only a traditional English Christmas but a traditional English mode of travel, which developed after road surfaces were improved in the latter half of the eighteenth century, and petered out with the advent of the railways in the nineteenth. This was the era of the mailcoach, for fifty years or more the fastest, the safest and the most reliable form of long-distance transport in Britain.

From the time the Romans went back to Rome, nobody had been very good at building roads. In fact, nobody really built them at all. They were basically just beaten tracks which got a little more beaten as the centuries went by. Lords of the Manor sometimes got their serfs to clean them up a bit, but that was about it. Then in 1555 parishes were authorized to appoint a 'waywarden' each year, who could call on all able-bodied parishioners to do four days' work on the roads. That should have improved things, but it has been suggested that each waywarden was only interested in keeping his own little stretch of road in good order and, anyway, if a main road passed through the parish, the heavy traffic soon chewed it up again.

The coming of the turnpikes in the seventeenth century produced regular money for road maintenance at last, but there still seemed to be no one around who could build a decent road to maintain. It was a hundred years after the first Turnpike Act that the first stretch of turnpike road was properly laid, with a surface of stone and gravel set on a firm, well-drained foundation. The man who built it, and who went on building good roads for another thirty years, was not Thomas Telford or

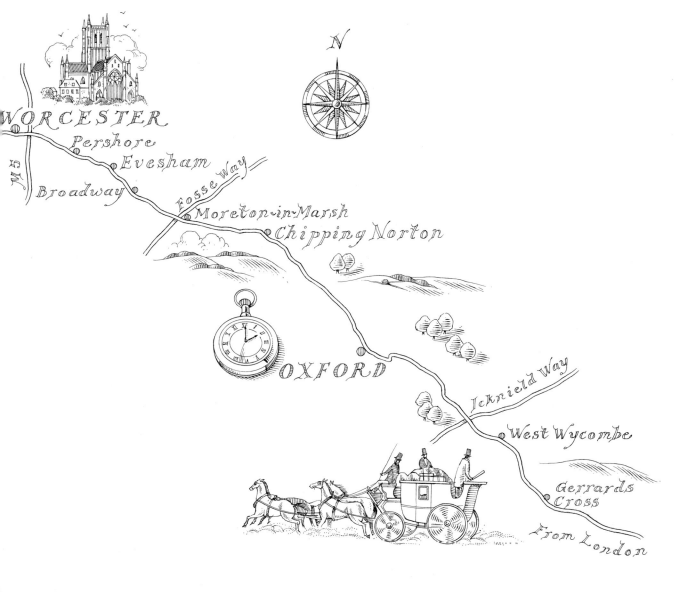

John Macadam, who generally get all the credit for this sort of thing, but a former fish-dealer, hosiery salesman and musician from Knaresborough called John Metcalf – who was also blind.

'Blind Jack' Metcalf was born in 1717, forty years before Macadam and Telford, and in spite of his blindness he led the field in roadbuilding. He must also have been a very persuasive talker, to convince a turnpike trust that he could build a road without being able to see it. But he assessed the lie of the land by riding and walking across it, and he developed his own system of covering the subsoil with bundles of heather before laying the stone and gravel, to improve the drainage. He built 180 miles of first-class roads in and around his native Yorkshire before he retired in 1792 – by which time Macadam and Telford were building their own roads elsewhere. As one historian commented: 'For the first time for nearly two thousand years, the speed of long-distance land transport in Britain was limited by the capacity of the horse, rather than the condition of the road.'

Enter another enterprising character called John Palmer. He must have matched Blind Jack's eloquence because in his early twenties he persuaded Parliament to grant a licence for his father's theatre in Bath – the first to be granted outside London. He and his father, now in partnership, acquired another theatre – and another licence – in Bristol, and they now faced the problem of transporting actors and props speedily between the two. John Palmer set up a shuttle of post-chaises, which worked so well he decided the same system could be used to transport the mail around the country.

Until then the mail was carried by postboys, and the service was not only slow but extremely vulnerable, to such an extent that the Post Office recommended that banknotes sent by mail should be cut in half, and each half sent by different deliveries. In 1784 the Bath mail took nearly two days to reach London; Palmer reckoned that a fast coach, using Telford's brand-new road from Bristol, could do the complete Bristol-London run in sixteen hours, stopping at Bath on the way.

Again his eloquence prevailed. In spite of scepticism at the Post Office he persuaded William Pitt, then Chancellor of the Exchequer, to let him have a go. His coach left Bristol at 4.00 p.m., called at Bath at 5.20, and arrived in London at eight o'clock the next morning, bang on time. Mr Pitt was delighted – and Mr Palmer found himself in the mailcoach business. In six months he was running mail services to Norwich, Liverpool and Leeds; six months later there were eight more. Other coach proprietors joined in, and by 1835 nearly thirty mailcoaches were leaving London every night for all parts of Britain, as far afield as Edinburgh and Aberystwyth.

The Edinburgh service was one of the first, thanks to the Great North Road. It was inaugurated in 1786, and the coach did the 400 miles in sixty hours. But there was no equivalent of the Great North Road through the Welsh mountains to Aberystwyth, and in the early days the London coach terminated at Worcester, with an assortment of connecting coaches taking different routes into Wales. It was not until 1835 that the turnpikes over the mountains had improved sufficiently for the Postmaster-General to authorize a through service from London to Aberystwyth.

The first mailcoach to make the run, known simply as *The Aberystwyth*, set off from London one morning in May of that year. On board were the regulation number of passengers – four inside, two on top – the Royal Mail, and an armed guard on the rear seat. Let's call him Bill the Blunderbuss…

Some stretches of the old mailcoach route are now bypassed by modern traffic.

The Aberystwyth, like all the other mailcoaches, is scheduled to leave London at 8 o'clock in the evening. It is due to arrive soon after eight o'clock the following night, so it is stretching things a bit for one guard to cover the complete journey. He would probably go as far as Oxford, like the coachman, and a new couple would take over from there. But this is a very special inaugural journey, so let us assume that Bill the Blunderbuss is very keen to keep the honour all to himself; or maybe he just needs the overtime. Unlike the coachman, he can at least snatch a nap along the way.

So shortly before 8.00 p.m., Bill emerges from the Post Office yard at St Martin's-le-Grand on a little two-wheeled mailcart drawn by a pony, one of a procession of carts which are heading for the various starting points of the mail routes. Each coach proprietor has his own base – invariably a pub – and when the previous coaches only went as far as Worcester they started from the Green Man on Oxford Street. Most of the western-bound mails, however, leave from the White Horse Cellar in Piccadilly, and on this occasion, having joined the premier league of long-distance mails, I think *The Aberystwyth* would be in Piccadilly too. After all, it is one of the sights of London, like the changing of the guard, to see the mailcoaches lined up for their 8 o'clock start.

Bill the Blunderbuss arrives in style on his mailcart, looking rather dashing in his regulation scarlet coat with blue lapels, gold braid and white ruffles, and black hat with a gilt band. Unlike the coachman, who is employed by the coach proprietor, Bill is a government employee in a government uniform – and with a long list of government rules and regulations to obey. One of them, for instance, instructs him 'on no account whatever to be wantonly discharging his blunderbuss or pistol as the carriage is going along the road, or through a town.' It is not clear what he does if the coach is being pursued by a highwayman, or a footpad tries to leap on board as the coach passes, but it is nice to know the Post Office had such a concern for the environment.

As it happens – and I know this spoils the plot of many a romantic novel – there is no evidence in the Post Office archives (which helpfully provided much information on this subject) that a highwayman ever held up a mailcoach on the open road. They preferred to attack unarmed postboys on horseback and unprotected mailcarts. Advocates of armed security guards would no doubt draw a lesson from that.

As well as his regulation blunderbuss, pistol and sword – there were no qualms about weapons then – Bill is also armed with a regulation horn, not just to give a triumphant toot at journey's end, as illustrated on the Christmas cards, but to warn other road-users to get out of the way. The Royal Mail has right of way over everyone else, and the horn has the same effect as a police siren. He also blows it to warn turnpike keepers to open their gates; it is another little perk of the Royal Mail to be exempt from tolls. Then comes the Christmas card bit – the horn is sounded when approaching a staging inn, to warn the ostlers to have fresh horses ready. For a mail guard, in fact, it is all blow...

Bill's other principal item of equipment is a timepiece.

Mailcoaches have a reputation for being so punctual that people set their watches by them, and the guard has to record meticulously the times of arrival and departure at each stop. This is not as simple as it sounds. Britain will not have standard time throughout the country until the middle of the century, and the guards have to adjust their time-pieces as they go along. It is not just a matter of a few seconds; the time in Bristol, for instance, is twenty minutes behind London. Judging by the pace of life in Norfolk, Norwich is probably behind by several hours...

Bill's official luggage does not stop there. 'It is a guard's duty to always have a bag of tools complete,' wrote the Surveyor and Superintendent of Mails, more interested in split pins than split infinitives. The bag has to include a screwdriver, a wrench, a cord and chain, wheel clips, nails, worms and screws, and a 'shackle perch bolt', whatever that may be – 'and if they do not produce all and every one of the above articles, clean and in the most perfect repair, they will not be paid...'

Bill the Blunderbuss – who also seems to be Bill the Maintenance Engineer – locates the black and maroon *Aberystwyth* among the waiting coaches, and transfers all this gear to his seat on the back of the coach. Followers of westerns would expect guards to ride shotgun beside the driver, with the mailbags under their feet, but the bags went in the boot at the back, and the guard sat above them, on his own. This could cause problems on a bumpy road; it was not unknown for a guard to be bounced off the back without anyone noticing. Perhaps on such occasions he was permitted to let off his blunderbuss...

With everything safely on board, Bill climbs on his seat, takes out his timepiece, and at the stroke of eight he slams the lid on the boot, the signal for the coachman to start. Other bootlids are slammed too, and the mail is on the move. They always get a cheer, and I hope there is a particularly loud one for *The Aberystwyth* as it sets off on the inaugural run to the Welsh coast, more than 200 miles away. Bill the Blunderbuss, while forbidden to loose off his weapon, must surely give a celebratory blast on his horn.

The coach heads west past Tyburn Gate, where Marble Arch now stands, and on through leafy Bayswater, Shepherd's Bush (still harbouring the odd shepherd), Acton and Hanwell, to the first change of horses at Southall. They will be changed every ten miles, four fresh horses at each stage. Multiply that by all the mailcoaches operating every day throughout the country, and it must be enough horses for the Charge of the Light Brigade. The logistics of having the right numbers of horses in the right places at the right times would test even the Fat Controller…

The route follows the line of the present A4020 through Hayes and Hillingdon, open country in Bill's day but now a suburban sprawl, with Heathrow Airport filling the final gap. It is only beyond the M25 motorway that the country-side opens up – and at last there is a reminder of the old coaching days. The Bull Hotel at Gerrards Cross has the Jack Shrimpton Bar, named after one of the highwaymen who did *not* hold up the mailcoach.

Gerrards Cross is where Judge Jeffries would have turned off the coach road to go home to Bulstrode Park. It has since been the home of a German commune and the Worldwide Evangelical Crusade, but to me its most interesting feature is its name. It goes back to a family called Shobbington who were lords of the manor at the time of William the Conqueror. When he and his army turned up at Gerrards Cross the family rode out on bulls to confront him.

William saw the funny side of it, and instead of getting involved in a bizarre bullfight he said they could keep their estate and rode off, chuckling. The Shobbingtons had a bit of a laugh too, and decided to change their name to Bulstrode, to commemorate the bulls they had straddled. They also put a bull's head on their family crest, and no doubt, in due course, the Bull Hotel was named in their honour.

The Aberystwyth changes horses again here, then presses on through Beaconsfield, past the two coaching inns at the crossroads. The George Hotel is supposed to have sword-marks on the stairs, made when the highwayman George Duvall – who also did not rob the mailcoach – was arrested. The stairs certainly have marks – what old stairs haven't – but whether they were made by a sword, and Mr Duvall's sword at that, only he can confirm. The section of wattle and daub near the entrance arch is quite genuine, however – part of the original wall.

The next change of horses is at High Wycombe, which even in Bill's day was famous for its furniture – there were thirty-three chairmakers registered in the town. Today there are over a hundred furniture factories, and they still

OPPOSITE *A surviving milestone on the coach route at Gerrards Cross.*

BELOW *The staircase at the George, Beaconsfield; swordmarks on the post, or just scratches?*

talk of the rush order for nearly 20 000 chairs, for a mass meeting addressed by the American evangelists Moody and Sankey. The chairmakers of High Wycombe combined forces and produced them on time; I expect there were even a couple of spares for Moody and Sankey.

Bill the Blunderbuss has a chance to sit on a Wycombe-built chair himself in the Red Lion Hotel, while the horses are changed, but he would have quite a jolt if he tried to walk in there today. The handsome portico on the front, where Disraeli sat on the red lion on the roof to make an election address, has been carefully preserved, and there is still a red lion on top – albeit a replica of the original -- but the doorway is now part of Woolworth's. Full marks for conservation, to a company which rarely deviates from its universal shopfronts of red and gold.

Other buildings, however, remain unchanged – the Guildhall in the Market Place, and the Little Market House opposite, still displaying the list of toll charges for the stalls. Bill would recognize Wycombe Abbey too, though Lord Carrington's family have moved out and a private girls' school has moved in.

The girls may be encouraged, or perhaps just depressed, when they see a stained-glass window in the parish church devoted entirely to famous women through the ages. None of these ladies, so far as I know, was born or lived in Wycombe, but maybe they passed that way. One of them, Elizabeth Fry, may even have been on Bill's coach, travelling to Oxford or Worcester to check on the prison conditions. The women in the window range from St Hilda and St Bridget to Emily Brontë and Queen Victoria – nearly a score of them altogether. In the male-orientated world of Bill the Blunderbuss I doubt the window would have been too popular and, indeed, it was only installed in 1933 – by a woman.

Much of the heavy traffic that used to pass through High Wycombe switched to the M40 motorway some years ago, but not before a lorry managed to demolish the old toll-house which lay on Bill's route. The rubble remained there for some time, a silent reproach to passing juggernauts.

Lacking the benefit of the M40, *The Aberystwyth* takes the old main road to West Wycombe, and Bill would find a familiar setting if he took that road today. The whole village is owned by the National Trust, and its basic character remains unchanged; only two new houses have been built this century. The most conspicuous survivals from Bill's day are Sir Francis Dashwood's church and mausoleum, perched on the hill overlooking the straight stretch of road which Sir Francis also built, using material from what became the Hell-Fire Caves. He went into roadbuilding, he said, to provide work for the unemployed – but it also meant that the road was considerably further away from his house.

The famous feature of the church is the great golden ball on the tower, in which the Hell-Fire Club played cards. In spite of their lurid nickname, they actually called themselves the Brotherhood of St Francis. There is no evidence they practised black magic, even though the caves now have names like the 'Robing Room' and 'Inner Temple'. After all, Sir Francis was a Cabinet minister, and a number of the club members were MPs.

'So what?' you may cry – and indeed every member was allowed to introduce one lady at their gatherings 'of a cheerful lively disposition, who disposes a general hilarity'. But black magic? Probably not.

The mausoleum on the hill was built to accommodate the hearts of the club members after their deaths, and there are urns in the alcove for that purpose. I am assured, however, that the urns are empty; the mausoleum's main feature is a monument to two of Sir Francis's four wives. In spite of the ladies of cheerful disposition dispensing hilarity, members of the Hell-Fire Club went in for wives as well. 'Nothing changes,' I hear you murmur…

The club has long since been disbanded when *The Aberystwyth* bowls through West Wycombe and takes a good run at the steep hill to Stokenchurch, where today a massive communications mast dominates the Chilterns. A pause to let the horses get their breath, then a downhill run to Tetsworth on the plain below, crossing a much earlier Timepath running along the hillside, the Icknield Way.

Tetsworth is midway between High Wycombe and Oxford, and the Swan Hotel is a convenient halfway house. Nearly thirty coaches passed this way each day, and most of them stopped at the Swan; there was stabling for forty horses in the yard. One woman traveller was fascinated by the sight of a horse being rubbed down with a besom, a sort of broomstick. 'At first we thought the horse would have been affronted, but no, quite agreeable. The dried flakes of

The coach road through West Wycombe; the whole village comes under the National Trust.

West Wycombe church, crowned by the golden ball in which the Hell-Fire Club played cards.

yellow mud, first besomed and then brushed, raised such a dust that, in the dust, man and horse were lost.' Presumably the horse preferred being dusty to muddy.

It conjures up a delightful picture, which is difficult to visualize at the Swan today. When I saw it, the building had been closed and on the market for some time. The agents say there is permission for restoration and refurbishment, which I suspect is sorely needed. They also say it is 'available for a variety of uses', which does not bode well.

The M40 has caused considerable alterations to the roads beyond Tetsworth, and it is quite tricky to rediscover the coach road and follow it to Wheatley, where *The Aberystwyth* turns off the route taken by the earlier Worcester coaches. That went past the village's cone-shaped lock-up – designed, I assume, for prisoners with pointed heads – and climbed on to Shotover Plain. Then it descended Headington Hill into Oxford, which was so steep that passengers travelling in the opposite direction had to get out and walk. This was too much for one unfortunate passenger, a Doctor Mathew Slade, who collapsed and died from the effort. No doubt there was something in the small print on the back of his ticket to exonerate the coach company. There is still a mounting stone at the top of the hill, which helped the surviving passengers to climb back on board.

Bill's coach makes a gentler descent into Oxford down the new turnpike.

It must be an eerie experience to ride into Oxford on a mailcoach in the early hours of the morning, the townsfolk asleep, the streets deserted, only the coaching inns showing signs of life. *The Aberystwyth* pulls into the yard of the Angel Hotel at two o'clock, exactly on time. It has covered 54 miles, about a quarter of the journey, in six hours. Bill notes the time – with some satisfaction, no doubt – on his timesheet, unloads the Oxford mailbag, and has a celebratory bowl of soup while the horses are changed.

There were a number of coaching inns in Oxford – the Star, the Angel, the Mitre, the Roebuck – but the mailcoaches favoured the Angel. Certainly it seemed to be the main coach-station, as it were, for the city. It took great pride in its daily there-and-back service to London, six hours each way, leaving at 7.30 a.m. and arriving back at 8.00 p.m. This allowed just thirty minutes in London, which

The conical lock-up at Wheatley – for felons with pointed heads?

cut down a bit on the shopping, but the timing was to connect with other coaches leaving London for the south, and I imagine only coaching fanatics made the double trip.

Alas, there is no trace of the Angel today. It stood in the High Street, opposite Queen's College, and the stagecoaches timed their departures by the college clock. A coffee shop later occupied the site, but that has gone too. In fact, all that Bill would recognize in Oxford today, I suspect, are the colleges themselves; and he would find the traffic quite appalling…

The change of horses is so speedy that Bill has to rush his soup. The Angel would only be popular among coachmen if it had an efficient team of horse-handlers, who could change horses faster than pit-stop mechanics can change wheels. One coach-guard wrote: 'The change of horses was like magic; sometimes – if no interference from a passenger with coachman, guard or horse-keeper – in less than a minute… Refreshed with a glass or foaming tankard of real, sparkling, home-brewed beer, made from real malt and hops, the horn sounded to "take your seats", and on we go.'

Suitably refreshed, then, either with real malt and hops or just soup, Bill and the mailcoach head out of Oxford and on to the Chipping Norton road. It would still be dark as they pass Blenheim Palace, but dawn is breaking as they enter Chipping Norton and change horses at the White Hart Inn. If Bill is a smoker he has a chance to replenish his pouch from the brass tobacco box at the inn, one of the earliest automatic vending machines. The instructions, dating from the eighteenth century, are written on the side:

> *A halfpenny drop into the Till,*
> *Press down the Spring and you may fill.*
> *When you have filled, without Delay,*
> *Shut down the Lid, or Sixpence pay.*

Back on the road, *The Aberystwyth* passes the site where Chipping Norton's most prominent building now stands. Bliss Mill, a Victorian woollen factory, is renowned for the lofty chimney which protrudes so bizarrely from the top of the central tower. The building has now been expensively converted into flats – so expensively, in fact, that two developers have been bankrupted in the process – but at least the residents may have the tallest television aerial in the Cotswolds.

The Mitre Hotel, one of Oxford's principal coaching inns.

The White Hart Royal at Moreton-in-Marsh, patronized by Charles I.

The Four Shires Stone, where four counties meet near Moreton-in-Marsh.

The next change is at another White Hart, this time in Moreton-in-Marsh. The inn has had a 'Royal' added to its name since Bill was there, and its sign across the road depicting a huntsman, hounds and a deer has long since been removed. The driveway into the courtyard which *The Aberystwyth* used is now the entrance hall, but the cobbles remain and there is still a game hook in one of the beams. The lounge with its vast open fireplace is much the same, and so is the bedroom where Charles I is supposed to have slept. A verse on the wall reads:

> *When friends were few and dangers near,*
> *King Charles found rest and safety here.*

But not for long...

Across the road from the White Hart, the Curfew Tower remains unchanged too. It was the sound of the curfew bell which guided a local squire, Sir Robert Fry, when he got lost on his way home from London across Moreton Moor, and he was so grateful that he left an endowment to pay the bellringer. It was rung every evening until 1860, when the bellringer, who doubled as the parish constable, had his leg broken in a struggle with a drunk, and never managed to pull the bellrope again.

The White Hart and the Curfew Tower lie on the junction with another early timepath, the Fosse Way, and *The Aberystwyth* crosses this to follow the coach road to Evesham. There is a steep climb to test the horses up to Bourton-on-the-Hill, which has a much pleasanter ambience about it than the better-known – indeed, far-too-well-known – Bourton-on-the-Water. The stables at the Horse and Groom must look inviting to the horses after their climb but the next change is not far away, at Broadway, where the road is distinctly downhill.

On the way they pass a distinctive signpost which still acts as a reminder of the coaching days. The arms are set about 10 feet above the ground, which is not much help to motorists but just the right height for a coachman. At the top of Fish Hill, however, which leads down into Broadway, the Fish Inn is now an unremarkable private house, standing in the dead end which used to be the coach route. These days the road zig-zags down the hill – and it is still pretty steep – but in Bill's day it went down in a straight line. Extra horses were needed for the climb, which were taken off at the Fish Inn. It must have been a horse's nightmare (or do horses have nightwomen?) to climb Fish Hill; as for the descent, Bill may be quite happy that he is facing backwards.

In Broadway, which is now saddled with the reputation of being the best-preserved village in the Cotswolds, and hence the most visited, *The Aberystwyth* changes horses at yet another White Hart, which all those tourists now know as the Lygon Arms. Squire George Lygon appointed his steward as innkeeper in 1839, and it has been the Lygon Arms ever since, catering for upmarket travellers who wax ecstatic about the service and the food. As the White Hart it was a more modest establishment, but it had its fans even then. One traveller wrote: 'There cannot be a cleanlier, civiller inn than this is.' And you can't say civiller than that.

Bill the Blunderbuss, however, only has time for a quick taste of real malt and hops, perhaps, before they are off again to Evesham. It is only 5 miles away and not worth another stop, but I hope he catches a glimpse of the splendid fifteenth-century Booth Hall, all black-and-white timber and plaster. It probably looks even better today than it did then, because it has been meticulously restored. It stands four-square in the centre of Evesham, without a vestige of a curve to its walls, yet curiously it is known as the Round House. One day I shall discover why.

Not so meticulously restored – in fact, considerably altered – is the Crown Hotel, an old coaching inn which now resounds to heavy metal instead of horses' hooves; part of the building is a night-club. *The Aberystwyth*, perhaps foreseeing this metamorphosis, changes horses in Pershore instead.

The old bridge across the Avon at Pershore shows signs of repair work when Bill crosses it, and the signs are still there. It happened after Charles I knocked down the central section to thwart his pursuers. Unfortunately it also thwarted some of his own followers, since he was in such a hurry to demolish it that they were caught on the wrong side, and thirty of them were drowned, trying to cross. A contemporary writer also records that 'some eighty countrymen, whose hats were picked up floating in the river', were drowned too, but it is not clear why eighty countrymen all rushed across the damaged bridge and fell in the river. Did they perhaps just throw

Moreton-in-Marsh's Curfew Tower; the bell once guided the squire safely home.

ABOVE *Looking down on to Broadway from Fish Hill, one of the steepest descents on the road to Aberystwyth.*

OPPOSITE *Pershore Old Bridge, damaged in the Civil War – some parts are older than others.*

Pershore's tollhouse, a reminder of the coaching days.

their hats in the air to welcome the King – and they all came down in the river? The bridge was later repaired with chunks of sandstone from nearby Elmsley Castle, and these still contrast with the original Cotswold stone.

The Aberystwyth probably changes horses at the Angel Inn, which still announces itself as a posting house. As he leaves the town Bill sounds his horn as usual for the tollgate to be opened. The difference at Pershore is that the tollhouse still stands today, the only one to survive on the route so far, and almost exactly halfway between London and Aberystwyth. A plaque on the wall announces that this is the Pershore Division of the Evesham Turnpike Trust, 1743–1877. Unlike some tollhouses it does not display a list of charges, but for Bill the Blunderbuss this is immaterial; one blast on the horn and he's through.

Now he is off on the last 10 miles to Worcester, crossing the present route of the M5 motorway. As he approaches the town he passes the public gallows, which I hope, for the sake of the passengers, are vacant at the time. The site is said to be marked by a cross in a garden, but one hardly likes to peer over people's garden fences. Then the coach passes the site of the Battle of Worcester – Charles II is involved this time – and arrives in the yard of the Star and Garter for an eight o'clock breakfast, 116 miles and twelve hours from Piccadilly.

Worcester was a major junction for coach routes, and over a hundred coaches were based in the town itself. They used four coaching inns – the Crown, the Bell, the Hop Pole and the Star and Garter – but only the Star (now Garterless) survives. The Hop Pole must have been the most upmarket; Princess Victoria chose to stay there in 1830, a few years before she became queen. The Star and Garter, however, shared some illustrious company in Foregate Street. Just along the road at Number 43 was Sir Charles Hastings, who founded the British Medical Association; and, when *The Aberystwyth* arrives, they are building the Shirehall.

This is not a patch, however, on the Guildhall, built over 100 years earlier. Inevitably Charles I is featured on it; there is a statue of him on one side of the entrance, and Charles II is on the other. Between them, over the doorway, is a carved head with large, Spock-like ears. This is the head of Oliver Cromwell, nailed to the wall by his ears; there are no doubts over Worcester's sympathies in the Civil War…

But the city has a much earlier royal link than the Stuarts. King John is buried in Worcester Cathedral, that splendid backcloth to so many county cricket matches. He is tucked between the shrines of St Wulfstan and St Oswald, and his tomb has the oldest royal effigy in England. That is a nice little tourist attraction for the cathedral, but I am not sure why he was so keen to be buried there. Maybe he just wanted a good view of the cricket.

King John's tomb is not the only unexpected memorial in Worcester. In the churchyard of St John's, Bedwardine, there is one of the very few tombstones in England, and certainly the earliest, to incorporate a photograph of the deceased. The body of twelve-year-old John Garmstone Hopkins, dressed in a dark suit and lying on a sofa, was photographed in 1871, arms folded across his chest, and draped with a shroud. The glass cover over the photograph was sealed so effectively that it remains in almost perfect condition – much better, in fact, than the stonework around it. The idea is fairly common on the Continent but unusual in England; I rather hope it stays that way.

Certainly it is an unusual discovery in such a typically English city as Worcester, whose residents included the typically English composer, Edward Elgar. As a fourteen-year-old, Edward was a relief bellringer at another of Worcester's churches, St Helen's, where the elderly ringer was sometimes incapacitated by the rheumatics. The curfew bell was tolled at eight, then another bell was rung for the same number of times as the date of the month. The story goes that young Edward liked to add one or two extra, just to cause a little confusion, thus pre-empting Jack de Manio by nearly a century...

All of which is of little consequence to Bill the Blunderbuss, tucking into his bacon and eggs at the Star and Garter, several years before John Garmstone Hopkins died or Sir Edward Elgar was born. He is more interested in planning the second half of the Aberystwyth run, which will take him into unknown territory; in a word, Wales.

There is still a sizeable chunk of Hereford and Worcester to drive through first, and the road is now winding and hilly, with few villages and only a couple of towns along the route. So this is a restful stretch for Bill, because in more populated areas he has to toss out the right mailbag at each place he passes through which warrants a post office. The local postmaster, or 'letter receiver', stands by the road to catch the bag and throw back another in return. If his aim is bad, either the coach has to stop, which is very unpopular with the coachman, or more likely, the bag has to wait for the next coach.

To avoid this problem, some postmasters who know their own limitations as bag-hurlers prefer to hold aloft a hooked pole with the bag dangling from it, and Bill has to grab it a he goes by. Alternatively, the bag is dropped from an upper window on to the coach. Either way, Bill has to be quite a slip-fielder, with bags coming from all directions – and there is always the prospect of falling off the coach if he reaches too far. Perhaps that is what the 'shackle perch bolt' in his toolbox is for – the coaching equivalent of a safety belt, shackling him to a bolt on his perch?

Anyway, there is no need for these acrobatics between Worcester and Bromyard, where the horses are changed at the Falcon Inn, still one of the finest half-timbered buildings in the town. The road bypasses it these days, but *The Aberystwyth* has to negotiate the steep and narrow streets to reach the Falcon. The other notable black-and-white building in Bromyard is Tower Hill House, where King Guess-Who found shelter in 1644...

Bromyard to Leominster is another quiet run. Again the town is bypassed now, but the coach goes through the centre and stops at the Red Lion, presumably on the site of the present Lion Yard. Leominster has its share of timbered buildings too, but Bill would be startled to find that one of the largest, the old town hall, has been moved bodily to a different site. In his day it stood on the main crossroads, but the Victorians wanted a new one, so they sold it for £95 and built the present Italianate town hall in its place.

The enterprising buyer of the old building managed to shift it to a less prominent position and gave it a new name, Grange Court. The only obvious change in its appearance is the ground floor, where the butter market used to be held behind the oaken colonnades; there is now a wall filling the gaps between the pillars. But everything else remains, including an inscription saying that the oak columns support the building 'as noble gentry support the honour of a kingdom'. That was carved in 1633 by the original builder, John Abel, who held the title of King's Carpenter – yes, *that* King – which explains his loyal sentiments. He could hardly have visualized that those wooden columns would march off with their burden to a new site.

It nearly happened again in the 1930s, when an American wanted to transfer the whole building to the States. Mercifully the local authority, with a higher regard for historic buildings than their Victorian predecessors, stepped in and took over Grange Court for use as offices.

Smaller relics from Bill's day have been moved too, notably the old toll sign from Knowle Gate, which is now in the museum. As a postscript to those days, the museum also has the notice announcing the sale of the tollhouses and gates by auction, when the turnpike was done away with in 1869. Of course they would only be of academic interest to Bill, who paid no tolls anyway.

After Leominster the mailcoach takes the old main road through Eardisland. This has been downgraded now, and the trunk road bypasses the village, which may be good for the peace and quiet of the villagers but deprives through travellers of seeing one of the most attractive villages in the county. It consists almost entirely of traditional black-and-white buildings, many dating from the seventeenth century, some even older – and one or two much younger, like the Tudor-style façade of Burton Court, which dates all the way back to 1912. It was erected by the same man who built Portmeirion, the bizarre Italianate village in Wales featured in *The Prisoner* series. To be fair, behind the bogus façade is a genuine medieval great hall.

Eardisland Bridge was damaged in the last war – not by bombs, just an American convoy.

Some of the most delightful old houses are up a side lane to the church, but one group carries quaintness perhaps a little too far. A terrace of tiny cottages bears the names 'Niche', 'Nutshell', 'Noggin', 'Nutmeg', 'Nook' and 'Nest'. Beatrix Potter, eat your heart out…

The Aberystwyth enters Eardisland across an old bridge which has already been rebuilt in 1800, and was to be rebuilt again after being damaged in the last war. It was not enemy action, incidentally, just a passing American convoy. There are two inns, but the coach has only come 5 miles from Leominster and another inn lies ahead at Pembridge, a village which is just as attractive as Eardisland but not so peaceful, since it still lies on the main trunk road.

It does have the bonus, however, of a medieval market hall with the notches still in the pillars where the old stalls used to fit, and a quite astonishing pagoda-like bell tower in the churchyard, its interior a forest of massive timbers criss-crossing between the stone walls. It served a secondary purpose as a mini-fortress. It commands a splendid view across the Welsh Marches to spot border raiders, and the slits in the walls are just large enough for shooting arrows. The defenders were not always successful; the west door of the church is still scarred by bullets, not from the Welsh, but from Cromwell's men. The spirit of Charles I is never too far away…

There are other spirits in Pembridge too. At the New Inn – which, like so many 'new' inns, is hundreds of years old – Bill the Blunderbuss may encounter a ghostly red-coated soldier, armed with a sword, wandering the corridors. There is a ghostly girl too, but she can only be seen by women. Perhaps one day they will get together, and the New Inn will hear the patter of tiny ghostly feet…

The Aberystwyth does not linger long in Pembridge, because something rather special awaits it at Kington, only a few miles ahead. London mailcoaches have been coming to Kington since 1821, but this one will be the first to keep on going. *The Aberystwyth* means that Kington is replacing Presteigne as the main route into mid-Wales.

I feel rather sorry for Presteigne, though perhaps it has benefited in recent years from being off the trunk road; the tourists probably much prefer it that way. But it lost its importance as a coaching route, and the Radnorshire Arms lost its principal source of income. It had been a coaching inn since 1792, when it was converted from the country retreat of one of Queen Elizabeth's great friends, Kit Hatton; for a change it was not Charles I who slept here. The hotel is busy again now, the oak panelling and beams are still there and the log fires still burn, but it has found, one might say, a new Forte.

For old times' sake I did try to follow the old main road from Presteigne to New Radnor, and a very tricky journey it must have been for a coach-and-four, steep and twisting, with an alarming drop on one side. These days it has a gate across it again, not with a tollkeeper but with some unfriendly-looking bullocks on the far side. If I had been Bill the Blunderbuss I would no doubt have blown my horn and sailed through, but it may be private land now, and anyway I didn't fancy those bullocks…

Back on the trunk road *The Aberystwyth* is within a mile

or two of Kington when it passes a most remarkable old building, now known as Penrhos Court. It has a vast expanse of timber and plaster, and the main building has an ancient cruck hall built about 1280, when Edward I took Kington away from the Welsh. More living accommodation was added around 1400, then a group of barns to create a courtyard, and when Bill drives past it is a prosperous farm. A fire seriously damaged the building in 1880, and although it was patched up, it continued to deteriorate. When it was bought by the present owners in 1975 it was completely derelict, but they created a restaurant in the cow byre and spent the next fifteen years restoring the main buildings. The cruck hall is now a banqueting hall again, the barns are bedrooms, and Penrhos Court has become a comfortable hotel – though all those stone flags can be a bit chilly. Although it has been virtually rebuilt, it is still much like the farmhouse complex which Bill sees as he rides past to Kington – and a hero's welcome.

There has been a long campaign at Kington for a through service to Aberystwyth, not merely to achieve a better mail service, one suspects, but to take trade away from Presteigne. It is only because the town has invested in a new turnpike to New Radnor that the Postmaster-General has authorized the new service.

'Great praise is due to the spirited inhabitants of Kington for the establishment of so desirable an object,' gushed the local paper, and the spirited inhabitants lived up to the occasion. They turned out in force to wait for *The Aberystwyth*, and when they hear Bill's warning blast, 'children shrilled with delight and there were cheers from young and old.' The coachman remained unmoved, indicating that this sort of thing happened to him all the time, but Bill the Blunderbuss must have been sorely tempted to fire a triumphant volley.

At the Oxford Arms, where the horses were changed, a group of young men managed to get hold of the coach and haul it to the Swan coach office, to rapturous applause, but the coachman was as dour as ever. 'The driver would not be diverted from his timetable by such frivolity.' No doubt Bill was thinking about his timesheet too. Without even sampling the local real malt and hops, they set off again to the cheers of the crowd, drove past the Royal Oak – 'the last pub in England' – and joined the new turnpike to New Radnor.

Behind them the inhabitants of Kington were as spirited as ever. A celebration dinner was held at the Commercial Inn, 'where the wines were of a superior vintage, and mirth and harmony prevailed until a late hour.' These days they don't get quite so excited when the mail van appears, and while I was in the town the inhabitants seemed more somnolent than spirited, but I am sure they could still whoop it up if another inaugural mailcoach came their way.

Just outside Kington *The Aberystwyth* passes the new tollhouse, which still stands there today. It only collected tolls for about fifty years before the turnpike system came to an end, and local rates were levied instead to keep the roads in repair. As it happens, Kington is one of the few towns in the country where tollhouses still survive on all the roads that lead out of it – though some of them are failing fast.

Halfway between Kington and New Radnor the mailcoach crosses the Welsh border, and Bill finds himself in Wales for the first time. It is much the same as England to start with, and New Radnor seems an English sort of place. It was, in fact, founded by an Englishman, Harold Godwinsson, to replace Old Radnor as a stronghold against the Welsh. A couple of years later, as King Harold, he came to an unfortunate end at the Battle of Hastings. The Normans took over and built a castle at New Radnor, but it was 'dismantled' by Cromwell's men after defeating its Royalist defenders; yes, Charles must have passed this way too. It is no more than a grassy mound when Bill arrives, much as it is today.

The town has since dwindled into little more than a village, and the prison of Bill's day has been replaced by the Eagle Hotel. The most forbidding edifice now is a massive and singularly unattractive Victorian monument, on much the same scale as the Albert Memorial in London, commemorating a local MP. His admirers, I fear, had more money than taste.

Bill is spared the sight of this in 1835. Instead he may well spot a milepost as he leaves New Radnor which says 'Penybont 7, Presteign 10½' – a reminder that until the arrival of *The Aberystwyth* from Kington, Presteigne was the destination for most of the traffic coming out of Wales, continuing straight on along the old road instead of turning sharply in the middle of the village, as the main street does today.

The Oxford Arms at Kington, where the locals took over from the horses.

One of the tollhouses which still guard the approaches to Kington.

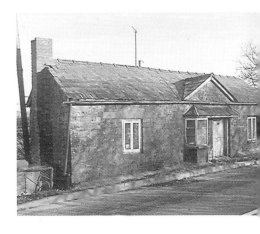

ABOVE *A milestone from the days when Presteigne, not Kington, was the main coaching town.*

OPPOSITE *The spectacular – and hazardous – mailcoach route through the Elan Valley.*

The road starts climbing now, and Bill can see the Welsh mountains ahead, rising to more than 2000 feet; the most spectacular part of the journey is about to begin. Only Penybont lies between, once a busy centre for sheep and cattle fairs, but its importance gone these days, along with that extra 'n'. It still has the Severn Arms, however, on the bank of the river, where Bill's horses are changed for the climb to Rhayader.

The scenery is becoming more impressive all the way, but the road itself is not too difficult yet. It is at Rhayader where, at one time, the most dramatic and indeed most dangerous part of the journey began. The old Aberystwyth road from Rhayader to Devil's Bridge can still be quite an experience, even in a car; on a mailcoach it must have been quite heart-stopping at times as it wriggled and twisted across the mountains, often with a sheer drop close by. Then it drops into a desolate landscape of old leadmines, passing between crumbling mine buildings, and there is a uniform greyness everywhere.

One early passenger spoke of his 'perpetual alarm' throughout the journey. Another wrote tremulously about the 'dreadful steep pitches and frightful precipices'. The Fountain Inn at Cwymystwyth, where there was a respite while the horses were changed, was renowned for its 'strong liquors' – and the passengers relished every drop.

Bill the Blunderbuss, however, is too late for all this drama. By 1812 the Aberystwyth Turnpike Trustees had heard so many horror stories about this road, and received so many complaints from nervous passengers and from local tradesmen losing valuable business, that they decided to build a new road to link up with the much less dramatic turnpike to Llangurig. In 1829 it was extended up the Wye Valley from Llangurig to Rhayader, and by the time *The Aberystwyth* arrives on its inaugural through run, all the local coach services have switched to the new route – 'thereby avoiding the dangerous precipices on the old road, which deterred many visiting a bathing place so improving and healthful,' as one writer put it, referring to the new fashion for sea-bathing which Aberystwyth was trying to encourage.

The hardier passengers may have regretted the change of route, because once the tricky part was over and the leadmines were passed, the scenery changed suddenly to attract-

Thomas Johnes's arch, a memorial to an early Welsh conservationist.

ive forestry land. An arch over the road was erected in 1810 by the man largely responsible for the transformation, Thomas Johnes. He found that 'there hath been great digging for Leade, the melting whereof hath destroid the woodes that sumtime grew plentifulli thereabout' – and his pioneering efforts to replace the lost woodland brought back life to the countryside. The Ministry of Agriculture's nearby Experimental Husbandry Farm took up where he left off.

Johnes also founded the Hafod Arms at Devil's Bridge, much frequented these days by tourists who come to explore the gorge and photograph the bridge. It is in fact three bridges, one on top of the other; the lowest, a simple stone arch, is the one attributed to the Devil. The story goes that an old lady's cow wandered across the river and she could not cross to retrieve it. The Devil conveniently built the bridge for her, but warned that he would take the first living thing to cross it. So the shrewd old lady threw a crust across the bridge, and her dog – who must have rated lower in her affections than the cow – duly chased after it. The Devil got the dog, the old lady got the cow, and the tourists got the bridge.

I hate to spoil the fun, but I have found precisely the same story attached to another Devil's Bridge in the north of England, and no doubt it occurs elsewhere too. It is rather more likely that this bridge was built by monks from the nearby abbey of Strata Florida, which may sound like a Roman road in Disneyland, but was once known as the Westminster Abbey of Wales because so many Welsh princes were buried there.

There was another notable burial too, recorded as 'Henry's left leg and thigh'. Henry was an eighteenth-century cooper, and like a Cooper called Henry who came much later, he was a very fit man – until a beer-barrel dropped on to his leg and it had to be amputated. He must have had a high regard for the leg because it was given its own burial service and interred in the cemetery. Henry hobbled off to seek his fortune in America, and the other leg, with the rest of Henry, is buried somewhere on the other side of the Atlantic.

The abbey is today reduced to one Saxon arch and a few segments of wall, but the Devil's Bridge has multiplied over the centuries, and now has two more on top of it. The middle bridge, built in the 1700s, was the one used in the coaching days; the iron bridge on top was added early this century. As for the gorge which runs beneath it, George Borrow called it 'a profound hollow with all the appearance of an extinct volcano', but it must have mellowed a bit since then; to me it just looks like a gorge.

Bill the Blunderbuss, of course, sees none of this. We have left him in Rhayader while the horses are changed at the Red Lion. The innkeeper is a Mr Evans – we are well into Wales by now – who is renowned for his sumptuous meals. One satisfied customer would certainly have recommended it for the 1835 *Good Food Guide*: 'a couple of very fine roast fowls, a hare, a dish of veal cutlets, a piece of cold roast beef and excellent tarts, for all of which, including about a quart of strong beer per man, we paid only a shilling each.' Bill, I fear, has to make do with a little real malt and hops.

The crossroads in the centre of Rhayader now has a clock tower in the middle, erected as a war memorial, which would have been quite a hazard for a coach-and-four. Arriving from New Radnor, earlier coaches would have crossed the junction to take the old Aberystwyth road. *The Aberystwyth*, however, turns right to follow the much gentler new turnpike beside the river to Llangurig. When it was built it destroyed an area once used by the Druids, where a spring called St Mary's Well ran into a basin chiselled out of the rock, which bore Druidic inscriptions. There were other Druid remains around it too. Roadbuilders in the early nineteenth century, however, had no great worries about preserving the nation's heritage, and all that remained after they had hacked out the new road was an unromantic trickle of water by the roadside.

When Bill rides into Llangurig he finds a very different place from the pre-turnpike era. In 1813 the *Cambrian Travellers' Guide* called it 'melancholy and wretched, and offering no accommodation to the traveller'; the road was 'inexpressibly laborious and frightful'. The new turnpike, completed in 1892, had the same effect on Llangurig as the railways later had on other Welsh towns. Hotels blossomed, shops opened, tourists poured through. Business, in short, boomed.

The church was transformed too. The *Cambrian Travellers' Guide* described it as 'a mixture of meanness and negligence' but new ideas for church design came with the

The original Devil's Bridge now has two more on top of it.

219

turnpike, and the vicar and churchwardens decided to bring it up to date by ripping out the ancient rood screen to put in new pews. Parishioners were allowed to take any piece they fancied. Fortunately, a visiting antiquarian had made drawings of it, and the present screen, installed in 1878, is based on his drawings.

The new screen was part of a restoration carried out by a remarkable 'squarson', Chevalier Lloyd, who became a Roman Catholic, was made a Knight of St Gregory by the Pope, then switched back again to become the squire and parson of Llangurig. According to his memorial by the coach road he was not merely remarkable but positively saintly. It was erected by tenants and friends 'as a mark of gratitude and esteem for his unbounded liberality, extraordinary charitableness, and his restoration of the church. A friend to the poor, a father to the afflicted, and a benefactor to all.' Unlike most memorials, it was erected while he was still alive; he must have found it gratifying reading.

When *The Aberystwyth* arrives in Llangurig the town is already making the most of the extra trade brought by the new turnpike, but Bill may scent a certain unrest in the air because it has brought extra tolls as well. Turnpikes trusts and local landowners could charge whatever they fancied, ostensibly to keep the roads in good repair but often to keep their own finances in good repair too. Eight years later the unrest bubbled over into rioting throughout mid-Wales, and Llangurig joined in with the rest. Some ingenious rioter with a comprehensive knowledge of the Old Testament dubbed these outbreaks the 'Rebecca Riots', based on a line in Genesis: 'And they blessed Rebekah, and said to her, "...may your descendants possess the gates of those who hate them."' Gates, after all, were what the riots were all about, though in a rather different context. To add to the aptness of the biblical reference – and to confuse the authorities, no doubt – many of the rioters dressed in women's clothes and the leading lights were addressed as Rebecca – the Welsh preferred the 'cc' spelling. Gates were destroyed, tollhouses attacked, tollkeepers injured; one elderly woman at a tollhouse on the old Aberystwyth road, for instance, was blinded by a shotgun. The Yeomanry and a body of Home Office constables had to sort things out, and some of the ringleaders were transported. I trust they were allowed to retrieve their trousers first.

However, it was not all in vain. A commission was set up which revised the turnpike regulations to ensure a fair, uniform toll, and gates had to be at least 7 miles apart. Those ringleaders, in fact, turned out to be the Welsh equivalent of the Tolpuddle Martyrs – the commission chairman said it had been 'a creditable portion of Welsh history' – but the Turnpike Martyrs never achieved the same fame.

All that is in the future, though, as *The Aberystwyth* changes horses for the climb up the Wye Valley to Pant Mawr, 1500 feet up in the Cambrian Mountains. The source of the Wye is only a couple of miles away, the source of the Severn a few miles beyond that. The scenery is bleak – and breathtaking.

Then the road descends into the Rheidol Valley, which the romantics called the California of Wales – not because of the climate, but because of the silver mines, which are just approaching their boom years as *The Aberystwyth* passes through. There are three mines in the valley itself, and a hundred more in the surrounding area. They were to reach their peak in the 1860s, then gradually die out by the early years of this century, but Bill would be impressed to find today that one of them, near Ponterwyd, is apparently working again, just as he would remember it.

The waterwheels are turning, a tram-waggon is being pushed along the rails, people are wheeling barrows, panning for silver in the stream, tramping in and out of the mine itself. But the 'miners' are actually tourists; the mine has been restored as a working museum and, although they can go through all the motions, they will no doubt get their mineral samples the easy way – from the gift shop.

From Ponterwyd the mailcoach starts its final stage to Aberystwyth, 11 miles ahead. It is still daylight as it completes the run down the Rheidol Valley, and the end of the long haul is in sight, the town stretched out in front of them and the sea beyond. A hundred years earlier, Daniel Defoe condemned Aberystwyth as 'a dirty smoky place', but that was before British holidaymakers discovered the delights of sea-bathing, and the town was cleaned up for their benefit. The clean-up of the town has continued ever since, to such an extent that today Aberystwyth looks much like any other big holiday resort, with hardly a Welsh accent to be heard among all the visitors and university students in the main streets.

In the Rebecca Riots, tollhouses and gates were attacked and demolished.

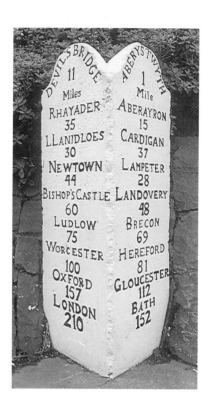

DEVILS BRIDGE
11
Miles
RHAYADER
35
LLANIDLOES
30
NEWTOWN
44
BISHOP'S CASTLE
60
LUDLOW
75
WORCESTER
100
OXFORD
157
LONDON
210

ABERYSTWYTH
1
Mile
ABERAYRON
15
CARDIGAN
37
LAMPETER
28
LANDOVERY
48
BRECON
69
HEREFORD
81
GLOUCESTER
112
BATH
152

A highly informative milestone; you name it, this has got the mileage to it …

Most reminders of the coaching days have been wiped out in the process, and the old coaching inns mostly survive in name only. One of the principal ones, for instance, was the Bellvue, which ran a regular stagecoach service to Shrewsbury, but the present Belle Vue Royal on Marine Parade, with its sunlounges and picture windows, could be on any seafront from Sidmouth to Scarborough, and no self-respecting horse would give it a second glance. The original Bellvue must have had a very shrewd proprietor, because when his coach service was threatened with competition he cut his fares to half-a-crown for the 80-mile journey, and hinted he would throw in a free breakfast too. The competition collapsed – whereupon he put up his fares to 24 shillings…

Similar price wars took place between other operators, and if Bill the Blunderbuss is hoping for the sort of welcome he had in Kington, I fear he will be disappointed. The townsfolk of Aberystwyth see plenty of coaches, and to the coach proprietors the new service to London just means more competition.

So there are no cheering crowds as *The Aberystwyth* turns into the yard of the Talbot Hotel at 8.15 p.m., at the end of its inaugural run. Bill makes the final entry on his timesheet, hands over the last of his mailbags to the post office messenger, and lays aside his blunderbuss, his pistol and his sword. It must be something of an anti-climax after more than 200 miles and twenty-four hours on the road, but I hope he enjoys a liberal supply of real malt and hops, even if he celebrates on his own.

Alas, even that celebration turned out to be a little hollow. Railways were being built all over the country, and the days of the mailcoach were numbered. The first mail service by rail had already started when *The Aberystwyth* made its run, and by the 1840s many of the London-based mailcoaches were being withdrawn. The last regular service out of London was in 1846, only eleven years later. Its destination, appropriately, was Norwich, in the heart of a county which I am glad to say has always been reluctant to move with the times.

So, back at the Talbot Hotel in Aberystwyth, what next for Bill the Blunderbuss? We may just possibly have the answer. The Oxford Historical Society has the memoirs of a coach-guard who later became a janitor at the University.

He wrote them in 1883, giving them the all-embracing title: *Coaching In and Out of Oxford from 1820 to 1840, by a Chip of the Old Block (with anecdotes and reminiscences) in his 75th Year.*

The name of the 'Chip', whose father had been a guard too, was William Bayzand – known to his friends, I am sure, as Bill – and it is thanks to his recollections that we know so much about the early stages of the Aberystwyth route. He spent much of his service on the *Mazeppa* coach from London to Hereford, via Oxford, and he was able to set down the details of the journey, which I have drawn on considerably, until his route diverged at Oxford. William Bayzand does not write about every journey he made or every route he served on, and I like to think that in 1835 he took a break from the *Mazeppa* to become Bill the Blunderbuss on the unaugural run to Aberystwyth.

Whether he did or not, his farewell comment is appropriate enough. 'Coaches, coachmen, guards, horse-keepers, inns and tollgates are all gone for ever, and if the rollcall were sounded for the muster of the old ones, the lovers of coaching, the ranks would be very short indeed.' And he adds:

'If I have given any amusement to my readers, I shall be perfectly satisfied that I have achieved success in my feeble attempt to describe the coaching days.'

I couldn't put it better myself.

Modern seafront hotels now mark the end of the road for The Aberystwyth.

THE MALLAIG EXTENSION

The Iron Road to the Isles
with Sandy the Steam

THE EARLY HISTORY of the railways is such a chapter of accidents and disconcerting experiences that it is amazing the idea ever caught on. It was not so bad back in the seventeenth and eighteenth centuries, when the rails were made of wood and the waggons were pulled by horses; no doubt the odd waggon tipped over, or ran downhill to overtake

the horse, with unpleasant results, but not much else could go wrong. We do know, however, that England's oldest surviving railway bridge, the Causey Arch in County Durham, built in 1727 to link the Tansfield colliery with the River Tyne, got off to an unfortunate start. The builder, a Mr Ralph Wood, whom a chronicler

PREVIOUS PAGES *The line to Mallaig – this is the most westerly railway curve in Britain.*

described unkindly but perhaps accurately as 'a common mason', built a wooden bridge first, which promptly fell over. He started again using stone, but the memory of the mishap must have preyed on his mind because, before the second one was completed, he leapt to his death from the parapet – perhaps expecting that this one would fall down too. He need not have worried; it stands there still.

The first moving vehicle to be powered by steam was not so durable. This was not a George Stephenson product; he was not due to build 'Locomotion No. 1' or *The Rocket* for another sixty years. The first 'steam road carriage' was built by a French mechanic called Nicolas Cugnot in 1770.

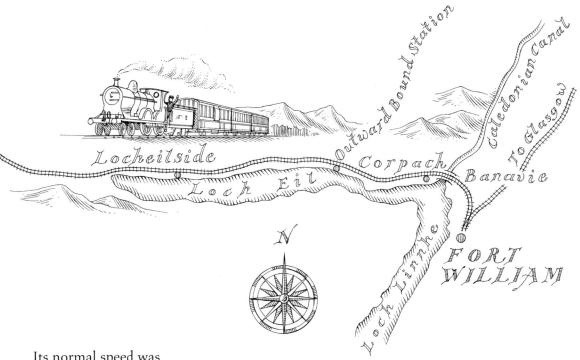

Its normal speed was 3 miles an hour, but when he took it to Paris for a demonstration it decided to travel rather faster down the final hill. M. Cugnot may have been hot on steam but he was not so bright on brakes. His steam carriage ran away, overturned, and knocked down several spectators. M. Cugnot himself was unhurt, but he conceded that the demonstration had not been entirely successful and went back to being a mechanic.

On this side of the Channel, James Watt also managed to transfer steam power to a wheel, but only for turning machinery, not for travelling. It was some time after M. Cugnot's catastrophe that a Cornish engineer called William Murdock developed a model steam carriage. He waited until late in the evening to try it out along the church path, perhaps choosing the late hour and the unlikely test-ground to thwart any industrial spies. He certainly thwarted the spies, but he also completely unnerved the Vicar, who saw a glowing, steaming shape puffing towards him through the dusk and was convinced it was a demon. He seems to have exorcized it very effectively, however, because Mr Murdock's steam carriage followed M. Cugnot's into oblivion.

However, a fellow Cornishman, Richard Trevithick, pursued the idea with better luck. When he tried out his full-size version near his home in Camborne,' she went off like a little bird'. It was he who had the idea of running a steam locomotive on rails instead of the road, and in 1804 he borrowed the use of a track in a South Wales colliery and pulled 10 tons of iron and seventy passengers for a distance of 9 miles. He must have been delighted but the passengers, I imagine, were glad when it was over; those 9 miles took them four hours.

At about the same time, young George Stephenson was looking after a pumping station in a colliery near Newcastle upon Tyne – and learning about steam. He persuaded the colliery owners to finance his first steam locomotive, curiously named *Blucher* – luckily it was 1814, not 1914, or the choice would hardly have been popular. Even in 1814 *Blucher* never achieved public acclaim, even though it successfully pulled a 30-ton load at a brisk 4 miles an hour. In fact, nobody seemed too bothered about steam engines at all, and George had five frustrating years and was on the point of emigrating when his luck changed; he was appointed engineer of the proposed Stockton and Darlington Railway.

His job was primarily to lay the track – the proprietors planned to use horses to pull the trains – but he talked them into using steam instead, and built 'Locomotive No. 1'. Ten years later he completed the Liverpool and Manchester Railway and *The Rocket* beat all comers. George Stephenson was home and dry at last, and the railway era had begun.

By 1870 there were 13 000 miles of main-line railways in

Britain; then came the branch lines, and the figures nearly doubled. But the internal combustion engine started a decline in the railways, and Dr Beeching's famous Axe completed it. In the 1960s, branch lines were lopped off without mercy, so that Norfolk, for instance, was left with just two main lines to the east and west of the country, and nothing in between. On the map they look like two mocking fingers pointing up from London. All over the country derelict railway tracks joined derelict canal beds as fading reminders of Timepaths that had fallen out of grace.

Happily a few unlikely survivors still defy the accountants and all the odds – saved by British nostalgia and the tourist trade. The Carlisle and Settle is perhaps the most famous, but the most spectacular – and many argue, the most beautiful line in Britain – is the West Highland Extension to Mallaig. It was never expected to pay, and it never has; it was built at the turn of the century – one of the last in the country – to provide a subsidized service to the isolated communities in the West Highlands, rather than as a commercial enterprise. So its current survival seems all the more miraculous.

The West Highland Line from Glasgow to Fort William was finished in 1894. The proprietors had always intended to extend it to the coast – the fish traffic from the herring boats was the only faint hope of making a profit – and a terminal was planned at Roshven Harbour. The local landowner, however, a Professor Blackburn, complained that the terminal and pier would spoil the view from his mansion. 'The whole thing is abominable,' he cried. Worse still, his 60 000 acres would be invaded by 'insatiable tourists'. He was supported by another eminent academic, Sir William Thomson, who said the harbour would be too small for herring boats because he could hardly sail his yacht into it – university professors obviously had a rather different lifestyle in those days.

As it happens, the Admiralty charts described Roshven as the best harbour on the west coast of Scotland, but the Old Professor Network went into action, strings were pulled, and the Parliamentary committee threw out the scheme. It took years to get an alternative plan approved, this time with the terminal at Mallaig. Work began on the 40-mile extension in January 1897, through some of the most difficult terrain in Britain; it was completed in just over four years.

On the morning of 1 April 1901, the passengers buying their tickets at Glasgow Queen Street for the 0555 train to Fort William were told there were several new stations they could book to, further along the line.

'April Fool to you too' they may well have said – or 'April gowk', if they were true Scots. They knew that the line to Fort William made a wide loop and entered the town from the north. If it kept going, it would either disappear into Loch Linnhe or carry on southwards, back to Glasgow.

But of course it was true. When the train arrived at Fort William station at 0950, a new driver – let's call him Sandy the Steam – attached a fresh engine to the rear, ready to haul it back to the junction with the new line. The turn-round took just ten minutes, and at ten o'clock precisely the guard waved his flag, Sandy sounded a celebratory blast on the engine whistle, and the first passenger train from the south sets off for Mallaig, on the new Iron Road to the Isles.

THE STATION AT FORT WILLIAM which Sandy is leaving is not the one we know today. It stood between the town and the loch, handy to transfer goods and passengers to the boats; one of the platforms actually extended beyond the station to the jetty. But in 1975 the new station was built a few hundred yards up the line, so that a ring road could be built on the original site. Only the Station Bar, and a faded notice saying 'Station Hotel' still remain. The ring road not only obliterates the old station, it cuts off the new one from the town; passengers have to reach it through a subway or across a lethal roundabout. It all provides as unprepossessing an approach to the town from the north as the serried ranks of 'Bed and Breakfast' signs along the main road from the south.

Sandy takes his train along the shore of the loch and over the site of the fort which later became Fort William. General Monk built it in 1654 and called it Inverlochy; the 'William' came much later with William of Orange. The general would no doubt consider it poetic justice that the railway which flattened his fort has now had its own station flattened too.

But the main feature of this part of the route remains unchanged. The passengers on Sandy's train have a splendid view of Ben Nevis, towering above Fort William, with a weather observatory on the summit reached by a pony track. If they come back in three years' time they will find the observatory closed; it cost £1000 a year to operate, and the government would only grant £350. This happened to be the time when two brothers called Wright were developing their heavier-than-air machine, the first to fly under its own power. The age of the aeroplane was just dawning, and the science of weather observation was to be a vital part of it, but the observatory was shut, and now only its ruins remain. The government had got it wrong again…

At Mallaig Junction signal-box Sandy leaves the main line to Glasgow and forks off along the single line to the west. A little further on there is another fork, where a short branch line runs to Banavie Pier on the Caledonian Canal. It links passengers and freight from Fort William with the canal steamers to Inverness on the east coast, and Sandy has done that little run many times before. It is at this second junction that the new track to Mallaig begins, and indeed this is where he passes milepost zero, because to a railway engineer this is the start of the Mallaig Extension. To anyone else it means they have to add 2 miles to all the mileposts along the line, to get the correct mileage from Fort William. Only an engineer would assume that anyone starts a journey from a set of points.

The little line to Banavie Pier, only half a mile long, has disappeared. By 1939 it carried just one train a day, and even by pre-Beeching standards that was hardly a practical proposition. The station announcer at Fort William gave out the departure of the last passenger train to the pier on 2 September 1939; it did not have quite the same impact as that other announcement by Neville Chamberlain next day.

Just beyond the junction Sandy steams into the new Banavie station, the first stop on the Mallaig Extension. Today the station is still there but the buildings have been demolished – what was left to be demolished after the station staff were withdrawn and the vandals took over. A brief stop, then he is on the move again, easing the train gently across the new swing bridge over the Caledonian Canal. In Sandy's day it was opened and closed manually; today it is electrically operated. Modern technology has come to the signalling system too. Beside the bridge the present signal-box may look like the one that Sandy knew, but

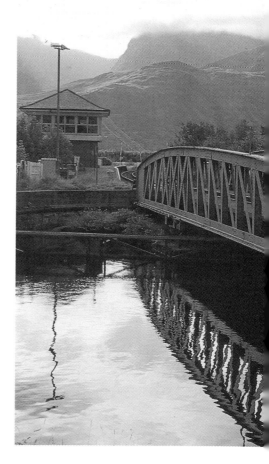

The start of the Mallaig line – the swing bridge over the Caledonian Canal.

it contains the control centre for something called Radio Electronic Token Block signalling, and the two people in charge control the entire West Highland network.

All this would be a mystery to Sandy. He just exchanges his brass token at the bridge for the next stage, and steams on to Corpach, where the first construction camp was set up and Lady Margaret Cameron of Lochiel – whose family were more railway-minded than Professor Blackburn of Roshven – cut the first sod in 1897. The 500 navvies based at Corpach cut the rest.

Corpach has gone through various transformations since then. After the navvies packed their shovels and left, nothing much happened until a naval repair yard was established there during the Second World War. Two hundred concrete houses were built on the golf course for the staff – accommodation which had more amenities than the navvies' camp of forty years before, but was hardly more pleasing to the eye. But the yard and the houses brought new and much-needed business to the Mallaig Extension, and so did the equally unlovely pulp and paper mill which was built there in the 1960s, just in time to save it from the Beeching Axe. The pulp mill chewed up 350 tons of logs a day, all brought by rail. It has closed now, but the mill remains, as unattractive as ever to the passing tourists but as indispensable as ever to the railway.

There is not much so far to justify the claim that this is the most beautiful railway line in Britain, but things can only improve – and they do. Sandy the Steam can speed up now along the fairly straight and level shore of Loch Eil and leaves the unsightly huts of Corpach behind – just as the paper mill is left behind today. He has no need to stop at the Loch Eil Outward Bound station because it doesn't yet exist. This was the only station to be added after the line was finished – eighty-four years after, in fact. It was fairly basic at first, built out of sleepers by the youngsters from the Outward Bound Centre as a change from climbing mountains and paddling canoes. Later they added a rather jolly log-cabin waiting-room, a distinct improvement on the standard metal-box architecture favoured by British Rail on its unattended stations.

Sandy does stop at the next station, Locheilside – though today trains only stop on request. Then he is climbing up the glen at the end of the loch, and the mountains close in.

ABOVE *The papermills at Corpach help to keep the line going. Then the scenery improves …*

OPPOSITE *The spectacular Glenfinnan Viaduct, built by 'Concrete Bob' McAlpine.*

BELOW *Loch Eil station. The log cabin waiting-room was built by Outward Bound youngsters.*

The first tunnels appear, and beyond is the head of Loch Shiel, with the broad valley of the River Finnan leading into it. Across the valley is the showpiece of the Mallaig Extension, 'Concrete Bob's' Glenfinnan Viaduct.

Concrete Bob, the renowned Sir Robert McAlpine, was the man who built the Extension – helped by two of his sons and 3000 navvies. He had been using this newfangled building material for houses, but he had never tried it out before on a viaduct nearly a quarter of a mile long and 100 feet high. Its proportions are so large that it is said a horse and cart being led along the unfinished superstructure fell into one of the hollow piers and was never seen again.

All the piers are safely sealed, however – with that unfortunate horse still inside one of them – as Sandy the Steam takes his train on to the crescent-shaped viaduct and drives it across the valley. Far below him, on the shore of the loch, is the monument marking the spot where Bonny Prince Charlie unfurled his standard in 1745, proclaiming a reward of £30 for the person of the usurper, King George; there were no takers.

With the loch in the background the monument looks more like a lighthouse, except for the carved highlander who stands where the lamp ought to be. But this is a memorial to 'those who fought and bled in that arduous exercise', and this is very much Jacobite country so one does not joke about lighthouses here.

Inevitably a tourist centre has been established nearby, and the place is full of Americans and Japanese in tartan caps, but from the windows of a train on the viaduct they look mere specks in an otherwise magnificent panorama of green mountains and blue water. The view is still there as Sandy climbs the steep hillside beyond the viaduct, where the fugitive Prince Charles hid with just three companions, all that was left of the army that had rallied to him at Glenfinnan eleven months before.

Ahead is Glenfinnan station, and the first passing loop since Sandy left the main line, 16 miles away. But even on its busiest days, two trains meeting on the Mallaig Extension is quite a rare occurrence, and all is quiet at Glenfinnan.

It would be quieter still today without the museum which has been created in the unwanted station building. A railway enthusiast called John Barnes, who worked in a local government planning department in the Midlands, negotiated with ScotRail for over two years before getting permission to set up an exhibition and display centre on the station in 1991. He left the Midlands behind to tuck himself away in this remote station in the West Highlands, and today the tourist trains prolong their stop at Glenfinnan. Passengers visit the museum and explore the 'McAlpine Tunnel', in which he has recreated the conditions of McAlpine's navvies worked under, ninety-odd years ago.

Glenfinnan station, now a railway museum containing a replica 'McAlpine Tunnel'.

Sandy the Steam merely stops long enough to pick up and deposit his passengers, then his fireman has to stoke hard as he sets off to complete the climb to the highest point on the Mallaig Extension, up in the hills which divide Loch Shiel from Loch Eilt. Then it is downhill all the way to the shore of Loch Eilt, the track zig-zagging gently down the hillside through a couple of tunnels, the views magnificent all the way – except inside the tunnels, I suppose I should say, but even these are impressive.

The main road – indeed, the only road – has been roughly following the route of the railway, but they take opposite sides of the loch until they meet again at Lochailort – and here, at Lochailort station, Sandy gets quite a surprise. After deserted Highland hills and glens he is suddenly surrounded by a horde of navvies, waving their shovels above their heads. This is not a repeat of the '45 Rebellion; the shovels are highly polished, as navvies' shovels always were when not actually shovelling – they used them as frying-pans to cook their meals – and they are being waved, not in menace, but in greeting. These are all who remain of the 1500 men who have been living at McAlpine's biggest construction camp of Lochailort off and on for the past four years. Sandy's arrival marks the fruition of those four years' work on the most isolated section of the Mallaig Extension.

The construction camp was very like an army barracks. Each hut had one big room with forty beds, with a separate room at the end for the ganger – in the Army's case, the corporal. Robert McAlpine was one of the more benevolent employers, and he provided washbasins, but no hot water; the only supply came straight from the river nearby. He also provided a bakery and arranged with a grocery firm to open stores at all his camps, where the men could buy good quality provisions at reasonable prices. This was not philanthropy, just sensible labour relations. The men needed this

kind of incentive to work in such remote areas; if they became dissatisfied there was plenty of work elsewhere. A good many of them did get fed up anyway with the isolation and the weather, and headed for more convivial surroundings in the south.

McAlpine's most important gesture, as it turned out, was to convert the old schoolhouse at Polnish, just outside Lochailort, into a hospital. It had eight beds, two nurses and a resident doctor. This was quite revolutionary; no construction camp in Britain had ever had its own hospital before. McAlpine's virtue had its own reward; when his son Malcolm was injured in a blasting accident, his life was saved at the hospital.

Malcolm was only twenty-one at the time, but he had already made a valuable contribution to the Mallaig Extension project. One of the biggest problems it presented was boring the tunnels and excavating the cuttings; the West Highlands have some of the hardest rock in Britain. Blasting was quickest but the most dangerous – as Malcolm later discovered. Pneumatic drills were safer, but they were operated by steam power, which meant using a lot of coal – and while the West Highlands have plenty of rock, they are pretty thin on coal. To get the coal to the remoter sites they needed a railway – to build the railway they needed the coal.

Young Malcolm came up with the answer. He was in a dentist's chair at the time, a situation not normally conducive to inspiration, and what inspired him was the dentist's drill, which again seems slightly bizarre. But he noticed that it was switched on by pressing a knob on the floor, and when the drill was removed from his mouth he took the chance to ask how it worked. The dentist stopped talking about the weather and explained the knob opened a valve in a water pipe under the floor, and operated a water turbine. It dawned on Malcolm that, while the West Highlands are short on coal, they are running with water.

As soon as he escaped from the chair he returned to the site and told the chief engineer about the dentist's drill. A dam was built across a handy loch, a pipe was laid to a turbine, the compressed air was piped to the drills, and the drills dug the tunnels – four times faster than they had dug before. In 1898 there were sixty drills being operated in this way, saving the labour of 500 men with picks and shovels – and all because Malcolm had had a spot of toothache...

OPPOSITE *The Glenfinnan monument is on the spot where Bonnie Prince Charlie unfurled his standard.*

Unfortunately for Malcolm, there were still some situations where blasting was required, and in the following year he suffered a lot more than toothache. He was supervising a blasting operation near Lochailort when he was hit by flying debris; the fragments of rocks were like shrapnel, and his injuries were appalling.

This was when the camp hospital came into its own. The company doctor examined him there and found he had a shattered pelvis, several broken ribs and severe haemorrhaging. It was too complicated for him to operate himself, but at least he was able to look after his patient in reasonable conditions until help came. Happily, McAlpine had also provided all his camps with a telephone link to the site office at Corpach. From there, Malcolm's brother Robert was able to send a telegraph to his father's home outside Glasgow, and a dramatic rescue operation was launched.

Robert senior was quite a remarkable man. He managed to persuade a famous Glasgow surgeon, Professor Sir William Macewan, to travel north with him immediately. He then persuaded – some say bullied – the staff of the West Highland Railway to run a special train through the night from Glasgow to Fort William, long after the line had closed down and the signalmen had gone to bed. This meant the fireman and driver had to take the train on a single track without any certainty there was nothing on the line ahead, and they had to operate all the points themselves. I can visualize Concrete Bill standing on the footplate, urging them on, while their solitary passenger sat in the coach behind them, boning up on shrapnel wounds …

They reached Fort William at 5.00 a.m. Even at that hour, McAlpine found a coachman, got him out of bed, and pointed him in the direction of Lochailort, along the picturesque but appallingly surfaced Road to the Isles. Seven hours later they arrived at Lochailort and the camp hospital. Sir William, in spite of his long and uncomfortable journey, then performed a major operation on young Malcolm McAlpine, and stayed by his bed for four days and nights.

But Malcolm was still not out of the wood. Sir William decided he would have to be moved to Glasgow, but his memory of that coach journey was still very fresh, and he knew that the jolting would be fatal. So, amazingly, he taught eight navvies how to carry a stretcher without tilting it or jogging it. Working in shifts, they carried Malcolm for

2 miles across country to Loch Eilt, where they boarded a boat. It was towed to the other end of the loch, then they carried him another 4 miles over the hills to Glenfinnan. They stopped there overnight, then completed the trek to the railhead, the most westerly point of the newly built Mallaig Extension.

McAlpine had organized an engine and waggon, and to stop these jarring against each other when on the move, the stretcher-bearers sat facing each other, four on the back of the engine and four on the front of the waggon, with their feet touching, so that their legs acted as human buffers.

Fortunately they did not have to sit like this all the way to Fort William, or they might never have walked normally again. The little train stopped at the head of Loch Eil, the stretcher was transferred to a steamer, the steamer took it down the loch to Banavie Pier, and a special train took it to Glasgow. The stretcher-bearers, now thoroughly hooked on the job, went with it, and carried Malcolm's stretcher themselves through Glasgow to Sir William's nursing home.

Malcolm McAlpine made a complete recovery. In due course he became a partner in the firm with his brothers and built, among other places, Wembley Stadium and the Dorchester Hotel – in concrete, naturally. Sir Malcolm, as he became, died in 1967 at ninety. I wish those eight stretcher-bearers had still been around to carry his coffin…

At Lochailort today I could find no trace of that vast construction camp, nor anybody who knew anything about it. I did come across a lonely walled burial ground on the moors, but the graves were occupied by the family of the local laird. However, the camp hospital, originally a school and now a private house called Polnish House, still stands by the road out of the village. It ought to have a plaque saying, not the usual 'So-and-so lived here' but 'Malcolm McAlpine nearly died here'.

There has been more blasting since Malcolm's day. The road itself has been widened and straightened for a short distance, until it reduces again to its customary single-track, and a new road was built around the coast in the 1960s to open up an area which could previously only be reached by boat. It was consequently very popular with Bonnie Prince Charlie, and near Loch Moidart a row of seven beech trees, 'The Seven Men of Moidart', recalls how he landed in Scotland with only seven followers, confident that he would

The old schoolhouse at Polnish, used as a camp hospital, now a private house.

ABOVE *Lochailort station, on the 'Iron Road to the Isles'.*

OPPOSITE *The line should have come to Roshven, but the landowner said it would spoil his view.*

The Prince's Cairn, where the defeated Young Pretender re-embarked for France.

soon assemble an army. As one of these trees dies or is blown down, a fresh one is planted. The new road continues to the far end of Loch Shiel, where Charles embarked from the home of his friend, Macdonald of Glenaladale, and was rowed up the loch to rally the clans at Glenfinnan.

Ironically, the road also passes Roshven Harbour, which Professor Blackburn and his friends defended so effectively from the incursions of 'insatiable tourists'. The roadbuilders succeeded where the railway company failed, and this is now a popular sailing and walking centre, much frequented by caravanners, picknickers, ramblers and climbers, all of whom the good professor would doubtless find 'abominable'.

Sandy, meanwhile, is pulling out of Lochailort station, which these days is a rather sorry sight, with one platform derelict and an unlovely metal-box shelter on the other. He steams into the first of the nine tunnels between here and Arisaig, and each time he emerges, a new vista lies ahead; this is the most exciting and picturesque section of the Mallaig Extension. It skirts Loch Dubh, where Malcolm built one of the dams for his water turbines, and when it reaches Loch nan Uamh, 'the Loch of the Caves', it crosses another concrete viaduct, not as dramatic as the one at Glenfinnan but still an impressive sight with its eight 50-foot arches.

On the shore of the loch is another reminder that this is Jacobite country. 'The Prince's Cairn' marks the place where Charles landed with his seven friends, and where he sailed away again a year later, with not even seven men left, escorted by two French frigates which had brought him money and arms but arrived too late to be of help. As they sailed out to sea they were engaged by English ships, one of whose captains later became Earl Howe, but this was not one of his better days and Charles made good his escape.

Sandy's fireman has some more hard work ahead as they approach the winding 1½-mile climb up Beasdale Bank, where British Rail's stock excuse of 'leaves on the line' can be quite justified. This is heavily wooded country, and Sandy is grateful that this is spring and not autumn. At the top of the gradient is the private station at Beasdale for the use of Arisaig House – folk were allowed to have their own stations in 1901. Today it is still private, in that the station building has been converted into a holiday home, but in fact the station has always been open to the public and it is still a request stop.

Beasdale station is now a private house – but the trains still stop there.

Borrodale bridge was built with one wide span to save money on the stone facing.

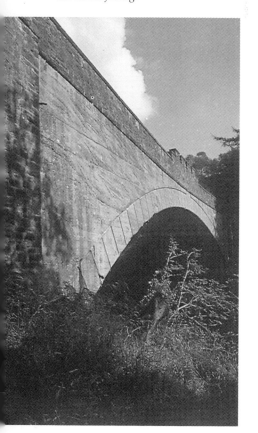

After a stop at Beasdale to let his fireman get his breath back, Sandy enters the longest tunnel on the Extension at Borrodale, which Malcolm McAlpine's water-powered drills have carved for nearly 350 yards through the West Highland rocks. It leads straight on to another of Concrete Bob's viaducts, but the concrete is not quite so apparent. The local landowner was not as keen on this new material as McAlpine, and insisted that the piers should be clad in granite. McAlpine checked the price of granite and decided that, instead of building his standard 50-foot spans he would cut down on the number of piers and build a single span instead. It turned out to be 127 feet, the longest single concrete span at that time in the world. With some of the money he saved, Concrete Bob added a few fancy battlements along the parapet, to the delight of the traditionally minded landowner.

Sandy takes his train across the viaduct, over a wild hillside which was later used as a Commando training ground, and into the station at Arisaig, the most westerly station on British Rail. It is also the nearest to the Gulf Stream, and writers have waxed poetic about the mass of luxurious growth sweeping down to the sea, trees almost tropical in their brilliance, flourishing palms and gardens full of subtropical plants. There is even, according to one enthusiast, 'a hint of the South Seas about the scene – the islands sparkling on the polished surface of the ocean might well be Pacific islands, and Eigg, with its unreal, block-shaped Sgurr has a volcanic look about it…'

That's the good news. The bad news, of course, is that Arisaig has Scottish weather too, and even in summer the palm trees can be drenched with rain, the polished surface of the ocean is a dreary grey, and Sgurr is invisible in the mist – leaving our enthusiast, I fear, with Eigg on his face. There was a construction camp at Arisaig, and I doubt the navvies felt they were in the Pacific, as they toiled away in the tunnels. But those who remain are cheerful enough on this bright April morning as they wave to Sandy and his passengers at the station.

From Arisaig the line continues further westward, so it can claim its own record as the most westerly point on the British Rail network, then it turns north across Keppoch Bog. Bogs are nearly as bad news for railway-builders as West Highland rock, and to get a decent foundation

McAlpine had to lay a cover of brushwood, then build a layer of rocks, then add thousands of tons of ashes. Basically he floated the track on an enormous raft, and Sandy probably prefers not to think about it as he drives across it for the first time. He feels much safer, I am sure, on the viaduct across the River Morar; he has got used to McAlpine's concrete viaducts by now, though this one has an extra-wide span of 90 feet, and it is so close to the Falls of Morar he can almost feel the spray.

With the viaduct behind him, the last one on the Extension, Sandy reaches Morar station and the Silver Sands of Morar, famed throughout Scotland. All the sand on this coast is silvery, but Morar sand is more silvery than most, and Sandy gets a fine view of it from his cab. Alas, it is not so easy to spot the sand today. I found Morar's beautiful bay was being bridged by a causeway for the new road to Mallaig. Bulldozers were scrambling up and down the hills on each side, cranes were operating on the causeway and the beach was blotted out by the huts of the workforce – the latter-day equivalent of Concrete Bob's construction camps. The people of Morar, I understand, are not too happy about this, and who can blame them. The Silver Sands of Morar will never look quite the same.

The locals were a little put out also when the level crossing on the present road was converted to automatic working in 1985. Previously the rail timetable allowed six minutes for the train crew to open and close them, which the locals admitted was tedious, but reckoned it was much safer. They were confirmed in this view when, five weeks later, an American tourist managed to ram the Royal train. Fortunately the train was empty at the time – it had just delivered the Prince and Princess of Wales to Mallaig – and nobody was hurt, but the cries of 'I told you so!' might have been heard in Fort William. Nevertheless the gates remain automatic – even following an episode when the klaxon malfunctioned after a train went by and continued to blast away for fifteen hours…

Sandy does not have to worry about such problems as he takes his train on the final stage of its journey, an easy seven-minute run along the coast with no gradients – or bogs – to worry about. As he rounds the last bend, Mallaig harbour lies ahead, with the ferries waiting at the dockside for the passengers to the Western Isles.

Such is progress: the new causeway being built beside the Silver Sands of Morar.

OVERLEAF *Mallaig harbour, at the end of the Mallaig Extension.*

The latest threat to the Mallaig line; a new road is being built alongside it.

Until Mallaig was selected as the terminal for the Extension it was just a little fishing village with only a handful of inhabitants. The harbour was built by Concrete Bob – with concrete blocks, of course, and the help of a substantial government grant. He built the station on a shelf of rock which jutted into the harbour and is still, arguably, the windiest station in Britain, though he did put up a wall at the end to keep off the worst of the wind and spray. Fishing boats and ferries switched to Mallaig from other harbours, and the village has grown to 1000 people, but there are still those who remember their elders talking about how different it was before the railway came.

John MacDougall lived at Sandaig in those days, on the far shore of Loch Nevis from Mallaig, and he recalls: 'Before the railway there wasn't a slated roof in Mallaig, just a few old crofts. There wasn't even a chapel; the people came across Loch Nevis to Mass.'

The change is just beginning as Sandy brings his train into the station – and John MacDougall remembers when it arrived. 'I mind fine seeing the first train that ever carried passengers to Mallaig. I was watching it through the glass from the hill above my house in Sandaig. There was plenty of people and I saw the first steamers sailing away for Skye and Stornaway.'

The steamers are the *Clydesdale* and the *Lovedale*, which brought over the passengers from the islands earlier that morning to catch the first train from Mallaig to Fort William. They are waiting there now, and any celebrations on the station have to be brief, but I hope the through passengers pause by Sandy's cab to congratulate him on his inaugural run before they go on board. They must be looking forward, however, to the end of their journeys. Anyone from Glasgow who is travelling to Skye on the *Lovedale*, for instance, will have a total journey time of ten hours and thirty-five minutes. A Londoner who has come up from King's Cross on the sleeper and is booked through to Stornaway on the *Clydesdale* will have travelled for twenty-four hours.

Yes, the Mallaig Extension is magnificent, but it isn't fast. It would have seemed so, of course, to anyone who had to make the journey along the appalling road before the railway came, but the road has improved enormously and continues to do so, albeit at the expense of the scenery. Today it runs broad and straight alongside the final section of the line between Morar and Mallaig, a warning of the tough competition the railway will face when it is completed.

Beeching may have missed it with his Axe, but the knives have been sharpened ever since. In 1965 British Rail stopped carrying the fish traffic because they said it was no longer economical; the locals say they lost the trade because the trains kept missing their connections. The Corpach Pulp mill closed in 1980, and another source of revenue had gone. Staff were withdrawn from stations, buildings became derelict, the number of trains was reduced.

Then in 1984, someone at ScotRail had a brainwave. 'Let's run a steam train', they said. 'That should pull in the punters.' They did – and it did. Steam train excursions are now packed in the summer months, and they help to pay for the winter services, which are relied upon to take children to school in Fort William, and people to work or to the shops; the Mallaig Extension is still, basically, a community line. The automated signals have reduced staff, but they have reduced the costs as well. In spite of that new road, the Extension may yet avoid becoming just another Timepath that has disappeared into the history books.

As for Sandy, if he was anything like the steam drivers I have met, he relished every journey he made on the Mallaig line. For them, driving a steam engine is pleasure enough, but driving it in the midst of this magnificent scenery, through valleys and glens, past rivers and lochs, over wooded hills and alongside silver beaches, with the great crescent of the Glenfinnan viaduct providing a constant marvel – that must be the ultimate delight.

The return of the steam trains came much too late for Sandy, but when the Mallaig Extension celebrates its centenary in 2001 – new roads, privatization and market forces permitting – a special steam train must surely repeat that inaugural run, and I am certain that, watching it from somewhere, there will be Concrete Bob and his sons, a certain Glasgow surgeon, eight beefy stretcher-bearers, 3000 navvies – and Sandy the Steam.

The Morar crossing, where road and rail meet.

OVERLEAF *The last of the Timepaths – still steaming on …*

POSTSCRIPT

A S I WRITE, THERE ARE OTHER rural railway lines which
are not merely being rescued from the brink of
extinction, but being brought back from the dead.
There are plans in Devon to restore 6 miles of torn-up track
to Tavistock. In Wales the 8-mile Llynfi Valley link from
Maesteg to Bridgend is carrying passengers again for the
first time since 1970. In Norfolk a preservation society is
bidding to buy the disused line between Dereham and
Wymondham, to run commuter trains again to Norwich. In
Yorkshire passenger trains are about to run on the Ribble
Valley line after thirty years. Just as the canal era was followed by the railway era in the nineteenth century, so the
canal preservationists are being followed by their railway
counterparts in the twentieth.

And let us not underestimate their enthusiasm and influence. The latest news from the Chichester Canal Society, for
instance, is that the Sports Council, the National Rivers
Authority and the District Council have been persuaded to
back West Sussex County Council in a feasibility study, to
see if the old ship canal between the city and the harbour
can be re-opened for its entire length – in spite of two low
road bridges which now block the way. The study should be
in progress, if not completed, by the time this book is published. And since I finished writing it, the Wey & Arun
Canal Trust have restored another lock to working order,
and cleared another stretch of the canal.

I wonder, will the other Timepaths be revived in due
course as well? If I may quote Norfolk again, a horse-drawn
coach regularly meets passengers at Holt station to take
them to the town centre, half-a-mile away. So shall we see
the mailcoaches returning as well, to save the environment
from the fumes of the petrol engine? Let's face it, the deliveries would probably be just as fast as they are today.

We still see flocks of sheep and herds of cattle on our
rural roads. They are only driven for short distances at
present, but will farmers be told that 'set-aside' should
apply to cattle-lorries as well as to land? This, after all,
would reduce air and noise pollution – and bring drovers
back into their own.

I doubt we shall see too many corpses again on the

Corpse Trail, but pony-trekking is increasingly popular, and the riders could cover much longer distances if they had packhorses to carry their luggage as they followed the old packhorse trails.

Our navigable rivers are thronged with pleasure-craft; is there not an opportunity for merchant boats – even crewed by Norwegian traders – to ply among all those potential customers moored along the banks, in a modern equivalent of a Viking longboat?

As for the Fosse Way and the Icknield Way, they are already trodden by long-distance walkers, where the modern development and traffic permit, and they will ensure there are no more encroachments on public footpaths and rights of way.

So will the time come when all these latterday Stans and Lens, the Vics and Pauls, the Dais and Bens, the Bills and Sandys, will become such a force in the land that they bring all the Timepaths into Time-present?

No. Probably not.

FURTHER READING

1 THE ICKNIELD WAY
The Icknield Way, Antony Bulfield, Terence Dalton Ltd, 1972.
The Icknield Way Path, Ed. Alan Jenyon, Icknield Way Association, 3rd ed., 1993.
A Picture History of Goring & Streatley, Anon, Goring & Streatley Local History Society, c. 1986.
Portrait of the Chilterns, Elizabeth Cull, Robert Hale, 1982.
The Stonehenge Solution, George Meaden, Souvenir Press, 1992.
Victoria Glendinning's Hertfordshire, Victoria Glendinning, Weidenfeld & Nicolson, 1989.

2 THE FOSSE WAY
Along the Roman Roads, Geoffrey Maxwell Boumphrey, Allen & Unwin, 2nd ed., 1964.
Britain Before the Norman Conquest, Anon, Ordnance Survey, 3rd ed., 1973.
Ilchester, Peter Leace and Robert Dunning, Somerset County Council, c. 1990.
Roman Roads in Britain, Ivan D. Margary, John Baker.

3 THE RIVER OUSE
Jorvik – Viking Age York, R.A. Hall, York Archaeological Trust, 1949.
Shell Guide to Reading the Landscape, Richard Muir, Michael Joseph, 1981.

4 THE CORPSE TRAIL
The Dales of Yorkshire, Richard Muir, Macmillan, 1991.
Lyke Wake Walk, Bill Cowley, Dalesman Publishing Co., 11th ed., 1988.
Walking the Dales, Mike Harding, Michael Joseph, 1986.
The Yorkshire Dales, Geoffrey N. Wright, David & Charles, 1986.

5 THE WELSH ROAD
The Drovers, K.J. Bonser, Macmillan, 1970.
The Drovers Roads of Wales, Shirley Toulson, Wildwood House, 1977.
The Making of the English Landscape, W.G. Hoskins, Hodder & Stoughton, 1992.
The Old Roads of England, Sir William Addison, Batsford, 1980.
The Welsh Cattle Drovers, Richard J. Colver, University of Wales Press, 1976.

6 THE WEY TO THE SOUTH
Canals and Rivers of Britain, Andrew Darwin, Dent, 1976.
The Chichester Canal, Anon, Chichester Canal Society.
The Chichester Canal, F.D. Heneghan, West Sussex County Council, 1958.
London's Lost Route to the Sea, P.A.L. Vine, David & Charles, 3rd ed., 1973.
The South Downs and *View of Sussex*, Ben Darby, Robert Hale, 1976.
The Story of Restoring London's Lost Route to the Sea, Anon, The Wey & Arun Canal Trust.

7 THE MAILCOACH RUN
Coaching in and out of Oxford, William Bayzand, Oxford Historical Society Collection.
History of Oxfordshire, Mary Jessup, Phillimore, 1975.
Portrait of Buckinghamshire, John Camp, Robert Hale, 1972.
Roads and Tracks of Britain, Christopher Taylor, Dent, 1977.
Roads and Trackways of Wales, Dr Richard Colyer, University College of Wales, Aberystwyth.

8 THE MALLAIG EXTENSION
The Mallaig Line, Tom Weir, Famedram (Dunbartonshire), 1972.
Sir Robert McAlpine and Sons, Iain P. Russell, Parthenon.
The West Highland Mallaig Extension, Tom Noble, Haynes, 1989.
The West Highland Railway, John Thomas, David & Charles, 1976.

INDEX